T0369599

The Diary of Manu Gandhi

The Diary of Manu Gandhi

1943–1944

Edited and translated by

Tridip Suhrud

OXFORD
UNIVERSITY PRESS

Oxford University Press is a department of the University of Oxford.
It furthers the University's objective of excellence in research, scholarship,
and education by publishing worldwide. Oxford is a registered trademark of
Oxford University Press in the UK and in certain other countries.

Published in India by
Oxford University Press
2/11 Ground Floor, Ansari Road, Daryaganj, New Delhi 110 002, India

© National Archives of India, 2019

The moral rights of the authors have been asserted.

First Edition published in 2019

ISBN-13 (print edition): 978-0-19-949616-7
ISBN-10 (print edition): 0-19-949616-1

ISBN-13 (eBook): 978-0-19-909807-1
ISBN-10 (eBook): 0-19-909807-7

Typeset in Adobe Garamond Pro 11/14
by The Graphics Solution, New Delhi 110 092
Printed in India by Replika Press Pvt. Ltd

Contents

Contents

Foreword

The Diary of Manu Gandhi is among the most significant collections on Mahatma Gandhi in the Private Archives collections of the National Archives of India and are predominantly written in Gujarati. These diaries were written by Manubehn (Mridula) Gandhi, who was the youngest daughter of Gandhi's nephew, Jaisukhlal Amritlal Gandhi, and Kasumba. We are pleased that the National Archives of India is presenting the English translations of these Diaries to the general readers.

I would like to acknowledge and thank Professor Tridip Suhrud, former Director and Chief Editor of Sabarmati Ashram Preservation and Memorial Trust, Ahmedabad, for his painstaking efforts of translation and annotation of the volumes of *The Diary of Manu Gandhi*. Apart from the tremendous historical value of this unique source, hitherto inaccessible to the non-Gujarati readers, Professor Suhrud's work invites the readers to engage in a more authentic and deeper understanding of what these diaries mean and represent. Sifting through the rich material, this reflective work seeks to provide a context, a deeper understanding of the juxtaposition of the outward manifestations of Gandhian nationalism with Gandhi's relentless spiritual journey as a natural corollary. The trajectory of ideals, practices and introspection blend and intermingle, almost seamlessly.

I would also like to thank my colleagues for their assistance in bringing out this volume, viz. Shri T. Hussain, Deputy Director of Archives, Shri S.K. Misra, Hasan Raza, Assistant Director of Archives, Smt. Anumita Banerjee, Dr S. L. Sahu, Archivists, and Shri Vivek Ranjan, Assistant Archivist.

I am confident that this Diary will be welcomed by readers of Indian history and politics and those interested in learning more about Mahatma Gandhi and Manubehn Gandhi. The Department intends to bring out more such publications from the rich collection of the National Archives of India.

Pranav Khullar
Joint Secretary to the Government of India and
Director General
National Archives of India, Ministry of Culture
New Delhi
June 2019

Introduction

In this *yajna* I got glimpses of the ideal of truth and purity for which I
have been aspiring. And you have fully contributed towards it.[1]

Manu: The Apprentice

Manu Gandhi (1927–1969) bears witness. On 30 January 1948 as
MK Gandhi walked to prayer and martyrdom, Manu, a partner and
a contributor to his final yajna—a ritual of self-knowing and self-
sacrifice—walked by his side. Before the assassin could come face to
face with Gandhi he had to push aside Manu who blocked his path
of hatred. The diary—a constant companion since 1943—a spittoon
and a *mala* that she carried, fell and scattered and the next instance
she cradled the man she called her 'mother' as his body bearing three
crimson marks slowly sank to the ground.

Gandhi desired that Manu bear witness to his death so that she
could bear testimony to his striving. He told her in May 1947, 'I
wish to reach a stage of a perfect *sthitprajna* and attain perfect non-
attachment. The success of my attempt depends solely on how I meet
death… But if it occurs to me to utter the name Rama with my last

---

[1] MK Gandhi to Manu Gandhi, April 29, 1947, Patna. *Collected Works
of Mahatma Gandhi* (*CWMG*), vol. 87, p. 384.

breath it should be taken as a proof of a success of my attempt. And as you are a witness to this yajna of mine I do wish that you should be my witness in this and not go before me.'[2]

Gandhi had deep doubts about his striving to see God face to face, to attain self-realization and achieve *moksha*. As all humans moved by this quest, he knew that such striving could and must remain incomplete so long as the seeker was in the mortal body. Gandhi felt that it is at the moment of his death that the truth of his striving would be available for verification. And this verification would only be done by someone other than the self; a person such that had the capacity to bear witness and the authority to become a testator.

Gandhi once again gave this responsibility to Manu. In the same month of May 1947 he told her, 'But if I should die of lingering illness, it would be your duty to proclaim to the whole world that I was not a man of God but an imposter and a fraud. If you fail in that duty I shall feel unhappy wherever I am. But if I die taking God's name with my last breath, it will be a sign that I was what I strove for and claimed to be.' [3]

What was Manu's *adhikar*, her striving, that made her a witness? These diaries from 1943–1948 are a story of striving to acquire the adhikar, to become a partner in the yajna that gave Gandhi a glimpse of truth and purity that he sought.

Manu (Mridula) Gandhi was the youngest daughter of Gandhi's nephew Jaisukhlal Amritlal Gandhi and Kasumba.[4]

The first reference to Manu in Gandhi's writings is in a letter of 20 March 1941 to her father Jaisukhlal, 'Let Mridula cook and study at the same time. Her education will shine all the better.'[5]

---

[2] *CWMG* vol. 87, p. 462.

[3] *CWMG* vol. 87, pp. 521–2.

[4] Amritlal Gandhi was the son of Tulsidas, brother of Gandhi's father Karamchand. Manu had three elder sisters, Umiya (b.1912), Vinodini (b.1917) and Samyukta (b.1923).

[5] *CWMG* vol. 73, pp. 386–7.

By May 1942, Gandhi probably at the urging of Jaisukhlal had brought Manu to live at Sevagram. By that time her mother had died. Gandhi told Rajkumari Amrit Kaur of the latest addition of persons in the circle of his care. 'I brought along Jaisukhlal's little daughter.'[6] Manu's training began at Sevagram, it included both literary training—including Sanskrit and English—and training in seva, of service to others, particularly Kasturba and Gandhi. Gandhi reported to her father in July of that year, 'Chi. Manu is a very sensible and smart girl. She serves Ba devotedly. She has become friendly with all.

There are no complaints against her. She is quite good in her studies too. I see that she is happy. She comes every evening to massage my legs. Of course, she also accompanies me in my walks. There is no need for you to worry about her.'[7]

But in August of 1942 national events around the All India Congress Committee's call to the British to Quit India led to Gandhi's arrest and soon thereafter, of several principal workers of the Ashram. Gandhi, along with Kasturba, Mahadev Desai, Pyarelal, Dr Sushila Nayyar, Sarojini Naidu and Mirabehn were held in detention at the Aga Khan Palace at Poona. As the Quit India agitation raged outside Aga Khan Palace, prisoners faced deep personal tragedy. On 15 August 1942, Mahadev Desai fulfilled one of his two lifelong desires. One was to write a biography of Gandhi and the other was to die in Gandhi's lap. He fulfilled his second desire and met a 'yogi's death'.

With Gandhi, Ba and other principal Ashram workers already either in jail or preparing for it, the women at the Ashram decided to join the protest. Manu at 14, was the youngest. On 31 August 1942, Manu wore a sari for the first time and became a satyagrahi. She became a prisoner that day and was kept at Wardha jail and transferred to Nagpur Central Jail on 2 September 1942. Gandhi as a prisoner

---

6 *CWMG* vol. 76, p. 122.
7 *CWMG* vol. 76, p. 345.

was on a 21-day-long fast at Aga Khan Palace from 10 February 1943 to 2 March 1943. Kasturba, already frail and ailing, suffered greater privations. The Government decided to shift Manu from Nagpur to Aga Khan. After nine months in prison, Manu—still a prisoner—began her journey to join Ba and Bapu on 19 March 1943.[8]

From 20 March 1943 to 6 May 1944 Manu remained at Aga Khan, a period of devoted service to Kasturba who died a prisoner on 22 February 1944.

She began her diary on 11 April 1943.

Diary-keeping for Gandhi was an essential duty for all those engaged in pursuit of truth and hence obligatory for Ashramites and satyagrahis. He constantly urged the Ashram community and constructive workers to maintain one. 'I beg this of you.' He wrote to Prema Kantak, 'If you have not been writing up your diary, start doing so.'[9] A daily diary, he believed, was a mode of self-examination and self-purification; he made it an obligatory observance for all those who walked with him on the Salt march. He kept a diary himself, although with the passage of years his reliance upon the diary as a mode of self-examination lessened, he never gave up the practice altogether. He told the Ashram community, 'Thinking about a diary I feel that it is of priceless value to me. For a person who has dedicated himself to the pursuit of truth, it serves as a means of keeping watch over himself, for such a person is determined to write in it nothing but the truth.'[10]

---

[8] There is a discrepancy in the dates. According to Manu she reached Aga Khan on 20 March 1943. According to the *CWMG*, Vol. 77, p. 74, Gandhi wrote on Manu's diary on 13 March 1943, which seems to be an error. Kasturba suffered symptoms akin to a heart attack on the 17 March and the Government thereafter decided to transfer Manu. CB Dalal, the chronicler of Gandhi's daily life, also gives the date as 20 March 1943. See, Dalal C.B., *Gandhiji ni Dinvari* (Gandhinagar: Information Department, 1970), p. 496.

[9] *CWMG*, vol. 47, pp. 2156-217.

[10] *CWMG*, vol. 44, p. 39.

In the tradition of diary writing—not just of the Ashram tradition—*Diaries of Mahadev Desai* are unparalleled. Mahadev is the greatest chronicler of Gandhi's life. It was Mahadev's aspiration to bear witness to Gandhi's striving for truth. From 1917 to 1942 he maintained a diary of each day he spent with Gandhi, that is on that rare day he was not Gandhi's shadow he did not write the diary. All of Gandhi's associates, including Manu, aspired to write a diary like Mahadev did.

Twelve volumes of Manu's diaries are lodged in the National Archives of India. These diaries, written in ruled notebooks, contain six volumes of Gandhi's prayer speeches (which she wrote as he spoke), one volume of copies of letters written by Gandhi, one volume of her 'English work book' (from the Aga Khan period) and four volumes of diaries. The prayer speeches and letters of Gandhi have already been published as a part of the *Collected Works of Mahatma Gandhi*. The present work is based on the translation and annotation of the four volumes of the diary from 1943 to 1948 (the time that she was not with Gandhi, she like Mahadev, did not write a diary).

Gandhi made it a practice at Aga Khan to read, sign and at times comment on Manu's diary. The original manuscript of the diaries bear marks of Gandhi's corrections, comments and are signed 'Bapu'. Each such mark of Gandhi's intervention in the diary and his signature are marked in the present volume.

The diaries of 1943–4 differ from the diary of the period of 19 December 1946 to 31 January 1948. The first set of diaries are of an adolescent 15-year-old Manu, uncertain about her vocation, her place by Gandhi's side, and her literary abilities in writing the diaries unformed. Under Gandhi's constant guidance Manu's diary begins to change. The signs of this change are apparent in the present volume itself. Two days after she began to maintain the diaries, Gandhi wrote the first note in her diary, 'You must keep an account of the yarn you have spun. Thoughts coming into your mind should also be noted down. You should keep a record of all that you have read.'[11] Some

---

[11] *CWMG*, vol. 77, p. 74.

days later he advised: 'You should improve your handwriting, write down whatever you learn from others. It will show you how much you have digested.'[12]

As she wrote, hesitantly to begin with, her inner thoughts, she did not submit the diary for his scrutiny and signature. In the entry of 21 May 1943, she wrote, 'But, I do write the diary daily, but do not show it to him because I wrote about the day when he refused to allow me to apply ghee on his feet.' The next day she did give him the diary but took it away before he could read it. Having done so, she wrote in the margin, 'And yet, I will show it to him.'

The diaries of the second phase to be published as the second volume of this set are distinctly different. She is the partner in his yajna, a chosen witness to his striving and his principal caregiver. The diaries are either read to Gandhi or read by him regularly and they bear the mark of his authentication. But this mark of his sign, 'Bapu' is different from the earlier period when she is under his tutelage. The Manu of 1946 December onwards is no longer a pupil; she is a partner in his yajna.

In the earlier weeks of December 1946,[13] Manu showed signs of hesitation when Gandhi asked her to read aloud to him her diary. She told him, 'I am ashamed to read my confessions to you.'[14] But by the very second day of her coming to be with Gandhi in Srirampur, Manu began to craft the diary as she wanted it and not as Gandhi instructed. In those days of troubled times in Noakhali, their days

---

[12]   *CWMG*, vol. 77, p. 75.

[13]   Noakhali: In December of 1946 Gandhi went to Noakhali, now in Bangladesh, which had seen a systematic massacre of Hindus of the region. The killings were followed by a mass migration of Hindus from the area, a pattern that was to repeat itself during the violence related to the Partition of the subcontinent in August 1947. The violence of Noakhali was sought to be avenged by violence against the Muslims in Bihar, thus setting a pattern of communal violence that was to engulf the subcontinent for the next one year.

[14]   Gandhi, Manu; *The Lonely Pilgrim* (Ahmedabad: Navajivan, 1964), p. 14.

usually began at 3.30 a.m. and for many days ended after 10 p.m. Gandhi wanting to reduce her burden of the diary-keeping told her to study the brevity of his own style of writing and write only the central point. But Manu, like Mahadev before her, wanted to write down every word that Gandhi said. 'But, I objected 'don't you think it will be useful to me in the future if I can remember and write down every word you say?'

'Yes, agreed Bapuji, My heritage to you all can be preserved that way. Mahadev used to do exactly the same.'[15]

On 27 December he told her the importance of his signature in her diary while appreciating the style of her writing.

'I didn't know you could write such long detailed diaries, but I like them. You must make it a point to get your diary read and signed by me. You won't appreciate today the value of my signature in your diary. But it will bear a sure testimony to the fact that I pour fourth my whole heart in whatever I tell you.'[16]

She continued to write the diary which she shared with him. On 27 April 1947 she and her diary reminded Gandhi of Mahadev. 'I daily go through your diary which reminds me of Mahadev.'[17] He also wrote to Jaisukhlal, 'She has made a great progress in writing the diary. She takes great interest in writing notes and when I see them, Mahadev's face appears before my eyes.'[18]

On 10 November 1947 Manu demanded—she felt that she had acquired the right and the capability for such an unusual demand—that she would keep with herself the original writing in Gandhi's hand and send copies made by her to persons concerned. Gandhi assented to Manu's instinct of an archivist. 'Only on the condition

[15] Gandhi, Manu; *The Lonely Pilgrim* (Ahmedabad: Navajivan, 1964), p. 28.

[16] Gandhi, Manu; *The Lonely Pilgrim* (Ahmedabad: Navajivan, 1964), p. 47.

[17] *CWMG*, vol. 87, p. 384.

[18] *CWMG*, vol. 90, p. 468.

that you will not over-exert herself. Of course, I would very much like you to do so.' [19]

On 23 January 1948 Gandhi did something rather curious. He dictated a letter to Manu which was addressed to her, the letter was signed by him with a scribble, 'May your service bear fruit.' It was in some ways, Gandhi's final gift to Manu, a testament to her ability, her devotion, her purity and also a reminder of her duty.

'I have been looking into your diary for quite a few days. I am very pleased. You have shown great devotion in serving me. Whether in the family or outside I have not met a girl of your purity. That is why I become a mother to no one but you.' [20]

In the same letter he mentioned the bomb explosion in his prayer meeting of 20 January 1948 and his impending death. If she could bear witness to his death he said, 'she would have won a "total victory".' 'Who knows,' he wrote, 'but there may be another bomb explosion and with Ramanama on my lips I may be taken away from you. If that happens you will have won a total victory, only I shall not be there to watch it. But these scribbled words will remain and so will you.' [21]

Why should Gandhi's death at the hand of an assassin, with Rama-nama on his lips at the dying moment, be a total victory for Manu? The answer lies in what Gandhi called his final yajna, an offering towards purity, non-violence and realization of truth. A yajna so enigmatic that he failed to explain it to anyone, not even his family, his closest associates and probably his failure to do so would remain in case of the readers of these diaries. In order to understand this yajna, Gandhi insisted upon using the term 'yajna', a duty that could not be forsaken. We have to contend with Gandhi's quest for brahmacharya, not in the limited sense of celibacy and chastity but in its root sense as conduct (charya) that leads to truth (Brahman). Understood thus

---

[19] *CWMG*, vol.89, p. 515.

[20] *CWMG*, vol. 90, p. 481.

[21] *CWMG*, vol. 90, pp. 481–2

his 'Experiments with Truth' were in a fundamental way experiments with Brahma.

Search for Purity

'Jesus was, to my mind, a supreme artist.'[22]

It is not through the invocation of this beautiful, enigmatic and sublime image that I wish to begin this exploration in the possibilities of brahmacharya. Instead, I wish to draw attention to something that is opposed to the very idea of sublime beauty, an experience that is 'degrading', 'dirty', 'defiling', something that is deeply repugnant to the conscience of Gandhi. It is through the un-aesthetic or more aptly anaesthetic that one can capture something of Gandhi's striving to lead the life of a 'supreme artist'.

On 14 April 1938 Gandhi had an involuntary discharge. This was not the first time that he had involuntary discharge. Involuntary discharge was, if anything, a routine occurrence with him. In 1936 he wrote to an Ashramite, 'I have always had involuntary discharges. In South Africa they occurred at intervals of several years. I do not remember exactly. Here in India there have been months.'[23] In 1927 he had admitted to having a similar experience twice in two weeks. 'I had an involuntary discharge in sleep twice during the last two weeks. I cannot recall any dream.'[24] The 14 April incident was unlike all previous experiences. The emission occurred while he was fully awake and he was in such a 'wretched' and 'pitiable' condition that he could not control the discharge though fully awake. Some two years before this he had a similarly troubling, defiling experience. He had a sudden desire for intercourse. He narrated it thus: '…the experience in Bombay occurred while I was fully awake and had a sudden desire for intercourse. I felt of course no urge to gratify the craving, there

---

[22] *CWMG*, vol. 25, p. 255.

[23] *CWMG*, vol. 62, pp. 428–9

[24] *CWMG*, vol. 35, p. 379

was no self-forgetfulness whatever. I was completely master of my body. But despite my best efforts the organ remained aroused. This was an altogether strange and shameful experience.'[25]

He wrote of his feelings of utter despondency, 'That degrading, dirty, torturing experience of 14th April shook me to bits and made me feel as if I was hurled by God from an imaginary paradise where I had no right to be in my uncleanliness.'[26] Gandhi, through this unmistakable Biblical image sought to convey not only his imperfect brahmacharya but a deeper sense of inadequacy, a more fundamental failing. His submission to *Satya Narayan*, Truth as God, was incomplete and hence, he had no right to represent Truth and non-violence. He lamented, 'Where I am, where is my place, and how can a person subject to passion represent non-violence and truth?'[27]

Gandhi posited a relationship between submission and self-knowledge, between surrender and capacity to represent Truth and non-violence. It is in this relationship that his craving to lead life as a supreme artist emerges.

The walls of his house, *Hriday Kunj*, were bare, completely bereft of any mark, artistic or otherwise. Gandhi had no need for outward expressions of beauty created by human hands. He said, 'There are two aspects of things—the outward and the inward. It is purely a matter of emphasis with me. The outward has no meaning except in so far as it helps the inward.'[28] Gandhi argued that there are moments, however rare, when one's communion with oneself is so complete that one feels no need for any outward expression, including art. He asserted, 'There comes a time when he supersedes art that depends for its appreciation on sense perception.'[29] Gandhi described this beautiful moment of communion with oneself as a moment when

---

[25] *CWMG*, vol. 62, p. 429

[26] *CWMG*, vol. 67, p. 61

[27] *CWMG*, vol. 67, p. 58.

[28] *CWMG*, vol. 25, p. 248

[29] *CWMG*, vol. 29, p. 397

one acquires the capacity to hear that 'small, still voice within,' what he often described as 'the inner voice.'

This need, this desire and ability to hear the voice speaking from within was Gandhi's principal quest. It signaled to him his nearness or distance from *satya narayan*. In his autobiography, *An Autobiography or the Story of My Experiments with Truth*, Gandhi articulated his vocation and calling. He wrote: 'What I want to achieve—what I have been striving and pining to achieve these thirty years—is self-realization, to see God face to face, to attain *Moksha*. I live and move and have my entire being in pursuit of this goal.'[30] He emphasized that all his actions, including those in the political realm, were directed to this end. This remarkable desire to see God face-to-face, to attain moksha, is predicated upon one possibility: that it is possible for us to know our self, to attain self-realization. Without this possibility of self-realization, God would remain ever elusive.

He was equally aware that not all that was experienced by the self was fully comprehensible and even less communicable. He said, 'There are some things which are known only to oneself and one's Maker.'[31] The original Gujarati is more enigmatic. It reads in a literal translation: 'There are certain things that arise and find repose in the soul, it is beyond my capacity to write about them.'[32] It is in this realm that language fails. Gandhi's quest to know himself involved both these realms—a public realm of experiments and a private, intensely personal realm of *sadhana* that was known only to him and his Maker. Both these realms are spiritual, moral and religious in the

---

[30] Gandhi, M. K. *An Autobiography or The Story of My Experiments with Truth*, A Critical Edition, Introduced with Notes by Tridip Suhrud (New Delhi: Penguin Random House, 2018), p. 46

[31] Gandhi, M. K. *An Autobiography or The Story of My Experiments with Truth*, A Critical Edition, Introduced with Notes by Tridip Suhrud (New Delhi: Penguin Random House, 2018), p. 46

[32] Gandhi, M. K. *An Autobiography or The Story of My Experiments with Truth*, A Critical Edition, Introduced with Notes by Tridip Suhrud (New Delhi: Penguin Random House, 2018), p. 46

sense that religion is morality. It is a realm where the seeker and his quest are one.

The implications of this quest become apparent when we situate it in the site of the experiments, which is the Ashram; the modes of experiment, which are Truth, Ahimsa (non-violence or love) and Brahmacharya and their manifestation in Swaraj.

The Dweller Within

Ashram, or 'a community of men of religions'[33] is central to Gandhi's striving. He was to later claim: 'Ashram was a necessity of life for me.'[34] Ashram as a community of co-religionists, is bound together not only by a common quest but by a set of obligatory observances that make them the Ashramites. Ashram therefore is where there are Ashramites. Thus, Yervada prison-mandir or temple as he called it—the Aga Khan Palace prison were as much an Ashram as the Satyagraha Ashram at Sabarmati and Sevagram at Wardha. Thus, the Ashram went with him on his lonely pilgrim to Noakhali and to Bihar that was his Karbala.

Before establishing the Satyagraha Ashram at Kochrab on 25 May 1915, Gandhiji had established two Ashram-like communities in South Africa. He insisted on them being 'Ashram-like', and steadfastly refused to describe them as ashram. One was merely a settlement—the Phoenix Settlement—while the other a farm, the Tolstoy Farm. Phoenix was established in 1904 under the 'magic spell' of Ruskin's *Unto This Last* but acquired an Ashram-like character only after 1906. It was in 1906 that Gandhi took a vow of Brahmacharya, initially in the limited sense of chastity and celibacy. Gandhiji says, 'From this time onward I looked upon Phoenix deliberately as a religious

---

[33] Gandhi, MK, *Ashram Observations in Action*, translated from Original Gujarati by Valiji Govindji Desai, (Ahmedabad: Navajivan, 1955, 1998), p. v.

[34] Gandhi, MK, *Ashram Observations in Action*, translated from Original Gujarati by Valiji Govindji Desai, (Ahmedabad: Navajivan, 1955, 1998), p. v.

institution.'[35] Thus, observance of *vrata*, which is often inadequately translated as vows,[36] is the defining characteristic of the Ashram. It is only through the observances that a community becomes a community of co-religionists and a settlement becomes a place for experiments with truth.

This he hoped would allow him and his fellow Ashramites to attain the perfect ideal, 'when it is night for all other beings, the disciplined soul is awake.'[37] This was the ideal for himself and the Ashram. He said, 'Let us pray that we shall see light when all around us there is darkness… we should thus be ready to take upon ourselves the burden of the whole world, but we can bear that burden only if we mean by it doing *tapascharya* on behalf of the whole world, we shall then see light where others see nothing but darkness.'[38]

This desire to be awake, to feel the presence of light when surrounded by darkness is for Gandhi the only true sign of a *bhakta*, a devotee. A devotee is one for whom God is *ananya*, of which there is no other, as the devotee is imbued with the presence of Truth as God. This single-minded devotion comes from *parayana* by repetition, by *namasmaran* of God. The day at the Ashram began with the congregational morning worship at 4.15 a.m. to 4.45 a.m.,[39] and closed with the evening prayer at 7 p.m. to 7.30 p.m.. So central was this worship to the life of the community that Gandhi could claim: 'Ever since the Ashram was founded, not a single day has passed to

---

[35] Gandhi, MK, *Ashram Observations in Action*, translated from Original Gujarati by Valiji Govindji Desai (Ahmedabad: Navajivan, 1955, 1998), pp. v-vi.

[36] On 31 October 1930 Gandhiji explained the inadequacy to JC Kumarappa, 'The word "vow" is also an unsuitable equivalent for the original "vrata".' *CWMG*, vol. 44, p. 264.

[37] II: 69.

[38] *CWMG*, vol. 37, p. 122.

[39] The time of the morning prayer was subject to much experimentation and change but was finally fixed at 4.20 a.m., a time when the tiller of the soil and a true devotee of God woke up.

my knowledge without this worship.'[40] Gandhi would agree that full realization of the Absolute is almost impossible for an embodied being and hence they repeat the name of their *ishta deva*, the personal god. 'The Absolute is devoid of all attributes and thus difficult for men even to imagine. Therefore, they are all worshipers of a personal God, whether they are aware of it or not.'[41] For Gandhi his ishta deva was Rama.

This Rama was not the embodied Rama, he could not have a physical form. Hence, 'the Rama whom one wishes to remember, and to whom one should remember, is the Rama of one's own imagination, not the Rama of someone else's imagination'.[42] This Rama of Gandhi's imagination was the Perfect One, He was the one who saved and purified even those who had fallen and committed sin, He was *patit pavan*. It is such Rama that he sought to worship. 'We should worship Him, the Inner Ruler, who dwells in the hearts of all, yet transcends all and is the Lord of all. It is He of whom we sing: *Nirbalke bal Rama.*'[43] It was this formless and flawless Rama that Gandhi wished to see face-to-face. The Rama that he referred to and the name that he repeated all his life and at the moment of his death was not that Rama who we know as Dashrath's son.[44] It was that Rama whose name Dashrath gave to his son. That Rama was *Atmarama*, it was Truth. Truth is not merely that we are expected to speak. It is That which alone is, it is That of which all things are made, it is That which subsists by its own power, which alone is eternal. Gandhi's intense yearning was that such Truth should illuminate his heart.

---

[40] *CWMG*, vol. 56, p. 152.

[41] *CWMG*, 49, p. 136.

[42] *CWMG*, vol. 36, p. 164.

[43] *CWMG*, vol. 36, p. 164.

[44] The idea of Rama being a son of Dashrath also grew with time. If Rama is merely Dashrath's son he could not be all-pervasive, but if a devotee were to think of Rama as all-pervasive then his Dashrath too becomes all-pervasive. See, *CWMG*, vol. 85, pp.331–2.

Despite his awareness that Rama had come 'home' to him, He was not near enough, and hence he needed to keep the recitation of the name. He spoke of this distance and his need for utterance: 'Even now, although Rama is near, He is not near enough to me; hence the need to address Him at all. When He is with me all the twenty-four hours, there will be no need to address Him even in the singular.'[45]

The Name was the saviour, it was pure devotion. Gandhi liked to describe himself not as a man of learning but as a man of prayer. Prayer was the very core of his life. He had an intense need for prayer. It was not just repetition of the Ramanama; in fact, prayer was the expression of the definitive and conscious longing of the soul; it was his act of waiting upon Him for guidance and his want was to feel the utterly pure presence of the divine within. Only a heart purified and cleansed by prayer could be filled with the presence of God, where life became one long continuous prayer, an act of worship. Prayer was for him the final reliance upon God to the exclusion of all else. He knew that only when a person lives constantly in the sight of God, when in the heart every moment. Such a prayer could only be offered in the spirit of non-attachment, *anasakti*. Gandhi spoke beautifully of the power of namasmaran. 'You must learn to repeat the blessed name of Rama with such sweetness and such devotion that the birds will pause in their singing to listen to you—that the very trees will bend their leaves towards you, stirred by the divine melody of that Name.'[46] This namasmaran, this ananya bhakti required total self-surrender and all-embracing love.[47] He claimed that all his actions were undertaken with the object of generating such devotion within him.[48] This bhakti he hoped would lead him on the path of self-realization, make him a *jnani*, a self-knowing one. 'The true meaning of bhakti is search for the *atman*. When the atman realizes itself, bhakti is transformed into

---

[45] *CWMG*, vol. 24, p. 197.
[46] *CWMG*, vol. 57, p. 446.
[47] *CWMG*, vol. 49, p. 136.
[48] *CWMG*, vol. 54, p. 468

jnana.'[49] To be a seeker after this knowledge is to be a brahmachari. Gandhi preferred the term brahmachari over the term vidyarthi (one who strives for knowledge). 'In our languages, there is a beautiful word, equivalent for the word student, that is *brahamchari*. Vidyarthi is a coined word and a poor substitute for *brahmacahri*.'[50]

Body, *deha,* for Gandhi is an impediment to this state of jnana, of self-realization. In a curious transposition Gandhi altered one of the most well-known of couplets of poet Tulsidas. In a discussion on the nature of Soul-Force or Truth-Force in his 1909 text *Hind Swaraj* Gandhi invoked Tulsidas. He wrote: 'The poet Tulsidas has said "Of religion, pity or love is the root, as *egotism of the body.*[51] Therefore, we should not abandon pity so long as we are alive".'[52] This transposition is not accidental. It is a transposition expected of one striving for brahmacharya. Since 1906, Gandhi had begun to observe brahmacharya in a limited and restricted sense of chastity and celibacy. His relationship with his body had undergone a fundamental transformation and this observance was an external signifier of that. Brahmacharya, described as a mahavrata, came to Gandhiji as a necessary observance at a time when he had organized an ambulance corps during the Zulu rebellion in South Africa. He realized that service of the community was not possible without observance of brahmacharya. At the age of 37, in 1906, Gandhi took the vow of brahmacharya. The same year saw the advent of Satyagraha as an expression of Soul-Force, as Truth-Force and as a covenant between human and God.

---

[49] *CWMG,* vol. 12, p. 126

[50] *CWMG,* vol. 34, p. 422

[51] Emphasis added.

[52] *MK Gandhi's Hind Swaraj: A Critical Edition* (translated and edited by Suresh Sharma and Tridip Suhrud, Orient Blackswan, 2010), p. 72. The couplet cited in the original Gujarati reads:

'*daya dharam ko mool hai, deha mool abhiman*
Tulsi daya na chhadiye, jab lag ghatmein pran.' Gandhi's citation differs- *deha* (body) in place of *pap* (sin) – from the one prevalent in Hindi: ' *daya dharama ko mool hai, pap mool abhiman.'*

The day was 11 September 1906. The Jewish-owned Empire Theatre in Johannesburg was packed from floor to ceiling with men of Asiatic origin. Men, because there was not a single woman in that audience. They had come together to declare their opposition to the Asiatic Registration Act or the Black Act, which required every man, woman and child of eight years or upwards of Asiatic origin to submit to registration by providing prints of all ten fingers; failure to register was an offence under the law and the defaulter could be punished with deportation. The meeting was expected to pass several resolutions, the most significant of which was the Fourth Resolution by which 'The Indians solemnly determined not to submit to the Ordinance in the event of its becoming law in the teeth of their opposition and to further all the penalties to such non- submission.'[53]

Gandhi was to confess later that he had not understood all the implications of the resolution he had helped to frame. The resolution was duly proposed, seconded and supported by various speakers. Among the speakers was Sheth Haji Habib, an old and experienced resident of South Africa. Deeply moved, he invoked *Khuda*. He used two terms, *'Khuda Kasam'* (an oath taken in the name of God) and 'Khuda' as *'hazar nazar'* (within the presence of God and with God as witness.) When Sheth Haji Habib came to the solemn declaration, Gandhi was 'at once startled and put on my guard. Only then did I fully realize my responsibility and the responsibility of the community.'[54]

Gandhi was aware that it was part of public life all over the world to pass resolutions which were either amended or were not observed by all concerned. Gandhi seized the moment, as he was to do time and again, intervened in the meeting and clarified the true nature of the proposed manner of passing the resolution. 'To pledge ourselves to take an oath in the name of that God with him as witness is not something to be trifled with. If having taken such an oath we violate our pledge we are guilty before God and man.'

[53] *Satyagraha in South Africa*, p.95

[54] *Satyagraha in South Africa*, p.96

He ended the long intervention on a personal note. He spoke of his personal responsibility. 'I am fully conscious of my responsibility in the matter. It is possible that a majority of those present here may take the pledge in a fit of enthusiasm or indignation but may weaken under the ordeal, and only a handful maybe left to force the final test. Even then there is only one course open to someone like me, to die but not to submit to the law. It is quite unlikely but even if everyone else flinched leaving me alone to face the music, I am confident that I would never violate my pledge.'

This long reminder of the defining moment is to remember that Satyagraha in its moment of conception is a covenant, a covenant of the self with God and of the self with the embodied person, if they can be thought of as distinct from one another. This element of pledge would become a central feature of Gandhi's thought and practice of Satyagraha.

Three years after this event Gandhi in his seed text *Hind Swaraj* explained the meaning of the term Satyagraha or passive resistance, a term that was an inadequate rendering of the term Satyagraha. In the Gujarati original he used two terms which do not appear to belong to a shared semantic universe, these are Satyagraha (Truth force) and *Atma Bala* (Soul force).

Before we examine the significance of this usage let us examine the terms through which he explains the idea of Satyagraha. 'Satyagraha or soul-force, is known in English as "passive resistance". This word refers to the path of self-suffering chosen by men to secure their rights. Its intent is reverse of armed force. When I refuse to do what I do not approve of, in so refusing I make use of Satyagraha or soul-force.'[55] In his English rendering Gandhi invoked the idea of conscience thereby establishing a relationship of Satyagraha with soul-force. He said, 'When I refuse to do a thing that is repugnant to my conscience, I use Soul Force.' There are two notions which are foregrounded: idea of conscience and the practice of suffering.

---

[55] MK Gandhi's *Hind Swaraj: A Critical Edition*, p.74

Idea of conscience would play an increasingly larger role in Gandhi's life. On 30 April 1933, Gandhi made a public announcement to go on an unconditional and irrevocable fast. This was his purest fast, a fast of twenty-one days. It was a fast for self-purification. He declared that this resolution was made in submission to his inner voice. Gandhi undertook the fast and of course, survived it. Subsequently he explained the voice of the inner voice. 'The night I got the inspiration, I had a terrible inner struggle. My mind was restless. I could see no way. The burden of my responsibility was crushing me. But what I did hear was a voice from afar and yet quite near. It was as unmistakable as some human voice definitely speaking to me, and irresistible. I was not dreaming at the time when I heard the voice. The hearing of the voice was preceded by a terrible struggle within me. Suddenly the voice came upon me. I listened, I made certain that it was the voice; and the struggle ceased. I was calm.' [56]

Gandhi claimed that he heard a voice, a voice that he described as a voice of Lord. But two questions arise. One, how does one acquire the capacity to hear the voice, and two, how does one know, make certain that it is the voice of truth, of Rama and not of Ravana?

The voice that he heard came from within and not from a force outside of him. Gandhi made a distinction between an outer force and a power beyond us. A power beyond us has its locus within us. It is superior to us, not subject to our command or willful action, but it is still located within us. He explained the nature of this power. 'Beyond us' means a 'power which is beyond our ego.'[57] According to Gandhi, one acquires the capacity to hear the voice when 'the ego is reduced to zero.'[58] Reducing the ego to zero requires total submission to Satya Narayan, truth as God. This is the true meaning of a covenant made in the name of God, and with God as witness.

The other characteristic of Satyagraha is that it is a mode of suffering. Suffering requires a witness, a being that would bear

---

[56] *CWMG*, vol. 55, p.255.
[57] *CWMG*, vol. 53, p.483.
[58] *CWMG*, vol. 53, p.483.

witness to, provide testimony of suffering. Of course, the final act of bearing witness is that of God. He recognizes the suffering of human heart pining for Truth as none else. But it is equally possible for us, the embodied beings, to bear witness to both suffering and Truth.

The suffering of Satyagraha requires both those acts of bearing witness. A Satyagrahi, therefore, must recognize the goodness of others, especially of those whose actions are sought to be opposed and transformed through the act of Satyagraha. It requires a conception of human nature which accords to the others however evil, capacity to recognize good, virtue, suffering and truth. This is why Gandhi called Satyagraha as love force. Love as the way in which Christ lived, suffered and gave up his life for us.

Satyagraha is also predicated upon a conception of means and ends that is unique to Gandhi. Gandhi likened means and ends to seed and tree, 'there is just the same inviolable connection between the means and the end as there is between the seed and the tree.'[59] Satyagraha also presupposes another relationship between the means and ends and that is of purity of both. Satyagraha requires both pure means and pure ends, the purity of ends does not justify the use of impure means. Means brings us to the Satyagrahi. Means and ends are linked by the practices of the Satyagrahi. The question 'what are pure means' can be answered in two ways. First, we can posit the Satyagrahi at the centre. Pure means are those which are employed by a person cleansed through a process of self-purification. The other answer could be that pure means are non-violent means. The quest for ahimsa is central to the pursuit of truth and hence for Satyagraha. Gandhi approaches the question of pure means from both these routes.

Gandhi described Satyagraha as a *sarvadhari,* which means both, in all directions, all sided, and something that everyone can bear, or carry. It affects both the parties, those who wield it and on those it is wielded. Gandhi lists several attributes in the discussion on Satyagraha in *Hind Swaraj.* Courage, freedom from fear (*abhaya*)

---

[59] *Hind Swaraj: A Critical Edition*, p. 66.

adopt poverty (*aparigraha* and *asteya*—non-stealing), steadfastness to truth, and brahmacharya. These would later develop into Gandhi's *Ekadesh Vrata*, the eleven vows.

Before we go to the relationship of Satyagraha and the Ekadesh Vrata, it is necessary to examine Gandhi's insistence upon *ahimsa*, not as a mere technique, as instrumentality but the philosophical necessity for ahimsa. This we can do by meditating upon the categories, the terms through which Gandhi sought to understand the nature of violence and non-violence, as also the opposition between the two. First a clarification about translation, the term 'ahimsa' is often translated as non-violence, non-killing or non-injury. Gandhi was aware that these terms do not always capture or contain the meaning of ahimsa. However, in his letters on the Ekadesh Vrata to the Ashramites written from Yeravda prison he chose to translate ahimsa as love. And it is this meaning that should inform our reading of ahimsa.

Gandhi described violence as 'brute-force' (*Sharir bal* or *top-bal* in Gujarati) and non-violence as 'soul force' (*atma bal* or *daya bal.*)

The distance between the two, between the beastly and the human is marked by non-violence. The idea of brute-force locates violence in the body and the instruments that the body can commend to inflict injury or to cause death. It connotes pure instrumentality. By locating violence within the realm of the beastly, Gandhi clearly points out the absence of the conscience, of the normative. He wrote, 'Non-violence is the law of our species as violence is the law of the brute. The spirit lies dormant in the brute but that of physical might. The dignity of man requires obedience to a higher law—to the strength of the spirit.'[60] The term soul-force is indicative of the conscience, of the human ability to discern the path of rectitude and act upon this judgment. In a speech given before the members of the Gandhi Seva Sangh in 1938 he brought this distinction sharply in focus. 'Physical strength is called brute-force. We are born with such strength... But

---

[60] *CWMG*, vol. 18, p. 133.

we are born as human beings in order that we may realize God that dwells within our hearts. This is the basic distinction between us and the beasts.... Along with the human form, we also have the human power—that is the power of non-violence. We can have an insight into the mystery of the soul-force. In that consists our humanity.'[61] It is only by this capacity for ahimsa that we can fulfil the human vocation, which for Gandhi is the pursuit for self-realization. Violence for Gandhi creates an impregnable distance in the path of self-realization. Gandhi said, 'The more he took to violence, the more he receded from Truth.'[62] As we, by use of violence recede from Truth, Satyagraha is not possible, as Satyagraha is the essence of this quest and yearning.

Satyagraha as a quest for truth is linked to the quest for Swaraj and for a civilization wherein self-realization is not structurally precluded. Gandhi's ideas of civilization and Swaraj were rooted in this possibility of knowing oneself. Gandhi argued in the *Hind Swaraj* that modern Western civilization in fact de-civilizes, and characterized it as Black age (Kali Yuga) or the Satanic civilization. It was so because modern civilization sought to shift the locus of human worth, making it untenable to have any sense of religion or morality. He wrote, 'Its true test lies in the fact that people living under it make bodily welfare the object of life.'[63] By making bodily welfare the object of life, modern civilization had shifted the locus of judgement outside the human being. It made not right conduct but objects the measure of human worth. In so doing, it had closed the possibility of knowing one self. He wrote, 'Civilization is that mode of conduct which points out to man the path of duty. Performance of duty and observance of morality are convertible terms. To observe morality is to attain mastery over our mind and passions. So doing, we know ourselves.'[64]

---

[61] *CWMG*, vol. 66, pp.420–1

[62] M.K. Gandhi, *From Yeravda Mandir*, p. 5.

[63] *Hind Swaraj: A Critical Edition*, p. 31.

[64] *Hind Swaraj: A Critical Edition*, p. 53.

This act of knowing oneself is not only the basis of spiritual life but also of political life. He defined Swaraj thus, 'It is Swaraj when we learn to rule ourselves.'[65] This act of ruling oneself is not possible without knowing oneself. Knowing the self requires capacity for ahimsa, steadfastness to truth, a delicately tuned breast capable of listening to the inner voice. Swaraj cannot be conceived in absence of Satyagraha. Satyagraha, with its invocation of the soul force, is based on this. Satyagraha with its necessity of purity of means and ends as also that of the satyagrahi is in the final instance based upon the recognitions of one's own conscience, on one's own conscience, on one's ability to listen to one's inner voice and submit to it.

This necessity about the purity of the Satyagrahi brings us to Gandhi's Ekadash Vrata, or the eleven observances. These taken together constitute what Gandhi called his experiments with Truth. This ever-wakefulness, he hoped would allow him to hear the call of truth as distinct from voice of untruth. This would give him the capacity to wait upon Satya Narayana. Prayer was one made to express his intense yearning to merge with God. It was his mode of waiting upon him for guidance. Only a heart cleansed through prayer could feel the utterly pure presence of God, of Truth.

This need for Vrata should not be underestimated in Gandhi's conception of Satyagraha. Gandhi later saw that his self-purification through the practice of brahmacharya was a necessary precondition for Satyagraha. He wrote: 'I can now see that all the principle events of my life, culminating in the vow of Brahmacharya were secretly preparing me for it.'[66] This is the most significant glimpse that we get of the inward preparation that was required for Satyagraha. In absence of the self-conscious, self-purification Satyagraha as Gandhi understood and practised it would not have come to him. He also said that Satyagraha cannot be sustained without a lifelong and continuous striving for purification.

---

[65] *Hind Swaraj: A Critical Edition*, p.56.
[66] An Autobiography; *CWMG*, vol. 39, p. 254.

In this we have an understanding of Gandhi's experiment and his quest. His quest is to know himself, to attain moksha, that is, to see God (Truth) face-to-face. In order to fulfil his quest, he must be an Ashramite, a Satyagrahi and a seeker after Swaraj. Experiment with Truth in this sense is an experiment with self-knowledge, with attaining mastery over himself, with performance of duty and observance of morality, with Satyagraha, with Swaraj, with true civilization and with brahmacharya.

Since he never claimed to have attained it, truth had to be practised every day, at every moment of wakefulness and also of sleep. This quest is made possible by the means of Ashram and its observances. Satyagraha and Swaraj as modes of self-realization are based on Truth because without Truth there can be no knowledge. That is why the word *chit*, or knowledge is associated with *sat*. Hence, Truth becomes a primary observance, it constitutes the root of the Ashram. What can be known by Truth is knowledge, what is excluded from it is not Truth, not true knowledge. Steadfastness to Truth, even unto death, requires immense and inexhaustible faith in God of Truth. And yet, Gandhi would confess that such perfect self-knowledge, realization of perfect Truth might not be possible so long as we are imprisoned in a mortal body.

This impossibility leads the seeker to ahimsa or love. Violence and quest for truth cannot exist together; as Truth is not outside but within and as Gandhi said; 'Hence, the more he took to violence, the more he receded from Truth.'[67] If violence makes a person recede from truth, it also makes a person recede from self. Thus violence leads to self-forgetfulness, therefore neither Satyagraha nor Swaraj, which are based on self-realization are possible with violence. Thus Truth is the end and Ahimsa the means to it.

A man whose only object is Truth, his method Satyagraha cannot be faithful to anything but the Truth. 'The man, who is wedded to Truth and worships faith alone, proves unfaithful to her, if he

---

[67] Gandhi, MK; *From Yeravada Mandir*, translated from original Gujarati by Valiji Govindji Desai (Ahmedabad: Navajivan, 1932, 2003), p. 5.

applies his talents to anything else.'[68] This is the true conception of brahmacharya, *charya* that is mode of conduct that brings one closer to *Brahman*, that is Truth.

This conception of brahmacharya made all eleven observances essential to self-purification, integral to surrender. Towards the end of his life they lost all distinctiveness. He said, 'Therefore, it is essential that all the disciplines should be taken as one. This enables one to realize the full meaning and significance of brahmacharya. In practice he alone is a true brahmachari who observes, in thought, word and deed, the eleven-fold vow in its entirety.'[69] He asserted that there could be no hierarchy in vows, 'All vows have the same importance. Violation of anyone of them amounts to violation of all.'[70] Such an aspirant does not, according to Gandhi, need 'Walls of Protection'.[71] Gandhi claimed that he never observed the traditional rules prescribed for a brahmchari in India. He enumerated them: 'Thus he may not live among women, animals and eunuchs, he may not teach a woman alone or even in a group, he may not sit on the same mat with a woman, he may not look at any part of a woman's body, he may not take milk, curd, ghee or any fatty substances nor indulge in baths and oil massage.'[72] Gandhi believed that none of the above restraints was necessary, at any rate not for himself. He did give up animal substances, with some modification. Gandhi asserted, 'A true *brahmachari* will shun false restraints. He must create his own fences according to his limitations, breaking them down when he feels that they are unnecessary.'[73]

---

[68] Gandhi, MK; *From Yeravada Mandir*, translated from original Gujarati by Valiji Govindji Desai (Ahmedabad: Navajivan, 1932, 2003), p. 8.

[69] *CWMG*, vol. 88, p. 59.

[70] *CWMG*, vol. 88, p. 332.

[71] On 8 June 1947 Gandhi wrote an essay under this title for *Harijan*. See, *CWMG*, vol. 88, pp. 100–2.

[72] *CWMG*, vol. 88, p. 101.

[73] *CWMG*, vol. 88, p. 102.

Gandhi repeatedly spoke of his desire to become a brahmachari like Sukhadev, who it is believed experienced no passion whatsoever, so complete was his brahmacharya that those around him also were cleansed of their passions, they for the moment of that contact became pure and unsullied like him. This ideal is also the ideal of the *sthitpragnya*, one whose intellect is secure, as expressed in the Gita. Gandhi said that long before brahmacharya came to him as a necessary observance he was attracted to the Gita's sthitpragnya contained in the Verses 62 and 63 of the Second Discourse. They read:

> *If one*
> *Ponders on the objects of the sense, there springs*
> *Attraction, from attraction grows desire,*
> *Desire flames to fierce passion, passion breeds*
> *Recklessness, then memory—all betrayed—*
> *Lets noble purpose go, and saps the mind,*
> *Till purpose, mind, and man are all undone.*[74]

The essential training of the brahmachari is to learn to be indifferent to the pleasures which the senses provide. A sthitpragnya is one who puts away 'all the cravings that arise in the mind and finds comfort for himself only from the *atman*,'[75] and one 'whose senses are reined in on all sides from their objects,'[76] so that the mind is 'untroubled in sorrows and longeth not for joys, who is free from passion, fear and wrath,'[77] who knows attachment nowhere; only such a brahmachari can be in the world ' moving among sense objects with the sense weaned from likes and dislikes and brought under the control of the atman.'[78]

---

[74] Sir Edwin Arnold's translation. See, Gandhi, M. K. *An Autobiography: A Critical Edition*, p. 146.

[75] II:55.

[76] II:68.

[77] II:56.

[78] II:64.

One mode by which the mind is so trained is an act of fasting, not in the sense of mortification of the flesh but in the sense of *upvas*. Gandhi knew that according to the Gita, 'when a man starves his senses, the objects of those senses disappear for him, but not the yearning for them.'[79] The yearning disappears when one has a vision of the Supreme Truth.

Yajna

Gandhi argued that this verse in fact advocated fasting for self-purification. Fast as self-purification is upvas (to dwell closer to Him), upvas can be done only when fasting of senses is accompanied by a desire to see God, as 'there is no prayer without fasting and there is no real fast without prayer.'[80]

The other is yajna. The Gita declared that 'Together with the sacrifice did the Lord of beings create,'[81] and the world would sustain so long as there was sacrifice, as 'sacrifice produced rain'.[82] Gandhi found the word yajna full of beauty and power. He interpreted the word to mean sacrifice, an act of service. He saw this idea of sacrifice as basis of all religions. His ideal was Jesus Christ. It was he who had shown the path, Gandhi said that the word yajna had to be understood in the way Jesus lived and died. It was not sacrifice when other lives were destroyed, the best sacrifice was giving up one's own life. He wrote, 'Jesus put on a crown of thorns to win salvation for his people, allowed his hands and feet to be nailed and suffered agonies before he gave up the ghost. This has been the law of yajna from immemorial times, without yajna the earth cannot exist even for a moment.'[83] Yajna for Gandhi was service to others and in the ultimate sense sacrifice of self. He said, 'This body has been given to

---

[79] II:59.
[80] *CWMG*, vol. 53, p. 259.
[81] III:10.
[82] III:14.
[83] *CWMG*, vol. 20, p. 404.

us only in order that we may serve all creation with it. And therefore, says the Gita, he who eats without offering yajna eats stolen food. Every single act of one who would lead a life of purity should be in the nature of yajna.'[84]

But how does one perform such a sacrifice in daily life? Gandhi's response was twofold: for one he turned once again to the Bible and the other was uniquely his own.

'Earn thy bread by the sweat of thy brow,' says the Bible. Gandhi made this central to the life of the Ashram and borrowed a term 'bread labour' from Tolstoy to describe the nature of work. This was an eternal principle; it was dharma, duty, to perform bread labour, as those who did not perform this form of yajna ate, according to the Gita, stolen food. The other form of yajna was according to Gandhi peculiar to his times, as every age may and should have its own particular yajna, this was the yuga-dharma. Gandhi said that the yajna of his times was spinning; it was the yuga-dharma. Spinning was an obligatory Ashram observance; each member was required to spin 140 threads daily, each thread measuring 4 feet.[85] This spinning was called *sutra-yajna* or sacrificial spinning. As his conviction that sacrificial spinning was the only true yajna for his times deepened, he along with the Ashramites resolved to change the name of the Ashram itself. Ashram, hitherto called Satyagraha Ashram was renamed Udyog Mandir (literally, Temple of Industry) explaining the term Udyog Gandhi said, 'Udyog has to be read in the light of the Bhagavad Gita.'[86]

This striving to be a bhakta, a jnani, a seeker after Swaraj, an Ashramite, a Satyagrahi, whose only true devotion through an unceasing practice of brahmacharya was to Truth, was for Gandhi the only real part of him. 'What is of abiding worth is my insistence

---

[84] Desai, Mahadev; *The Gospel of Selfless Action or The Gita According to Gandhi*, p. 177.

[85] Initially spinning was time bound, half an hour; later the measure was changed to threads spun.

[86] *CWMG*, vol. 43, p. 203.

upon truth, non-violence and brahmacharya which is the real part of me. That permanent part of me however small, is not to be despised. It is my all.'[87] It was for this reason that Gandhi insisted that brahmacharya must remain inviolate in any condition. He sought through this the capacity to hear his inner voice, to submit to Satya Narayan and the power that purity of life, strict vigilance and ceaseless application produce. He believed and hoped that his submission to Truth would produce in him ahimsa that would touch and imbue others with similar ahimsa. He was conscious of the distance that he needed to walk in this quest. 'I have not acquired that control over my thoughts that I need for my researches in non-violence. If my non-violence has to be contagious and infectious, I must acquire greater control over my thoughts.'[88]

He, time and again, described himself as an imperfect brahmachari. The sense of imperfection, the awareness of one's sinfulness is mark of a bhakta. Bhakta is a sinful one and Gandhi like Tulsi and Surdas thought of himself as one. 'Tulsidas considered himself to be the most sinful person, "who is there so crooked, so wicked and so sensual as I?" sang Surdas.'[89] This was not a language of modesty but an expression of what the heart felt. What Gandhi claimed for himself was not to be known as perfect brahmachari, a claim that would sully brahmacharya and dim the lustre of truth. 'Why should it not be sufficient for the world to know that I am a genuine seeker, that I am wide awake, and that my striving is ceaseless and unbending?'[90] He therefore could assert that his life and thoughts tend towards that state. After his public admission of his discharge many associates questioned him on his seemingly unattainable quest. They argued that perfect brahmacharya that he sought cannot be attained by one who lives and serves the world. Gandhi argued that unattainability of the ideal is not a failing of the ideal but of the seeker. The quest

---

[87] *CWMG*, vol. 30, p. 16.

[88] *CWMG*, vol. 67, p. 197.

[89] *CWMG*, vol. 26, p. 33.

[90] *CWMG*, vol. 30, p. 15

for perfection is the only endeavour given to the seeker. He also argued that if the same measure were to be applied, cultivation of ahimsa would also be negated. 'A perfect brahmachari should remain unaffected by passion in any circumstance. If you say that nobody has ever been, and nobody will ever be, able to cultivate such freedom from passion, then it means that we should abandon the struggle to cultivate brahmacharya. If this is correct, then it follows that one can never cultivate perfect ahimsa.'[91] Gandhi was aware that in his self-chosen path there was no relative merit, either he had to succeed or accept failure as his lot. A close associate wrote reassuringly to him that Gandhi was too pure for sexual consciousness. He dispelled this impression quickly. 'I wish this was a true certificate. I am sorry to have to disillusion you. I am trying to lose that consciousness. But I have not lost it. Loss of that consciousness cannot be relative; it must be absolute. I do not know of any historical instance. It is difficult, I know, for history to record such instances.'[92]

It was also argued that Gandhi should eschew all contacts with all women under all circumstances and at any rate. This shifted the agency of his failings to women associates. Gandhi was quick to rebuke this: 'You miss the crucial point. It is not the woman who is to be blamed. I am the culprit. I must attain the required purity.'[93] He had another argument. His experiments in brahmacharya were done as a satyagrahi. An experiment of a satyagrahi cannot harm anyone else because the subject and the object of the experiment is the satyagrahi. 'If my experiment is that of a Satyagrahi, no harm at all can come to anyone.'[94]

In the final years of his life Gandhi gave himself up to the Ramanama. He was surrounded by failure and a raging fire. It was at once a sign of Gandhi's deep faith and his utter despondency and loneliness. Ramanama became the cure and perhaps the only form

---

[91] *CWMG*, vol. 67, p. 106
[92] *CWMG*, vol. 47, p. 9.
[93] *CWMG*, vol. 67, p. 118.
[94] *CWMG*, vol. 79, p. 192.

of cure that he came to rely upon. In the midst of intense debate about the nature of India's independence, Gandhi often retreated to Uruli-Kanchan, a naturopathy clinic. The retreat was a mode of finding a cure, a healing, not only for the diseased body of patients that he treated but also for the disease of India.[95] To one and all he asked to recite the Ramanama with a pure heart. The cure for the disease, both of the body and the body-politic of India, lay in the Ramanama. He spoke of Ramanama as infallible remedy, as he put it in Gujarati *ramban*.[96] Ramanama was no longer a symbol, nor was it a metaphor. Ramanama had become the thing itself. Ramanama alluded to no reality or presence outside of itself. It had become for Gandhi, real. It was incumbent upon him to prove this reality. He was convinced that the violence that surrounded him was due to his own failing, his imperfect ahimsa and imperfect brahmacharya. As he walked through the ravaged villages of Noakhali and Bihar, sleep eluded him. Even the chanting of Ramanama failed to bring repose. He lamented: 'Why can't I, who preach all healing virtues of Ramanama to others, be content to rely on it exclusively myself?'[97]

Surrounded by raging fire Gandhi embarked upon the final yajna. Manu Gandhi became a partner in this yajna, which involved sharing his bed. His closest associates termed this 'experiment' as immoral, as adharma. Gandhi responded to almost universal opprobrium with uncharacteristic spiritual arrogance. He argued that his endeavour was to expand the notion of brahmacharya itself. 'A reformer cannot afford to wait till others are converted, he must take the lead and venture forth alone even in the teeth of universal opposition. I want to test, enlarge and revise the current definition of brahmacharya, by which you swear in light of my observations, study and experience.'[98]

---

[95] The metaphor of the diseased India had stayed with him since the time that he wrote the *Hind Swaraj*; wherein he spoke of the need to find a physician for diseased India.

[96] Literally, the arrow of Rama, as infallible as the arrow.

[97] *CWMG*, vol. 86, p. 218.

[98] *CWMG*, vol. 87, pp. 90–1

He claimed to represent true brahmacharya better than any of his associates.[99]

His other argument was far more fundamental. He claimed that what he had embarked upon was yajna and not an experiment. An experiment has a beginning and an end, it is subject to human volition, while yajna being duty, being dharma was not so. '"Experiment" or *prayog* is an ill-chosen word. I have used it. It differs from the present in the sense that one could be stopped by me, the other being dharma could not be.'[100]

Gandhi seems to suggest that his submission to Truth had not left in him any vestige of autonomy. He hoped for this reason that his yajna would give him a glimpse of the ideal and if he were to have that even fleeting glimpse the world would be redeemed. 'I believe that even if only one brahmachari of my conception comes into being, the world will be redeemed.'[101] In this short-lived yajna he felt that his strivings had reached their culmination and that finally he had the glimpse of the pure state. He shared this with Manu Gandhi, his partner in the yajna. 'I have successfully practised the eleven vows undertaken by me. This is the culmination of my striving for the last sixty years.... In this yajna I got a glimpse of the ideal of truth and purity for which I have been aspiring.'[102] This is the most direct and clear statement of Gandhi's claim, never before this yajna did he ever claim to have had even the slightest, most fleeting glimpse of the ideal of truth and purity.

Dark Night of the Soul

Gandhi's quest to attain perfect brahmacharya and through that perfect ahimsa did not go unchallenged. It was argued by his associates at the Ashram—both at Sabarmati and at Sevagram—that he, as a

---

[99] *CWMG*, p. 91.
[100] *CWMG*, p. 104.
[101] *CWMG*, vol. 88, p. 348.
[102] *CWMG*, vol. 87, p. 384.

practising brahmchari, should eschew all contact with women and follow the nine-fold fortification[103] prescribed for a brahmachari. At Sabarmati, his co-workers, probably all male, told him that his practice of walking with his hands on shoulders of grown-up girls and women offended accepted notions of decency. But the practice continued after a discussion with inhabitants of the Ashram. The same question was brought before him again in September 1935, but this time those who argued against it were armed with evidence that his practice was encouraging others and they sought justification in Gandhi's practice. Gandhi, though unconvinced of the need of a practising brahmachari to erect 'walls of protection', decided through an open note published in *Harijan* of 21 September 1935 to renounce the practice. 'Whilst I do not believe in a *brahmacharya* which ever requires a wall of protection against the touch of the opposite sex and will fail if exposed to the least temptation, I am not unaware of the dangers attendant upon the freedom I have taken.'[104] This renunciation proved short-lived because the women in the Ashram, particularly Sushila Nayyar, Prabhavati, Raj Kumari Amrit Kaur and Mirabehn objected to such exclusion from his touch. In April 1938 Gandhi had that 'defiling', 'degrading' and 'dirty', experience that we have dealt with in the preceding section. As the news of his 'fall' and his despondency became widely known he was advised once again to eschew all contact with all women—including Kasturba and Dr Sushila Nayyar, his physician. Shaken, deeply perturbed and nursing fundamental doubts about his practice of brahmacharya, Gandhi was more receptive to suggestion than ever before and on 2 June 1928, he announced his decision to follow the traditional conduct expected of a brahmachari and eschew any physical contact with all women, including Ba who now was the recipient of his daily ministration. He addressed a confidential circular to the inhabitants of the Ashram

---

[103] These are i) co-habitation, ii) conversation, iii) proximity, iv) observation, v) absence of barriers, vi) memories of having been a house-holder, vii) control of palate, viii), avoidance of over-eating, ix) sloth.

[104] *CWMG*, vol. 61, p. 437.

wherein he called his conduct a violation of brahmacharya. He argued that, probably echoing the argument made to him, it was wrong of him to take freedoms that he forbade his co-workers.

'Yesterday it became clear to me,' he said, 'that it had been wrong on my part to forbid my co-workers to avail themselves, the freedom I had given myself. I cannot understand how I could have put up with it all these years. I feel my action was impelled by vanity and jealousy. If my experiment was dangerous, I should not have undertaken it. And if it was worth trying, I should have encouraged my co-workers to undertake in on my conditions. My experiment was a violation of the established norms of *brahmacharya*. Such a right can be enjoyed only by a saint like Sukhdevji who can remain pure in thought, word and deed at all times of day. Having thus deliberated I arrived at the decision yesterday.'[105] In another letter he berated himself and said that his conduct 'was a result of abysmal ignorance and certainly conceit, too.'[106]

In utter despair he sought succour from his many 'children', particularly his 'daughters' whose touch he had just renounced. He wrote to Mira, 'I shall feel pride in my being a parent to so many children, if any one of them will give me a lifting hand and pull me out of the well of despair.'[107]

There was a fundamental flaw in Gandhi's thinking which was made apparent to him by his 'daughters'. Gandhi had been led to believe that his involuntary emission while fully awake had been caused because he remained in close physical proximity to women. It is women, the argument went, who cause a brahmachari to fall from his exalted state, through temptation. As he gradually was 'pulled out of the well of despair' he re-awakened to the reality of his daughters, something that he had known but despair had led to amnesia. He knew that women were not the cause of his fall. No woman, including Kasturba, even during their years of sexual intimacy, had ever been a

---

[105] *CWMG*, vol. 67, pp. 104–5.

[106] *CWMG*, vol. 67, p. 132.

[107] *CWMG*, vol. 67, p. 61.

'temptress'. No woman, he was to say later 'had any attraction for me in the same sense that my wife had.'[108] He also realized that women whose touch he was asked to eschew, whose proximity was sought not only to be circumscribed but prohibited were all celibate—Sushila, Prabhavati, Mira, Amrit Kaur and others were nothing but as pure as him. He also realized that this exclusion, this absence, silence and marginalization of women from his life and of his from their lives was to deny his own striving, that is, to become mentally a woman. They had discussed together without any fear or inhibitions matters most personal and private like menstruation, bodily functions, child-bearing, breast-feeding and prison-going. In the Ashram and in the public domain women were his 'co-workers'. He knew that many Muslim women did not observe purdah before him. He and the women around him knew that Gandhi had consciously adopted many activities and self-practices traditionally associated either as feminine or belonging to the domain of women's work. Two self-practices that define him—spinning and fasting—belonged to women's work and ritual practices. His cherished self-image was that of a 'nurse'. As Gandhi re-awakened to his deeply held convictions he realized that he had professed an un-truth. Women cannot be blamed for his failings. He wrote, 'You miss the crucial point. It is not the woman who is to blame, I am the culprit. I must attain required purity.'[109] He admitted that 'The imperfection of *brahmacharya* in me has some other causes.'[110] As Gandhi re-established in his mind the parity of women as co-brahmacharis the need for walls of protection disappeared. On 17 September 1938, he gave up the repugnant practice of observing nine-fold fortification and resumed his natural conduct towards women and therefore towards himself.

On 23 November 1925, after two days of agony, Gandhi decided to go on a fast for seven days. There was a 'moral lapse' among young boys and some girls at the Satyagraha Ashram at Sabarmati.

---

[108] *CWMG*, vol. 70, p. 314.
[109] *CWMG*, vol. 67, p. 118.
[110] *CWMG*, vol. 67, p. 363.

For Gandhi the purity or impurity of the principal worker affected the community. If he were free from fault, the atmosphere would be affected by his innocence. Thus, untruth among those around him was a symptom of deep failing, a failing which could only be attributed to him. It was a sign that the light with which he aspired to lead his life still eluded him. What he was required to do was to reach deep within and seek to dispel the darkness.

In 1946 as Bengal and later Bihar erupted in a macabre orgy of violence and slaughter, Gandhi sank into deep despair. He began to deny his body food and went on a semi-fast. He wrote to Jawaharlal Nehru from Sodepur near Calcutta on 5 November 1946, 'And the cry came from within: "why should you be a witness to this slaughter? If your word, which is as clear as daylight, is not heeded, your work is over. Why do you not die?"'[111] The same day he wrote to Sardar Patel, 'My going on living depends entirely on complete peace being established in India.'[112] Even as violence suggested a deep and collective failure of ahimsa, of non-violence, Gandhi remained steadfast in his faith in ahimsa. He said to the people of Bihar, 'I am in no way ashamed of my ahimsa. I have come to Bengal to see how far in the nick of time my ahimsa is able to express itself in me.'[113]

Ahimsa had to express itself in him. And when it did, Gandhi believed, ahimsa would re-establish peace in India. To find that ahimsa in himself Gandhi decided to go into physical isolation in order to dwell within himself. 'Where do I stand? Do I represent this ahimsa in my person? If I do, then deceit and hatred that poison the atmosphere should dissolve. It is only by going into isolation from my companions, those on whose help I have relied all along, and standing on my own two feet that I shall find my bearing and also test my faith in God.'[114] On 20 November 1946 he declared to the people his resolve to live in a violence-ravaged village of

---

[111] *CWMG*, vol. 86, p. 78.

[112] *CWMG*, vol. 86, p. 79.

[113] *CWMG*, vol. 86, p. 92.

[114] *CWMG*, vol. 86, p. 134.

Srirampur with two companions: Professor Nirmal Kumar Bose, foremost anthropologist, his Bengali teacher and interpreter and Shri Parsuram, a stenographer. Never since his return to India in 1915 was Gandhi physically so isolated. Srirampur had 1450 Muslim and 650 Hindu inhabitants with most Hindus having left the village. Nirmal Kumar Bose described the hut in which they were to spend 43 nights from 20 November 1946 to 1 January 1947. 'The house where we had put up consisted of a few detached huts made of wooden frames, with walls as well as thatches of galvanized iron sheets. The floor was mud… Gandhiji occupied a spacious hut in the centre of a courtyard, surrounded on all sides by thick groves of areca and coconut.'[115]

In the statement in which he announced his resolve to live in isolation, Gandhi for the first and perhaps the only time in his life seemed to doubt the attributes of truth and ahimsa. He questioned whether truth and ahimsa would measure up to his faith in them. Hitherto, Gandhi had doubted his capacity, his striving to measure up to truth and ahimsa. His absolute faith in these values that he held as eternal and immutable is shaken. He said, 'I find myself in midst of exaggeration and falsity. I am unable to discover the truth. There is terrible mutual distrust, oldest friendships have snapped, truth and ahimsa by which I swear, and which have, to my knowledge, sustain me for sixty years, seem to fail to show the attributes I have ascribed to them.'[116] On the same day to the inmates of Sevagram he wrote saying that they should give up any hope of his ever returning to the Ashram. His belief that he would never return to the Ashram was to come true. In the same letter he doubted the power of satyagraha. 'Is the Satyagraha of my conception a weapon of the weak or really that of the strong? I must realize the latter or lay down my life in the attempt to attain in.'[117]

---

[115] Bose, Nirmal Kumar, *My Days with Gandhi* (New Delhi: Orient Longman, 1974, 1987 re-print), p. 50.

[116] *CWMG*, vol. 86, p. 138.

[117] *CWMG*, vol. 86, p. 143.

The dark night of the soul that Gandhi experienced was long and gloomy. He had in the same day doubted truth, ahimsa and satyagraha. He told Amiya Chakravarty, a long-time associate of poet Tagore, of his darkness, 'I am groping for light. I am surrounded by darkness, but I must act or refrain as guided by truth. I find that I have not the patience and the technique needed in these tragic circumstances, suffering and evil often overwhelm me and I stew in my own juice.'[118]

Nirmal Kumar Bose heard him muttering to himself, '*Kya Karun? Kya Karun?*'[119] A question that did not leave him till 30 January 1948, as he kept repeating it like a refrain, a *namasmaran*.

In a note to Pyarelal on 4 December 1946 he spoke of darkness and his inadequacy. 'I am still groping. I see I have not yet found the key to ahimsa. Here I am out to perform a stupendous yajna, but my unfitness for the task is being demonstrated at every step.'[120]

Although written in despair and speaking of darkness this note to Pyarelal shows a fundamental shift in Gandhi's perception. For the past several weeks he had spoken about the failure of the eternal values of truth, ahimsa and satyagraha to demonstrate, in some ways measure up to, the attributes that he had ascribed to them. This showed a fundamental doubt, a doubt so basic that it would have nullified his quest to attain truth, ahimsa and practice satyagraha, because they were found wanting. The solitude of Srirampur and his in-dwelling had made him aware that perhaps the locus of that failure and despair was within him. He found himself unfit for the task, he was unable to find the key to ahimsa. Once this shift in locus took place the nature of his own responsibility became clear to Gandhi. He must dwell within, find his communion with truth, search himself for violence within him, and purify himself of all desire that give rise to untruth and violence. He had to test his brahmacharya— not celibacy of which he was no longer anxious—as the only path

---

[118] *CWMG*, vol. 86, p. 192.
[119] 'What should I do? What should I do?, *My Days with Gandhi*, p. 63.
[120] *CWMG*, vol. 86, p. 195.

that would lead him to Satyanarayana. If he was found wanting in pursuit of such brahmacharya both truth and ahimsa would elude him and make his night of darkness even longer. He wrote, 'I do not remember to have experienced such darkness in my life ever before, and the night seems long.'[121]

It was at this never-ending night of darkness and despair that Manu, now a young woman of eighteen re-entered his life to become a partner in his yajna, to become the witness to his striving, to provide testimony to his utterance of Ramanama at the moment of his death.

Since their release from Aga Khan Palace detention Manu and Gandhi had been separated. Gandhi had come out of Aga Khan having cremated Kasturba and Mahadev a 'broken reed' and felt that he had nothing to give to Manu. She intermittently spent time in his company at Sevagram, Mahabaleshwar and Panchgani, acquired formal training in nursing at Sevagram from Dr Sushila Nayyar and later at Dr Dinshaw Mehta's clinic at Poona. She had decided against marriage and as security of her financial safety her father Jaisukhlal had made a provision of a trust fund—the deed of which was drafted by Gandhi.

Two days before he was to leave for Noakhali, on 4 November 1946, Gandhi received a letter from Manu and another from Jaisukhlal. In response, Gandhi wrote of his incapacity to bear witness to the violence in Bihar. Therein he wrote, 'These days, therefore, Manu should be with me. But it seems it is now impossible for her to come. May she be out of trouble and be happy.'[122]

By the time the letter reached Manu on 1 December 1946 at Mahuva in Saurashtra, Gandhi had decided upon his isolation and had scattered all his associates in the ravaged villages of Noakhali. Manu, moved by his words that her place was with him, wrote to him the same day placing a condition that she would come but would not want to be in a village away from him. 'I do not wish to come if you want me to work in some village away from you. I am

---

121 *CWMG*, vol. 86, p. 198.
122 *CWMG*, vol. 86, p. 73.

doing that work as best as I can at this end. On the other hand, I am eager and anxious to be with you, if only you will let me help you and look after you.'[123] Gandhi invited Manu and Jaisukhlal to Noakhali with a proviso that she could go back if she found the atmosphere dangerous. Manu accompanied by Jaisukhlal reached Srirampur on 19 December 1946 at 3 p.m., Gandhi welcomed her, 'So you *have* come.'[124] Indeed she had, never to leave his side till the moment of his death.

That night at 12.45 a.m. Gandhi woke up Manu and had a long talk with her and explained her dharma, asked her to consult Jaisukhlal and take a decision about remaining by his side or leaving. He noted in his diary that she remained steadfast.

We do not know the exact date but probably soon after she reached Srirampur Gandhi and Manu shared the same bed. And with that began what Gandhi called his yajna—a duty that could not be forsaken—and what all his associates and family without exception called adharma. The diaries pertaining to this and subsequent periods would be published in the second volume.

This practice for Gandhi was not without precedent. He had then called it an 'experiment', and as an experiment it was available for scrutiny to others and could be stopped either by his own decision or at times at the urging of others. That he had conducted such experiments in the past was public knowledge, not just within his close circle of associates but was publicly known as he had written about it in various letters and made public through his journals. Even in the face of wide-ranging criticism, Gandhi had continued with the practice. Gandhi's argument was that as a practising brahmachari he had a duty to examine himself of any trace of impurity, carnal desire and passion within him, and that he would continue the practice so long as such self-examination was necessary.

Nirmal Kumar Bose, who witnessed this yajna, speculated on the possible motives of Gandhi. 'Saints have lived in India who have been

[123] *The Lonely Pilgrim*, p. 5.
[124] *The Lonely Pilgrim*, p. 8.

able to rise above the impulse of sex by identifying themselves with those belonging to the opposite sex. In the case of the mystic Shree Ramakrishna, it is said that his psychological identification reached such a high degree that somatic changes followed, and discharge of blood through the pores of his skin appeared periodically during one phase of his life, as in the case of women. But Gandhiji, even within the secret recesses of his heart, never gave himself up with absolute abandon to an intensity of feeling.'[125]

Bose questioned Gandhi about the practice and also cautioned him that he had observed among Gandhi's women co-workers a tendency to view Gandhi as an 'exclusive possession'.[126]

Bose reported on the conversation: 'In explaining his position, Gandhiji said that it was indeed true that he had permitted women workers to use his bed, this being undertaken as a spiritual experiment at times. Even if there were no trace of passion in him of which he was conscious, it was not unlikely that a residue might be left over, and that would make trouble for the girls who took part in this experiment. He had also asked them if, even unconsciously, he had been responsible for evoking the least shade of evil sentiment in their hearts.'[127]

The first person to object to this yajna was Parsuram who, apart from NK Bose, was the only other person accompanying Gandhi. In a letter, he asked Gandhi to be relieved of duty as he did not wish to bear witness to a practice that he could not agree with. He probably asked Gandhi to immediately stop the practice. Gandhi replied, 'I cannot concede to your demands.'[128] Parasuram left Gandhi on 2 January 1947. Gandhi's closest associates, persons who were aware of Gandhi's spiritual quest, his experiments in all fields—not just brahmacharya—were deeply perturbed by Gandhi's response and approach to Parsuram. In February 1947 Kishorelal Mashruwala,

---

[125] *My Days with Gandhi*, p. 177.
[126] *My Days with Gandhi*, p. 115.
[127] *My Days with Gandhi*, p. 116.
[128] *CWMG*, vol. 86, p. 299.

Swami Anand and Narahri Parikh expressed deepest reservation and relinquished charge of the *Harijan* papers and all correspondence related to them. Sardar Patel and Gandhi's youngest son Devadas also objected; not just on the nature of the experiment itself, and not specific to Manu's participation, albeit it is likely that their unease also stemmed from the fact that Manu was in the place of a granddaughter to Gandhi. Their critique, as can be discerned from Gandhi's writings, was fundamental. They argued that Gandhi had come to regard adharma as dharma and the practice could only be regarded as a violation of brahmacharya. Their charge of adharma was the most fundamental charge that could have been levied against Gandhi. The very claim that Gandhi made for the necessity of the practice was based on his belief that his was not an 'experiment', but a yajna, which was his dharma, a duty that could not be forsaken. In a letter to GD Birla, Gandhi acknowledged the possibility that 'A Satyagrahi may end up as a *duragrahi* if he comes to regard untruth as truth.'[129] The only distinction between a satyagrahi and a duragrahi being the capacity to recognize truth from untruth. In such a case Gandhi felt, 'it becomes the duty of all friends to oppose me vehemently.'[130] He told Birla, 'Sardar is quite clear in his mind that what I look upon as my dharma is really adharma. Devadas of course has written as much.'[131]

Probably the unanimous opinion of his closest associates that he had lost capacity to distinguish between truth and untruth and that his practice was adharma and violation not only of moral conduct but also of brahmacharya motivated Gandhi to write and seek opinion of three persons whose spiritual training and quest he viewed with respect. These were Satish Chandra Mukherji (also known as Nanga Baba), who had also spent two months at Sabarmati Ashram, and the Bhave brothers—Vinoba and Balkrishna.

---

[129] *CWMG*, vol. 86, p. 464.
[130] *CWMG*, vol. 86, p. 464.
[131] *CWMG*, vol. 86, p. 464.

To Mukherji he wrote, 'And now I put before you a poser. A young girl (19) who is in place of a granddaughter to me by relation shares the same bed with me, not for any animal satisfaction but for me (to me) valid moral reasons. She claims to be free from passion that a girl of her age generally has and I claim to be a practised *brahmachari*. Do you see anything bad or unjustifiable in this proposition? I ask this question because some of my intimate associates hold it to be wholly unjustifiable and even breach of *brahmacharya*. I hold a totally opposite view.'[132]

To Vinoba he wrote: 'The friends in our circle have been very much upset because of Manu's sleeping with me. Kishorelal's agony is difficult to bear. He is so upset that he is on the verge of breaking down. ...My own mind, however, is becoming firmer than ever. For it has been my belief for a long time that that alone is *brahmacharya* that requires no hedges. My experiment arose from this belief... Manu's sleeping with me is not part of my experiment but it is part of the present *yajna*.'[133]

To Balkrishna Bhave he wrote: 'For me Manu's sleeping with me is a matter of dharma, and I am resolved to drive home the lesson that a person cannot give up what is a matter of dharma to him for love of those who are dear to him or out of fear of anybody. If in a situation like this I give up what I believe to be my dharma through false regard for friends or fear or love, my *yajna* would remain incomplete and bear no fruit. This is my side of the case. Kishorelal's side as far as I can understand it, is the opposite. He thinks that I have come to regard *adharma* as dharma and that, therefore, my practice dishonours my *brahmacharya* and sets a bad example to people.'[134]

From Gandhi's correspondence we know that Vinoba wrote to him a 'frank letter', most likely expressing disagreement with Gandhi's thought and practice. In March 1947 Gandhi wrote to

---

[132] *CWMG*, vol. 86, p. 414.

[133] *CWMG*, vol. 86, pp. 452–3.

[134] *CWMG*, vol. 86, pp. 475–6.

him, 'I have your frank letter. Somehow I am not convinced by your argument.'[135]

As 'small-talk', and 'whispers' acquired a life of their own, Gandhi decided to publicly acknowledge his yajna and invited people to bless the effort.

In a public prayer meeting on 1 February 1947 at Amishpara village Gandhi referred to 'small talks, whispers and innuendos' going around of which he had become aware. He told the gathering that in the midst of so much suspicion, distrust and falsehood he did not want his 'innocent acts' to be misunderstood and misrepresented. He told the gathering that he had his granddaughter with him. The Prophet had discounted eunuchs made such by operation. But he welcomed eunuchs made such through prayer by God. His was that aspiration. It was in spirit of God's eunuch that he had approached what he considered was his duty. It was an integral part of his *yajna* that he was performing and invited them to bless the effort.[136] This declaration of his yajna and his seeking of blessing from the people through those who had gathered for prayers at Amishpara was probably thought to be inappropriate by NK Bose whose task it was to translate the speech in Bengali for those who had gathered to pray and listen to Gandhi. He chose to omit this part in his translation, which was noticed by Gandhi who expressed his disapproval to Bose. These 'small talks', 'whispers' and 'innuendos' bothered Gandhi deeply. At no point had he conducted himself in secrecy and it was he who had informed colleagues and family of his practice. On the day of the prayer speech he told Manu to guard the diary, 'And don't let this diary fall into the hands of any and every person.'

In the midst of such mistrust, misunderstandings and his oldest colleagues turning away from him like never before Amritlal V Thakkar (Thakkar Bapa) travelled to Hamichar village in Noakhali, where he stayed for six days from 24 February 1947. A detailed note

---

[135] *CWMG*, vol. 87, p. 63.
[136] *CWMG*, vol. 86, p. 420.

on the discussion is available wherein Gandhi sought to explain the yajna and his need to undertake the yajna.

Thakkar Bapa opened the conversation with the obvious question: 'Why this experiment here?' Gandhi replied, 'You are mistaken Bapa, it is not an experiment but an integral part of my *yajna*. One may forgo an experiment, one cannot forgo one's duty. Now if I regard a thing as part of my *yajna*—a sacred duty—I may not give it up even if public opinion is wholly against me. I am engaged in achieving self-purification. The five cardinal observances are the five props of my spiritual striving. *Brahmacharya* is one of them. But all the five constitute an invisible whole. They are inter-related and inter-dependent. If one of them is broken, all are broken... I do not allow myself any divergence between theory and practice in respect of the rest. If then I temporize in the matter of *brahmacharya*, would it not blunt the edge of my *brahmacharya* and vitiate my practice of truth? Ever since my coming to Noakhali, I have been asking myself the question: 'What is it that is choking the action of my ahimsa? Why does the spell not work? May it not be because I have temporized in the matter of *brahmacharya*?'[137]

Through this conversation, Gandhi made two propositions. One, there was a failure of his ahimsa, as evident from the violence that surrounded him in Noakhali and Bihar. And second, this failure of ahimsa arose from the fact that he had temporalized the practice of brahmacharya. This requires some elaboration.

Gandhi states or more appropriately re-iterates in this conversation that his spiritual striving rested on five cardinal principals—truth, non-violence, brahmacharya, non-possession and non-stealing. He states that his failure lay in the belief that he could remain steadfast to all these practices and still view them as distinguishable from each other. Thus, the practice of ahimsa, Gandhi believed, is as much a practice of brahmacharya, as it is of non-violence in thoughts, words and deeds. All of these together lead to truth. Several months after

---

[137] *CWMG*, vol. 87, p. 14.

this conversation Gandhi reflected on his yajna through an essay in *Harijan*; called 'How Did It Begin?' in June 1947. This was his first essay after a long gap from writing for *Harijan* wherein he chose to write on eternal values.

He described brahmacharya as a way of life that leads us to Brahman. A perfect brahmachari, he reiterated, would have all the attributes of a sthitpragnya described in the Gita. Gandhi went on to describe the discipline required to attain brahmacharya, wherein he went beyond the traditional five observances as described by Patanjali in the *Yogsutra*. 'Patanjali has described five disciplines. It is not possible to isolate any one of these and practise it. It may be possible in the case of truth, because it really includes the other four. And for this age the five have been expanded into eleven.'[138] These eleven observances are truth, non-violence, brahmacharya, non-possession, non-stealing, bread labour, and control of the palate, fearlessness, equal regard for all religions, swadeshi and removal of untouchability. These are the *Ekadash Vrata*, the eleven observances that constitute the Ashram life. Gandhi claims that brahmachari as a way of life, as conduct that leads one to Brahman, is possible only by observance of the ashramic life. Having established the necessity of the Ashram observances, Gandhi argued that they constitute one indivisible whole, and that they cannot be practised in isolation. 'It is well to bear in mind that all disciplines are of equal importance. If one is broken all are broken... when it is isolated even an elementary observance becomes difficult, if not impossible. Therefore, it is essential that all disciplines should be taken as one. This enables one to realize the full meaning and significance of *brahmacharya*. In practice he alone is a true *brahmachari,* who observes, in thought, word and deed, the eleven-fold vow in its entirety.'[139]

Gandhi's yajna becomes clear with this. The failure of ahimsa was to him the failure of his brahmacharya, that is not of his celibacy but

---

[138] *CWMG*, vol. 88, p. 58.
[139] *CWMG*, vol. 88. P. 59.

his observance of the Ashram life. Gandhi believed that only if he were not found wanting in his observance of all eleven ashram vows that ahimsa that had been 'choked' could find its full expression. Gandhi's yajna was to be an Ashramite and not test either his or Manu's celibacy.

Gandhi was unwilling to accept the argument that a perfect brahmachari, that is, a perfect Ashramite, is an unattainable ideal. 'Rejecting the possibility of perfect *brahmacharya* is like saying that there is no God because we have not seen Him face-to-face or met men who have had that experience.'[140]

Gandhi failed to communicate the necessity of his yajna, his desire to be an ideal Ashramite and cultivate the possibility of perfect brahmacharya either to AV Thakkar or other associates of the Ashram.

AV Thakkar's visit and stay at Himchar had from his point of view and from the perspective of all those who had characterized Gandhi's yajna as adharma an unexpected outcome.

Manu decided to withdraw her consent to be a partner in this yajna. With Manu's withdrawal of consent the yajna or the experiment ceased. Pyarelal has described the moment of Manu's communication to Gandhi about her detachment from the practice—this was a concession she made to Thakkar Bapa and other elders who had objected to the practice. 'The conversation had an unexpected sequel. Manu came and told Gandhiji that although to begin with Thakkar Bapa had doubts about the propriety of what Gandhiji was doing, his six days' close contact and observation had completely dispelled his doubt and he was convinced that there was nothing wrong or improper in his practice or with anyone concerned with it and had written to that effect to his friends, too. He had further told her that what, more than anything else, had brought about this conversion was the sight of their perfectly innocent and undisturbed sleep, as he watched them from day to day, and her (Manu's) single-minded and tireless devotion to duty. She, therefore, saw no harm in conceding

---

[140] *CWMG*, vol. 88, p. 234.

Thakkar Bapa's request to suspend the practice for the time being, provided Gandhi agreed. She made it absolutely clear that mentally she was entirely at one with Gandhiji, that *she had renounced nothing, surrendered not an iota*.'[141]

Infallible Proof

With Manu's decision not to be a partner in the yajna, the practice of sleeping in the bed stopped, but not Gandhi's quest to attain truth. As his loneliness became deeper, Gandhi realized that the only true test of his truth, his ahimsa, his brahmacharya, his observance of the eleven Ashram vows would be the manner of his death and his own conduct at the moment. The yajna he felt had brought him nearer to God and truth. On 29 April 1947 he told Manu, 'I am surrounded by exaggeration and untruth. In spite of my search, I do not know where truth lies. But I do feel that I have come nearer to God and truth… I have successfully practised the eleven vows undertaken by me. This is the culmination of my striving for the last sixty years… In this yajna I got a glimpse of the ideal of truth and purity for which I have been aspiring. And you have fully contributed towards it.'[142] He believed that their purity—their, not only his—would allow for atonement of sins of others. 'As against the sins of crores of men, perfect purity of even two persons will certainly have an effect. Yes, there is this, that these two persons will be severely tested.'[143]

Manu's ill-health, which was later diagnosed as appendicitis and intestinal tuberculosis, made Gandhi realize that he had again been found wanting in his devotion to Ramanama. If Rama were enshrined in his heart in such a way that even recitation of the name became unnecessary, Manu would be free from ailment. In a letter he shared his agony. 'Her health would improve to the extent she

---

[141] Emphasis in the original. Pyarelal, *Mahatma Gandhi: The Last Phase*, part 1, Book II, p. 226, (Ahmedabad: Navajivan, 1956, 1997 (reprint)).

[142] *CWMG*, vol. 87, p. 384.

[143] *CWMG*, vol. 88, p. 212.

and I are able to enshrine Ramanama in our hearts. This girl is my partner in this yajna. I have not a shadow of doubt that whatever her thought, word and deed, they are bound to interact on my actions and the purity or impurity of my thought, word and deed will have a bearing on her actions. Therefore, the more sincere I am in reciting the Ramanama the greater will be her improvement.'[144] To Dr BC Ray he wrote in similar vein: 'After all I have made her my partner in this *yajna*. If Ramanama is firmly rooted in my heart, this girl should be free from ailment.'[145]

On 15 May 1947 Manu was operated for appendicitis by Col Dr Dwarka Prasad Bhargava at Patna. Gandhi put on a surgical mask and watched the entire operation. He came home and wrote to Jaisukhlal that his 'pride had been humbled.' He had felt closer to god like never before, glimpsed purity that he had been striving for and yet he was found wanting in his devotion to Rama. He confessed to Jaisukhlal: 'Thus it is that God humbles man's pride. I do not know what new lessons He is still going to teach me.'[146]

For Gandhi, Manu's operation was an infallible proof that his striving was incomplete and any proof of his striving would be available at the moment of his death. Manu would bear witness to that death and would either proclaim him an imposter or bear testimony to his striving. On 22 May 1947, the day she was released from hospital, he told her that she was to be the witness. 'During the last eight days, since I sent you to the hospital, I have been thinking where I stand, what God demands of me, where He will ultimately lead me... If I should die of lingering illness, it would be your duty to proclaim to the whole world that I was not a man of God but an imposter and a fraud. If you fail in that duty, I shall feel unhappy wherever I am. But if I die taking God's name with my last breath, it will be a sign that I was what I strove for and claimed to be.'[147]

[144] *CWMG*, vol. 87, p. 401.
[145] *CWMG*, vol. 87, p. 468.
[146] *CWMG*, vol. 87, p. 476.
[147] *CWMG*, vol. 87, pp. 521–2.

A Poser

We have hitherto followed Gandhi's striving, his yajna and the deep and abiding disapproval of his closest associates at his adharma through a close reading of his writing and when available, that of his associates.

Two aspects have not emerged in this introductory essay. One is Manu's writings. The two volumes of her diary presented here are in Manu's hand. The translation does not omit anything from the source, and at places where the source is damaged or undecipherable, it has been indicated. The translation is presented with editorial notes which seek to provide context, biographical details of persons whose presence has faded from our memory, and at places the notes draw attention of the reader to other sources. A similar exercise has been done with the Gujarati original, which would be published almost simultaneously with the English translation by Navajivan Trust, a publishing house established by Gandhi and which has published all of Manu Gandhi's writings.

The other aspect is equally fundamental. This is about the nature of consent, the question of authority and power.

Gandhi consistently described Manu as a 'partner' in the yajna, despite the palpable and obvious hierarchy that defined their relationship. The word 'partner' signifies parity, equality, exercise of free will and autonomy.

We should underline that the current formulations of consent would not accept this idea of parity that the term 'partner' posits between Gandhi and Manu.

We know that Manu consented to be a partner in this yajna and the practice stopped when she withdrew her consent. There is no indication in either her diaries or in Gandhi's writings or the writings of NK Bose and Pyarelal that once she communicated her desire to discontinue the practice, that Gandhi sought to persuade her otherwise.

But, we are looking at consent in an accepted but a very narrow and, limited sense. The question of consent has to be posed in a sense in which it would or better still, ought to make sense to Gandhi, however a-historical, counter-factual and hence speculative the exercise is.

We know that Gandhi did not share the traditional view of male brahmacharis that women are the cause of breach or failure of brahmacharya. Only once in his life did he succumb to this view, but soon he realized the deep falsehood of this proposition and re-affirmed that any failure of his brahmacharya or any shortcomings in his realization of perfect brahmacharya lay only within himself. This allowed him to recognize the quest of women brahmacharis.

And for this reason the question of consent from within his worldview that we need to ask is this: Would Gandhi have consented to be a partner in a yajna sought to be undertaken by a woman brahmachari? Would he have consented to become a partner where the primary striving to see God face-to-face, to attain self-realization, to achieve moksha by becoming an ideal Ashramite and a perfect brahmachari was that of a woman co-worker?

If he were so willing, that would be true consent and partnership. But if his answer were to be negative, he would from within his own worldview be committing adharma, not only as violation of morality, of right conduct and duty, but also in his incapacity to recognize truth from untruth, he would cease to be a satyagrahi of his own description.

Bapu: My Mother

Manu saw Gandhi as her Mother. She was the only one who claimed that she saw him as a woman, as a mother, while for all others he remained Bapu. She exclaimed—and it should be noted during the period of yajna—in joy of having him as her mother.

'And, oh, joy! I am actually *having* that experience! It is *I* who am that beloved child of Mother Bapu! I am immensely happy at my rare good fortune!'[148]

---

[148] *The Lonely Pilgrim*, p. 111. Tridip Suhrud. June 2019.

Note on Translation

This diary is a translation of Manu Gandhi's original Gujarati diaries, currently lodged with the National Archives of India. Manu Gandhi was at this time an adolescent of 14–15 years, with uneven and at best irregular education. The Gujarati diary is written in a hand that is yet to be formed, her orthography is uncertain and inconsistent, her grammar ill-formed. The diary writing itself is a part of her education with M. K. Gandhi. The later part of the diary and the second volume that is scheduled to be published bear evidence to the refinement she attained in the craft of writing diaries, being a chronicler to Gandhi and at times acting as his secretary and managing correspondence.

And yet, this volume, particularly the entries of the initial months bear cuneiform like marks of her apprenticeship. The translation aspires to fidelity to the original in two ways. The editor/translator has not omitted any part of the diary or any entry therein. The translation seeks to retain the staccato quality of her prose and the un-chiseled language. The footnotes on the text indicate faulty orthography, particularly if Gandhi had corrected the same word in a previous entry. This in a hope that the translation is able to capture the process of diary writing that is so evident in Gujarati. The English translation is to be followed by a publication of the original Gujarati diaries by Navajivan Trust.

The Diary of Manu Gandhi

1943–1944

Date: 11.4.43 Sunday[1]

Today, got up at 5:30 a.m. for prayer, brushed my teeth, used the latrine and joined in the prayers. The prayers were over at 6. I bathed for twenty minutes from 6 to 6:20. Then till about 6:45 read and wrote a bit of English.

6:45 to 7	Squeezed[2] some juice for Bapuji[3] and then[4] drank my milk and prepared tea for Ba.
7 to 7:30	Cut vegetables, cleaned utensils and did other sundry work.
7:30 to 8	Read the Gita and Gujarati grammar.
8 to 8:30	Walked with Bapuji.
8:30 to 9:30	Gave a massage to Ba and washed her hair.
9:30 to 11:30	Prepared lunch for Ba, cooked khakhara and other things.

---

[1] Manu Gandhi reached the Aga Khan Palace prison on 20.3.1943.

[2] 'Squeezed' added by Gandhiji in pencil.

[3] She always wrote 'Pujya Bapuji' and 'Pujya Motiba' for Gandhiji and Kasturba.

[4] 'And then' added by Gandhiji in pencil.

11:30 to 12:15	Cooked my meal and had lunch with Ba.
12:15 to 1	Read a little.
1 to 2	Applied ghee on Bapuji and Ba's feet.
2 to 2:15	Completed homework for English lessons.
2:15 to 3	Had English lessons with Murabbi[5] Sushila-behn[6].
3 to 3:15	Read the newspapers.
3:15 to 4	Could not spin today. Took some rest and read.
4 to 4:30	Gita and grammar lessons with Bapuji.
4:30 to 5:30	Applied oil in Ba's hair, read the Ramayana and newspapers to her.
5:30 to 6	Made tea and cooked meal for Ba.
6 to 6:30	Folded the washed clothes, prepared the twig for brushing teeth and cleaned utensils used by Bapuji.
6:30 to 7:45	Darned Ba's clothes.
7:45 p.m. onwards,	played, walked till 8 p.m.
8 to 8:30	Prayers.
8:30 to 10	Finished all the remaining work, gave a massage to Ba, read to her for a while, she could not sleep, hence stayed in her service.
10:15	Went to bed[7].

---

[5] Murabbi: 'Respected,' henceforth it will not be indicated. It has been marked only in the first instance.

[6] Dr Sushila Nayyar (1914-2000), studied medicine at Lady Hardinge Medical College and joined the Sevagram Ashram, worked as MKG's personal physician and was imprisoned with him at the Aga Khan Palace prison. After Independence she served as a member of the Lok Sabha and Union Minister of Health. She is the author of several books including five volumes of a biography of MK Gandhi and the story of his last imprisonment, *Bapu Ki Karavas Ki Kahani*. She was Pyarelal Nayar's sister.

[7] Signed 'Bapu' in pencil.

Date: 12.4.43 Monday

Woke up at 6. Prayers completed at 6:30.

6:30 to 6:45	I brushed my teeth, used the latrine and did other daily chores.
6:45 to 7:30	Squeezed juice, made tea, drank milk, made the dough for khakharas and rotis, cut the vegetables.
7:30 to 8:30	Could not walk today, but gave a massage to Ba after bath.
8:30 to 9	Read a little (Gita and history).
9 to 11:30	Cooked khakhara, roti, vegetables, boiled milk, etc.
11:30 to 12:30	Made lunch, Ba's and mine, and wrote some English.
12:45 to 1	Cleaned the utensils, made Ba's bed, massaged her body.
1 to 2	Applied ghee on Bapuji's and Ba's feet.
2 to 3	Slept while trying to read.
3 to 3:30	Went to Mirabehn[8] to rehearse the song for 'Flag hoisting'.
3:30 to 4	Spinning (Since it was a day of silence[9] could not study).

---

[8] Mirabehn (Madeleine Slade) (1892–1981) left her aristocratic life in England to work with MKG and joined the Satyagraha Ashram at Sabarmati in 1925; she was detained at the Aga Khan Palace prison. After Independence she established Pashulok Ashram near Rishikesh, returned to Europe in 1959 and lived in Vienna pursuing her passion for the music of Beethoven. Her autobiography is titled *The Spirit's Pilgrimage* (1960). For her and Gandhi's correspondence see *Beloved Bapu: The Gandhi-Mirabehn Correspondence*, edited by Tridip Suhrud and Thomas Weber (New Delhi: Orient Blackswan, 2014).

[9] It was Gandhiji's day of silence, the practice of Monday as a day of silence commenced from 17 January 1921. From 9 September 1923, the

4 to 4:45	Read the Ramayana and the newspapers to Ba.
4:45 to 5:30	Made tea and prepared meals.
5:30 to 6:30	Prepared the twig for brushing teeth, folded washed clothes and cleaned utensils.
6:30 to 7:30	Played.[10]
7:30 to 8	Went for a walk.
8 to 10	Prayers, gave a massage to Ba and tended to her other needs. Completed other tasks, read (Gujarati grammar) and went to bed at 10:15.[11]

Date: 13.04.1943[12]

I woke up today at 5:15. The prayers concluded at 5:30. I wanted to read from 5:30 to 6:30, but fell asleep.

6:30 to 7	Read.
7 to 8	Juice, tea, cleaned utensils, etc.
8 to 8:30	Today being 13th April, saluted the flag[13] and went for a walk.
8:30 to 9	Applied oil to Ba's hair and combed it.
9 to 10:30	Gave massage to Ba, she and I bathed thereafter.
10:30 to 11	Prepared milk for Ba, tea leaves were over, so made tea with herbs.[14]

---

practice was modified. The silence commenced at 3 p.m. on Sunday and lasted for 24 hours.

[10] There is mention of a game of carrom and badminton elsewhere in the diary. See the entry of 30.8.43.

[11] Signed 'Bapu' in pencil.

[12] Day not mentioned in the diary, it would be mentioned only if it is in the original.

[13] The flag hoisting was in commemoration of the massacre at Jallianwala Bagh which took place on 13 April 1919.

[14] The term in Gujarati is 'medicines', suggesting herbs.

11 to 11:30	Wrote English.
11:30 to 12	Applied ghee to Bapuji's feet and cleaned some cotton.[15]
12 to 1	Applied ghee to Ba's feet. She had severe body ache, hence gave her a massage.
1 to 1:30	Read newspapers and rested.
1:30 to 2:30	Spun, read newspapers (and the Ramayana) to Ba.
2:30 to 3:30	Answered questions on grammar.
3:30 to 4:45	Cooked.
4:45 to 6	Prepared meals and we ate together.
6 to 6:30	Listened to the gramophone.
6:30 to 7	Folded the washed clothes, prepared the twig for brushing teeth and cleaned utensils.
7 to 7:30	Played.
7:30 to 8	Went for a walk.
8 to 10:30	Prayers. Gave massage to Ba, tended to her other needs, finished all the remaining work and went to sleep.

Note: Since today was the 13th April and conclusion of the 'National week'[16] all of us had observed a fast.[17] And we had distributed shiro, savouries and tea to the prisoners,[18] Bapuji himself

---

[15] To make slivers for spinning.

[16] The National Week was observed every year in commemoration of the National Week observed in 1919 as part of the movement against the Rowlatt Act.

[17] Corrected by MKG; 'had observed half a day fast'.

[18] Prisoners from the Yeravada Prison were placed on duty at the Aga Khan Palace prison. They were not required to tend to the personal needs of the prisoners of the Aga Khan Palace, but they served the officials and also tended the gardens.

served them. In the evening we gave them khichdi, vegetables, bananas and onions.[19]

Date: 14.4.43

Today I woke up at 5:15 for prayers which were concluded at 5:30.

5:30 to 6	After the prayers I made an attempt not to sleep, but sleep wins against me[20] and I slept.[21]
6 to 7:30	Bathed. Since I was late, Sushilabehn prepared the juice. I drank milk, prepared tea for Ba, prepared the dough for khakhara, cleaned the utensils, etc.
7:30 to 8	Combed hair, read the Gita, cut vegetables.
8 to 8:30	Went for a walk, had Darshan.[22]
8:30 to 10	Applied oil to Ba's hair and combed it, gave her a massage and made all preparation for Ba's bath, gave her a bath.[23]
10 to 11	Cooked khakhara, vegetables[24], boiled milk, etc.
11 to 12:30	Prepared the meal and had it.
12.30 to 1	Wrote English.
1 to 2	Applied ghee on Bapuji's and Ba's feet and gave a massage to Ba.

[19] Signed 'Bapu' with a note in Gujarati: 'The spinning count should be noted. The thoughts that occur should be written down. A note on reading of the day should be provided.'

[20] Corrected by MKG as 'wins over me'.

[21] Corrected by MKG as 'I go to the sleep'.

[22] Darshan refers to the Samadhi of Mahadev Desai who had passed away while in prison at 15 August 1942.

[23] MKG made two grammatical corrections. Instead of 'Motiba Ne Snan thi' to 'Motiba Na Snan Ni.'

[24] MKG, in pencil showed the correct for at the letter 'શ' (sh) for 'Shak'; i.e., vegetables.

2 to 2:30	Slept [could not spin], because I slept.
2:30 to 3	Wrote answers to questions of grammar[25] given by Bapuji.
3 to 3:30	Studied English.
3:30 to 4	Read the newspaper, prepared a bath.
4 to 4:30	Studied with Bapuji, studied the Gita and questions and answers of grammar.[26]
4:30 to 5:30	Today was Rama Navami, hence I read 10 chapters—five more than usual—of the Ramayana to Ba.
5:30 to 6:30	Prepared meals, made tea and fruits for Ba and cleaned the utensils.
6:30 to 7	Prepared the twig for brushing teeth, folded washed clothes and did other sundry chores.
7 to 7:30	Played.
7:30 to 8	Went for a walk, had Darshan.
8 to 10	Prayers, gave medicines to Ba and massaged her body[27] and pressed it.
10 to 10:30	Studied natural[28] geography with Murabbi Pyarelalji.[29] What is the shape of the Earth? What is the substratum? How do day and night occur? Does the Sun rotate or the Earth? These and similar

---

[25] MKG, corrected the spelling of Vyakran.

[26] Same as before.

[27] Manu distinguished between 'giving a massage' and 'pressing the aching body'.

[28] MKG, corrected the spelling, 'Prakritik'.

[29] Pyarelal Nayar (1899-1982), joined the Satyagraha Ashram at Sabarmati during the Non-Cooperation Movement and worked with Mahadev Desai in the Gandhi Secretariat. Some of his works are *Mahatma Gandhi: The Early Phase* (1956) and *Mahatma Gandhi: The Last Phase* (1956).

issues were discussed. It was deeply interesting. I lost my sleep, but went to bed at 10:30. I had also posed certain questions related to geography, which were resolved.

Date: 15.4.43 Thursday

Note: Last night Ba had severe body ache of which I came to know only this morning. At night I was enveloped by such deep sleep that I had no inkling of what happened. But, Ba, this morning, told me that I am not required to get up at night, as I work through the day and fall into deep sleep of tiredness. But I felt that she was in such pain, all others were awake and yet why could I not wake up? I resolved that I would get up at the first call from Ba. I went to bed with that resolve and I could keep that resolution. Around 1 o'clock in the morning Ba was in pain. I may not have got up at the first call but I did wake up and till about 1:30, I gently pressed her legs, hands, back, etc. I went back to sleep after that. I was satisfied that I got up on my own[30] and could serve Ba. How good it would be if I could likewise get up every time I am needed at night? I make this resolution and I also pray to God that I may not to be kept in such deep sleep. But today either my prayers bore fruit or my resolve did, only Rama knows, but I got up, which made me very happy.

15.04.1943

Today I woke up at 5:15, when the prayers were halfway through.

5:15 to 6	I slept again. I did not wish to sleep, but I had no pressing work. I had come late after my studies with Pyarelalji and had a slight headache. Hence I slept.

---

[30] MKG corrected her grammar.

6 to 7	Brushed my teeth, bathed, prepared juice[31], drank milk, made tea, cleaned the utensils, etc.
7 to 7:30	Prepared dough for khakharas and roti, cut vegetables, cleaned a cupboard, combed hair.
7:30 to 8	Read the Gita, read grammar.[32]
2:30 to 3	Prepared a bath for Ba, scanned through the newspapers, read to her Pujya Ramdaskaka's[33] letter, wrote a reply to him as dictated.
3 to 3:30	Studied English with Sushilabehn.
3:30 to 4	Spun (I have not counted the spun thread) I had to get up while spinning, hence did not spin for long. I shall count spun thread after two days of spinning.
4 to 4:30	Studied Gita and grammar[34] with Bapuji.
4:30 to 5:30	Read the Ramayana to Ba, also read to her the newspapers, pressed her feet.
5:30 to 6:30	Made tea for Ba, gave her medicines, tea and fruits. I ate my meal.
6:30 to 7	Prepared the twig for brushing teeth, made a ghee lamp, folded washed clothes.
7 to 7:30	Played.
7:30 to 8	Went for a walk with Bapuji.
8 to 8:30	Prayers.
8:30 to 11	Gave a massage to Ba, then pressed her body, gave her medicines, tidied up her bed and went to Pyarelalji for studies. But I was early and Pyarelalji was not prepared. He took the class for

---

[31] It is implied that she prepared juice for MKG.

[32] Despite MKG's correction in the entry of 14.03.43 she spelled 'vyakaran' wrong.

[33] Ramdas Gandhi (1897-1969). Third son of Kasturba and MKG.

[34] MKG corrected her spelling of 'vyakaran.'

only 20 minutes, which was in part a repetition of yesterday's lesson and he explained a bit about the solar system and latitudinal regions of the Earth. I went to sleep at 11.

Date: 16.4.43

Today I got up at 5:15 for the prayers. The prayers concluded at 5:45, but I did not go back to sleep. I gave Ba her drinking water and immediately went for a bath.

5:45 to 6	Bathed, brushed teeth, combed hair, etc.
6 to 6:30	Wrote English.
7:45 to 8	Made tea, drank milk, squeezed juice, prepared the dough.[35]
8 to 8:30	Went for a walk.
8:30 to 9:45	Massage, combed Ba's hair, etc.
9:45 to 11	Churned butter, made khakhara, roti, vegetables, boiled milk, etc.
11 to 12:30	Prepared my meal and ate it.
12:30 to 1	Read English.
1 to 2:30	Cleaned the utensils, applied ghee to Bapuji's and Ba's feet, prepared her bath, gave hot water to her, read to her Pujya Manilalkaka's[36] letter and also the newspapers.
2:30 to 3	Slept.

---

[35] In the margin, against this entry MKG had signed 'Bapu', indicating that he had read the previous day's entry. This day's entry has been signed at the end of the entry.

[36] Manilal Gandhi (1892-1956) was the second son of Kasturba and MKG. He edited and published the *Indian Opinion* from Phoenix in South Africa and played a significant role in the movement against Apartheid.

3 to 3:30	Studied English with Sushilabehn.
3:30 to 4	Spun (160 threads[37]) 60 of yesterday and 100 of today. I did not spin for half an hour continuously; I had to get up many times.
4 to 4:30	Studied the Gita and grammar with Bapuji.
4:30 to 5:30	Read the Ramayana to Ba.
5:30 to 6:30	Tea, meals, cleaned utensils, etc.
6:30 to 7	Folded washed clothes, prepared the twig, lamp, etc.
7 to 7:30	Played.
7:30 to 8	Went for a walk with Bapuji.
8 to 8:30	Prayers.
8:30 to 9:45	Gave medicines to Ba, gave her a massage and pressed her feet.
9:45 to 10:30	Studied with Pyarelalji. He showed me longitudes, latitudes and latitudinal zones in an Atlas. And briefly showed me as to where the War is being fought.
10:30 to 11	Wrote English and read grammar. I have been given a new chapter (of grammar) to read. I slept at 11.[38]

Date: 17.4.43

Today I woke up at 5 for the prayers.

5 to 5:30	Prayers were conducted.
5:30 to 6:30	I went back to sleep after giving water to Ba. Bapuji suggested that I should sleep.

---

[37] The length of the spun year depends upon the circumference of the wheel, the ideal circumference is four feet. 160 threads would make 640 feet of spun thread.

[38] Signed 'Bapu'.

6:30 to 7:30	Squeezed juice, made tea, drank milk, gave tea and medicines, cleaned the utensils and prepared dough for khakhara and roti.
7:30 to 8	Combed hair, darned my clothes.
8 to 8:30	Went for a walk.
8:30 to 9:30	Gave massage to Ba, combed her hair and made preparations for bath.
9:45 to 11	Cooked khakhara, rab, roti, vegetables etc.
11 to 12	I had my meal and served meal to Ba.
12 to 1	I read the Gita and grammar.
1 to 2	Applied ghee to Bapuji and Ba's feet.
2 to 2:45	Slept.
2:45 to 3:30	Read Pujyabhai's[39] letter, read it out to Bapuji and Ba and studied English.
3:30 to 4	Spun, have not counted.
4 to 4:30	Studied the Gita with Bapuji.
4:30 to 5:30	Read the Ramayana. Completed the Bal-Kanda today. Ba fell asleep, hence did not start the Ayodhya-Kanda but for a while read the fifth book of Gujarati.
5:30 to 6:45	Tea, meal, folded washed clothes, prepared twig for brushing teeth and other sundry chores.
6:45 to 7	Listened to records on the gramophone.
7 to 7:30	Played.
7:30 to 8	Went for a walk with Bapuji.
8 to 8:30	Prayers.
8:30 to 9:45	Gave a massage to Ba and pressed her body.
9:45 to 11	Was with Pyarelalji and wrote English. Slept at 11.[40]

---

[39] Her father, Jaysukhlal Gandhi.
[40] Signed 'Bapu'.

Date: 18.4.43

I woke up at 5 today. The prayers were conducted at 5:30.

5:30 to 6	Slept.
6 to 7:30	Bathed, squeezed juice, made tea and drank milk.
7:30 to 8	Gave medicines and tea to Ba. Prepared the dough for khakhara and read the Gita.
8 to 8:30	Went for a walk.
8:30 to 9:45	Massaged and combed Ba's hair.
9:45 to 11	Cooked.
11 to 12	Prepared my meal and ate it.
12 to 1	Read (wrote and read English).
1 to 2:30	Applied ghee to Ba and Bapuji's feet, pressed Ba's body.
2:30 to 3:15	Slept (I could not study English today).
3:15 to 3:30	Read newspapers to Ba.
3:30 to 4:15	Once again pressed Ba's body, spun 100 threads, prepared her bath.
4:15 to 4:30	Studied the Gita with Bapuji.
4:30 to 6:30	Prepared the twig for brushing teeth, folded washed clothes, cooked a meal, made tea and finished other sundry chores. Read 'Prasad'.
6:30 to 7:30	Played.
7:30 to 8	Went for a walk.
8 to 10:30	Prayers, gave a massage to Ba, pressed her body. Read a bit of grammar. Pyarelalji could not give time today, so I went to sleep.

Note: Even tonight, at around 2:45 Ba felt giddy and did not feel well at all. Today, I woke up at the first call. I gave her water and pressed her head, legs, back, hands, etc. till 3:30, I went back to sleep at 3:30.[41]

---

[41] Signed 'Bapu'.

Date: 19.4.43

Tonight at around 3:30[42] Ba felt uneasy and troubled, hence I had woken up. I sat with Ba from about 3:45 to 5. She had felt uneasy even before that. Before I sat with her, Pyarelalji sat with Ba. I went to Ba at 3:45 after which he left.

The prayers commenced at 5.

5 to 5:30	Prayers. After which I slept and could get up only around 7.
7 to 8	Brushed teeth, squeezed juice, drank milk, made dough for rotis, made tea for Ba and gave her medicines, cut vegetables, etc.
8 to 8:30	I had not bathed thus far as I had woken up late. I did not go for a walk; I did darshan and came back. I washed my hair and therefore took longer to bathe.
8:30 to 9:45	Applied oil to Ba's hair, combed them, gave her a massage and prepared her bath.
9:45 to 10:30	Cooked roti, vegetables, and boiled milk. Today I did not make khakharas.
10:30 to 11:30	Read English. Have started reading the *Anasakti Yoga*[43] but have not completed it.
11:30 to 12:30	Cooked my meal and ate it, cleaned utensils.
12:30 to 1	Read Gujarati grammar.
1 to 2	Applied ghee to the feet of Bapuji and Ba.
2 to 2:30	Slept.
2:30 to 3:30	Read the Ramayana.
3:30 to 4	Applied oil and combed hair, read the newspapers.
4 to 4:30	Studied English with Sushilabehn.

[42] In the previous day's entry it is 2:30 a.m.

[43] *Anasakti Yoga* is MKG's translation of the Bhagvad Gita into Gujarati. First published in 1930.

4:30 to 5	Spun (120 threads).
5 to 5:30	Went and bathed in the pool.
5:30 to 6:30	Made tea, gave medicines and tea to Ba. Played the Dilruba[44] and had my meal.
6:30 to 7	Listened to records on the gramphone.
7 to 7:30	Played.
7:30 to 8	Went for a walk.
8 to 8:30	Prayers.
8:30 to 11	Gave a massage and pressed Ba's body. Folded and put clothes at their proper place. Sewed two buttons to Ba's blouse. Studied with Pyarelalji, read a little and went to sleep.[45]

Date: 20.4.43

Today Bapuji woke me up at 5:15 for the prayers.

5:15 to 5:45	Prayers.
5:45 to 6:30	I went back to sleep after the prayers.
6:30 to 7:30	Prepared the dough for khakhara, squeezed juice, drank milk, gave tea and medicines to Ba, cleaned the utensils and bathed.
7:30 to 8	Combed hair, cut vegetables, read the Gita.
8 to 8:30	Went for a walk.
8:30 to 9:45	Gave a massage to Ba, applied oil and combed her hair, prepared her bath. Prepared enema for her.
9:45 to 11	Cooked khakhara, roti, vegetables, milk, etc.
11 to 11:30	Wrote English.

---

[44] A stringed musical instrument—cross between a sitar and a sarangi—very similar to the esraj. 'Dilruba' literally translates to 'the robber of the heart'.

[45] Signed 'Bapu'.

11:30 to 12:30	Cooked and ate my meal.
12:30 to 1	Read Gujarati grammar.
1 to 1:45	Applied ghee to Ba and Bapuji's feet.
1:45 to 2:30	Slept.
2:30 to 3:30	Prepared mud pack for Ba and applied it, prepared her bath and read the Ramayana.
3:30 to 4	Ate oranges, folded clothes and placed them in their proper place.
4 to 4:30	Studied the Gita and grammar with Bapuji.
4:30 to 5	Spinning (130 threads).
5 to 5:30	Studied English with Sushilabehn.
5:30 to 6	Made tea, served tea and medicines to Ba and went for my bath.
6 to 6:30	Cleaned utensils and had my meal.
6:30 to 7	Prepared twigs for brushing teeth, folded washed clothes and went to play.
7 to 7:30	Played.
7:30 to 8	Went for a walk with Bapuji.
8 to 8:30	Prayers.
8:30 to 10:15	Gave a massage to Ba and pressed her body. I studied with Pyarelalji and went to sleep.

Today it is a month since I came to Poona to be with Bapuji.

Date: 21.4.43

I remained more or less awake tonight because Ba had severe pain on her sides. But till about 3 o'clock Sushilabehn slept by Ba's side. After 3 o'clock I slept by her side. Ba caressed me with deep love. It has been four years since the death of my mother.

Four years ago, I would sleep by my mother's side and she would caress me affectionately and put me to sleep. I recalled that experience and felt that after four years Ba made me sleep by her side, just as my mother used to. And she touched me with her loving hand, it gave me limitless joy. And the memories of my mother, which had faded, came alive. It brought tears to my eyes. Today, it was as if my mother had caressed me, such was the joy.[46]

5:15 to 5:45	Prayers.
5:45 to 7	Slept again.
7 to 8	Made juice, bathed, drank milk, made tea, combed hair. Gave medicine to Ba, prepared the dough for khakhara and read one discourse of '*Anasakti Yoga*'.
8 to 8:30	Went for a walk.
8:30 to 9:45	Gave a massage to Ba and combed her hair.
9:45 to 10:30	Khakhara, milk, vegetables, rotis, etc were cooked.
10:30 to 11	Wrote English.
11 to 11:30	Ate my meal and served to Ba her meal.
11:30 to 12:15	Read grammar.
12:15 to 1	Helped Pyarelalji to arrange all the newspapers date-wise.
1 to 2	Applied ghee to Ba and Bapuji's feet.
2 to 3:15	Slept.
3:15 to 4	Read the Ramayana and the newspapers.
4 to 4:30	Studied with Bapuji (the Gita and grammar).

----

[46] This passage has been corrected by MKG. Manubehn's first rendering read as follows:

'And when she caressed me with her loving hand, at that time I felt that after four years this caressing gave me limitless joy. And I have not entirely forgotten the memories of my mother, but many of her memories had been forgotten, were revived. It brought tears to my eyes. But, today the joy was just as if my mother had caressed me.'

On the margin MKG made the following note.

'These corrections relate only to grammar and syntax. These should be understood.'

4:30 to 5	Bathed.
5 to 5:30	Made tea, squeezed juice for Bapuji and read the 'Vande Mataram' for a while.
5:30 to 6	Had my meal.
6 to 6:30	Cleaned the utensils, prepared the twig for brushing teeth, folded washed clothes and placed them at their proper place.
6:30 to 7:30	Played.
7:30 to 8	Went for a walk with Bapuji.
8 to 8:30	Prayers.
8:30 to 10:30	Gave a massage to Ba and pressed her body, prepared her bed and placed a mosquito net over it. I studied with Pyarelalji. Today I learnt about springs, falls and sulphur water. Slept at 10:30.[47]

Date: 22.4.43

Bapuji woke me up at 5 for the prayers today.

5 to 5:30	Prayers.
5:30 to 5:45	Slept again.
5:45 to 7:30	Bathed, squeezed juice, combed hair, made tea, drank milk and prepared the dough for khakhara and rotis.
7:30 to 8	Read *Gita Dhwani*,[48] read the Gita, and also the Marathi translation of the Gita[49]. (The first discourse in each.)
8 to 8:30	Went for a walk with Bapuji.
8:30 to 9:45	Gave a massage to Ba, applied oil to her hair and combed it.

---

[47] Signed 'Bapu'.

[48] Kishorelal Mashruwala's translation of the Gita into Gujarati verse.

[49] Marathi translation of the Gita in verse by Vinoba Bhave.

9:45 to 10:15	Cooked vegetables, milk, khakharas, roti, etc.
10:15 to 11:15	Wrote English.
11:15 to 12:30	Ba and I had our meals.
12:30 to 1	Gave massage to Ba.
1 to 2	Gave massage to Bapuji, cut the long sleeves of a frock and stitched them.
2 to 2:30	I did not sleep today. From today I am not ever going to sleep in the afternoon, unless on some day I have not had a regular night's sleep or I am unwell. Otherwise, I will not sleep even if I have no other work.
2:30 to 3:30	Spun for a while, as Ba woke up I gave her water and read to her the Ramayana and the newspapers.
3:30 to 4	Read Gujarati grammar.
4 to 4:30	Studied the Gita and grammar with Bapuji.
4:30 to 5	Spun (today I spun 200 threads).
5 to 6:30	Today Sushilabehn had some other work, hence I could not study with her. I bathed and had my meal. Soaked the twig for brushing teeth, folded washed clothes and placed them at their proper place, made tea, squeezed juice.
	Listened to music on the gramophone.
6:30 to 7:30	Played.
7:30 to 8	Went for a walk with Bapuji.
8:30 to 10:30	Gave a massage to Ba, pressed her body, gave her medicines and put her to sleep. Studied with Pyarelalji. From today: one, I will not sleep in the afternoon and two; I will not change my clothes for playing sports. I shall play in my saree and if that is not possible, I shall give up playing that game.[50]

---

[50] Signed 'Bapu'.

Date: 23.4.43

Today Bapuji woke me up at 5:15 for the prayers.

5:15 to 5:45	Prayers.
5:45 to 6:30	Slept once again.
6:30 to 7:45	Prepared the dough for khakhara and roti, squeezed juice, bathed, cut vegetables, drank milk, etc.
7:45 to 8	Combed my hair, studied the Gita and discourse from *Gita Dhvani*, *Gitai*[51] and the Gita.
8 to 8:30	Went for a walk with Bapuji.
8:30 to 11	Gave a massage to Ba, applied oil to her hair and combed it, cooked vegetables, made roti, khakhara, khir and bhakhari for Ba.
11 to 11:30	Soaked clothes in soap water, washed vegetables and other food and served a meal to Ba.
11:30 to 12:30	I ate my meal. Bapuji examined my English notebook and pointed out my errors. Cleaned the utensils, I observed the warder clean Bapuji's plate.
12:30 to 1	Wrote English.
1 to 2	Applied ghee to Bapuji's and Ba's feet.
2 to 2:30	Read Gujarati grammar.
2:30 to 3:15	Spinning (190 threads).
3:15 to 4:30	Studied with Bapuji.
4:30 to 5:30	Read the Ramayana and the newspapers to Ba.
5:30 to 6	Made tea and had my bath. I gave tea and medicines to Ba. Cleaned the glass bottle in which jaggery is stored. Cleaned the utensils and sat for a while with Bapuji.

---

[51] Marathi translation of the Gita in verse by Vinoba Bhave.

6 to 7:30	Had my meal, listened to songs on the gramophone. Today there was severe pain in my leg, hence I did not play. And I do not know as to where the time went. I wasted the time. I watched others at play for a while.
7:30 to 8	Went for a walk with Bapuji.
8 to 8:30	Prayers.
8:30 to 9:45	Gave a massage to Ba and pressed her body.
9:45 to 10	Studied with Pyarelalji.
10:10	I went off to sleep.[52]

Date: 24.4.43

Today Bapuji woke me up at 5:15 for the prayers.

5:15 to 5:45	Prayers.
5:45 to 6:30	Slept. Bapuji once again woke me up at 6:30.
6:30 to 7:45	Brushed my teeth, bathed, combed hair, made tea, drank milk, gave tea and medicines to Ba, prepared dough for roti and khakhara, cut vegetables, etc.
7:45 to 8	Read the third discourse from the *Gita Dhvani* and *Anasakti Yoga.*
8 to 8:30	Went for a walk with Bapuji.
8:30 to 10	Applied oil to Ba's hair and combed it, gave her a massage.
10 to 11	Cooked khakhara, roti and vegetables and made khir and bhakhari for Ba.
11 to 11:30	Wrote English.
11:30 to 12:30	Prepared Ba's meal, served her and had my meal.

---

[52] Signed 'Bapu'.

12:30 to 1	Read a story book.
1 to 2	Applied ghee to Ba's and Bapuji's feet.
2 to 2:30	Ba's brassiere was tight, so I loosened it up (opened the stitches made by the tailor).
2:30 to 3:15	Studied with Sushilabehn.
3:15 to 3:45	Spun (120 threads) completed one hank[53] today.
3:45 to 4:45	Studied with Bapuji.
4:45 to 5:30	Read the Ramayana and the newspapers to Ba.
5:30 to 6:45	I went for my bath. Made tea, prepared a twig for brushing teeth, made a wick for the ghee lamp, cleaned utensils, folded and placed away clothes and went for my meal.
6:45 to 7	Had my meal and finished some miscellaneous work.
7 to 7:30	Played.
7:30 to 8	Went for a walk with Bapuji.
8 to 8:30	Prayers.
8:30 to 10:30	Gave massage to Ba, pressed her legs, gave her medicines and studied with Pyarelalji.
10:30	Went to sleep.[54]

Date: 25.4.43

Woke up at 5:15 for prayers, Bapuji woke me up.

5:15 to 5:45	Prayers.
5:30[55] to 6:30	Slept again.

---

[53] The term is 'gadi', suggesting a knot; in spinning terminology it is called 'aanti' or hank. 375 lengths or strands would make a hank of 500 yards. See *CWMG*, vol. 24, p. 483.

[54] Signed 'Bapu'.

[55] Should be 5:45 a.m.

6:30 to 7:45	Bathed, squeezed juice,[56] made Ba's bed,[57] cleaned utensils, made tea, gave medicines and drank milk.
7:45 to 8	Stitched Ba's brassiere.[58]
8 to 8:30	Went for a walk.
8:30 to 10	Gave a massage. Today being Sunday,[59] gave a head bath to Ba and therefore it took a bit longer.
10 to 11	Cooked khakhara,[60] khir, vegetables, etc.
11 to 11:30	Prepared[61] meal for Ba and had my meal.
11:30 to 12:30	Finished work on Ba's brassiere. Button holes and button require work.[62]
12:30 to 1	Today the goat gave birth to kids,[63] I went to have a look at them.
1 to 2	Applied ghee to Bapuji's and Ba's[64] feet.
2 to 3:45	Finished stitching the button-hole and button of Ba's brassiere, wrote English and studied English with Sushilabehn.
3:45 to 4:15	Studied the Gita and grammar with Bapuji.
4:15 to 5:45	Applied oil to Ba's hair, combed her hair, read the Ramayana and the newspapers, made tea.[65]

---

[56] MKG corrected her orthography: 'શસ' to 'રસ'.

[57] MKG corrected 'પથારી'.

[58] MKG corrected her 'ખ', 's' and 'શ' made a note in the margin 'ડ, ઠ, ઢ (da, tha, dha) this difference should be kept in mind.

[59] MKG corrected 'રવીવારે' to 'રવિવારે', and corrected the form of 'થ'.

[60] MKG corrected the form of letter 'ખ'.

[61] MKG pointed out that word 'તૈયાર' would imply to prepare or cook, while the appropriate term would be to 'serve a meal' 'પીરસવું'.

[62] MKG corrected the form of letter 'ખ' and wrote a note in the margin 'ખ, ન, ખ,, the difference of.'

[63] The term is 'બચ્ચાં', was written as 'બરચાં', the letters were not conjoined. MKG made a correction.

[64] MKG corrected the form of 'બ', which read like 'ખ'.

[65] MKG corrected the forms of letters 'બ', 'ન', 'થ', 'ઘ'.

5:45 to 6:30	Prepared the twig for brushing teeth, cleaned utensils, folded and placed clothes at their proper place. Read the Gujarati fifth book for a while and made preparations for the lamp.[66]
6:30 to 7	Had meals.
7 to 7:30	Played.
8 to 10:30	Gave a massage to Ba and pressed her body, placed the mosquito net over her bed. After which I went to Pyarelalji. Today, he told me three stories. Today is Sunday, and we have made a rule that every Sunday he should tell me a story. For a while, he did not wish to tell the third story as he had a headache, I pressed his head, after which he told the third story. I slept at 10:30.[67]

Date: 26.4.43, Monday

Today Bapuji woke me at 5:30 for the prayers.

5:30 to 6	Prayers.[68]
6 to 6:30	Today I washed my hair and therefore took longer to bathe.
6:30 to 7:30	Squeezed juice, made tea, cut vegetables, prepared the dough for khakhara, cleaned the utensils, etc.[69]

---

[66] MKG corrected 'મુખ્યા' to 'મુક્યા', literally, placed.

[67] MKG changed 'દાખ્યું' to 'દાબ્યું' (pressed). Changed 'તેમને' to 'તેમણે', corrected letter 'બ' 'આપું' to 'આપ્યું', corrected letters 'મ' and signed 'Bapu'.

[68] MKG corrected the form of letter 'થ' in 'પ્રાર્થના'.

[69] The word 'etc.' translates 'વગેરે'. MKG wrote "Henceforth word etc. should not be used, details have to be specified. Word et cetera has no place in a diary."

7:30 to 8	Cleaned Ba's and my cupboards.
8 to 8:30	Went for a walk with Bapuji.[70]
8:30 to 10:30	Combed Ba's hair, gave her a massage, and prepared her bath and enema.
10:30 to 11:15	Cooked khakhara, vegetables, etc.
11:15 to 12:15	Made preparations for Ba's meal and had my meal.
12:15 to 1	Read the 'Vande Mataram' to Ba.
1 to 1:45	Applied ghee to Ba's and Bapuji's feet.
1:45 to 2:15	I slept.[71]
2:15 to 5:30	During this time read the 7th 'sarg' of Ramayana and newspaper, oiled my hair in the rest of the time. Since it was Bapuji's day of silence, I did not study with him, and Sushilabehn had some work, so did not study with her either. Did spin. But I do not know where the time went. Time passed in laziness.[72]
5:30 to 6:30	Prepared twig for brushing teeth, folded the clothes and placed them,[73] prepared the lamp, I had my meals, made tea for Ba, etc.[74]
6:30 to 7:30	Played.
7:30 to 8	Went for a walk.
8 to 8:30	Prayers.
8:30 to 11	Gave a massage to Ba, pressed her body and placed mosquito net over her bed. Went to study with Pyarelalji. He became so deeply

---

[70] MKG corrected the form of letter 'થ' in this entry.

[71] MKG corrected the form of letter 'થ' in this entry.

[72] She had written, 'Time passed like laziness', corrected by MKG.

[73] In her formulation it read 'placed the clothes in a folded place', corrected by MKG.

[74] The word 'etc' crossed by MKG.

engrossed in the map that we lost awareness of time. It struck 11 o'clock. Soon thereafter, I slept.

27.4.43 to 1.5.42[75] My eyes pained and hence I was prohibited from writing anything at all. Hence, could not write.

Date: 1.5.43

Today Bapuji woke me at 5 for the prayers. We did prayers from 5 to 5:30.

5:30 to 6:45   I slept.

I woke up again at 6:45 and ...

6:45 to 7	Brushed my teeth, squeezed the juice, cleaned table, etc., made tea.
7 to 8	Bathed, combed hair, drank milk, gave tea and medicines to Ba.
8 to 8:30	Went for a walk with Bapuji.
8:30 to 9:30	Gave a massage to Ba, combed her hair and prepared her bath[76] etc.
9:30 to 10	I had a severe headache; hence I closed my eyes, and laid down.
10 to 11	Went to the kitchen, made vegetables, milk, etc.
11 to 12	Read the 'Reader' for a while, made preparations for meals and ate.
12 to 1	I slept.
1 to 2	Bapuji woke me up. I got up. After reading the Ramayana, Bapuji lay down and I applied ghee to

---

[75] It should be 43.

[76] She had used the English word 'bath', MKG wrote over it 'स्नान'.

his feet. Today I could apply ghee to Bapuji with ease, otherwise he asks me to apply it only for five minutes so that I can sleep. But, today Ba did not want to have ghee applied to her feet. After which, in the remaining time, I cleaned my cupboard and arranged clothes properly.

2 to 2:30	I studied with Sushilabehn.
2:30 to 3	I gave water, etc. to Ba and read the newspapers.
3 to 4	Had eye-drops poured in my eyes. I studied with Bapuji with eyes closed.
4 to 4:30	Read the Ramayana once again to Ba.[77]
4:30 to 5	Ate oranges and sat down to write English.
5 to 7	Made tea, read and wrote some English, ate, lay down with my eyes closed. I went to play and bathed.
7 to 7:30	Played.
7:30 to 8	Went for a walk.
8 to 10	I gave a massage to Ba, pressed her body, studied with Pyarelalji and went to bed.

NOTE: Today's 'Vande Mataram' reports that Vijaya behn's [of Anandlal Bapuji] husband Prof. Prabhudasbhai died on 29.4.43 at night. He had cancer.

The headache that I had in Nagpur has started here as well.[78]

Date: 2.5.43

Today Bapuji woke me up at 5.

5 to 5:30	Prayers.
5:30 to 6:30	Slept again.

---

[77] MKG corrected the form of the letter 'વ'.

[78] Signed 'Bapu'.

6:30 to 7:30	Squeezed juice,[79] drank milk, bathed, made tea, arranged[80] the medicines, combed hair.
7:30 to 8	Read the Gita,[81] and cleaned Ba's room.
8 to 8:30	Went for a walk with Bapuji.
8:30 to 9:30	Oiled Ba's hair and combed it, gave her a massage and made preparations for her bath.
9:30 to 10:30	Cooked.
10:30 to 11	Wrote English.
11 to 12:15	I warmed up vegetables, milk, etc., made preparations for meals, I ate, cleaned the utensils, finished other sundry work and went to sleep.
12:15 to 1	Slept.
1 to 2	Applied ghee to Ba's and Bapuji's feet.
2 to 3:30	Today, I did not study with Sushilabehn as she had some other work. I read Ramayana to myself.[82]
3:30 to 4	Read newspapers.
4 to 4:30	Studied with Bapuji.
4:30 to 5:30	Spun, have not counted.[83]
5:30 to 6:45	Prepared twig for brushing teeth and lamp and lights,[84] made tea and after that went to bathe in the pool. Cleaned utensils after eating.
6:45 to 7:30	Played.

---

[79] MKG corrected the form of letter 'ક'.

[80] She has written 'રસખી' instead of 'સરખી'.

[81] MKG corrected GITAJI to GITA.

[82] 'Read to myself' translates a phrase that would literally translate as 'read it in my mind', indicating a difference between reading silently and reading aloud (not necessarily to others).

[83] MKG's question 'How much?'

[84] This term translates the Gujarati term 'diva batti', whereas the term light would indicate electrical light.

7:30 to 8	Because of strong winds we could not play for long. It was a time for walk as well. Walked with Bapuji.
8 to 8:30	Prayers.
8:30 to 10	There was a storm and it rained. Therefore, after the prayers we brought all the beds inside. Gave a massage to Ba and slept after applying ghee to Bapuji's feet.[85]

Date: 3.5.43, Monday

Today was the day to drink castor oil. I had thought much about ways to escape from the clutches of castor oil, one can escape from everything else but it is not an easy thing to escape away from Bapuji.[86] At exactly 5:15 a.m. Bapuji came to my bed with a glass of castor oil, another of water and lemon and woke me up. Today being his day of silence, he said nothing. I brushed my teeth and Bapuji handed to me the glass of castor oil. I was certain that I would vomit. But how is one to vomit in Bapuji's presence? Bapuji was ready to pour it down my throat, but I drank it with my own[87] hands. With great effort I gulped it down and immediately Bapuji gave me the lemon which I sucked. That gave me some relief. Till about nine in the morning the foul smell did not leave my mouth. I drank water thrice. I went to the latrine only twice. Today, for the first time in my life I drank[88] castor oil at the hands of Bapuji, otherwise I would never drink castor oil, no matter whatever the insistence. But Bapuji made me drink it. The other routine activities continued. Since it was Bapuji's day of silence, I did not study with him. At the time I

---

[85] Signed 'Bapu'.
[86] MKG corrected 'નથી' to 'ન હતી'.
[87] MKG corrected 'મારી હાથે' to 'મારે હાથે' (with my own hands).
[88] MKG corrected 'પધું' to 'પીધું' (drank).

was scheduled to study with Sushilabehn, I was asleep, therefore did not study with her either. I read ten 'sargs' of Ramayana, spread over twenty-five pages. These days Pyarelalji has much work and does not teach me. Today I wrote a letter to Murabbi Ramdaskaka. Even today there were heavy rains and a storm. For past many days I have not shown this book to Bapuji. I finished all my work at 10 and went to sleep. I did not spin today, but henceforth I will take out half an hour daily for spinning. Today, the headache was somewhat less. My head pained from morning till only about 2 p.m., after which I was cured.[89]

Date: 4.5.43

Today the day passed as per routine schedule. It was the day of weighing. My weight was 99,[90] Ba's was 88 and Bapuji's was 108.

Date: 5.5.43

Today the day passed like all other days. Additionally, I sewed a bed-sheet of mine and fastened three buttons to a blouse. From today I have decided that I shall improve my handwriting by whatever means. Today Ba examined this notebook of mine and pointed out one or two errors. Today wrote letters to Pujya Manilalkaka and Manubehn. I wrote to Pujyabhai[91] also. Tonight, Ba allowed me to massage her but not press her legs. I studied verses 8 to 17 of the fourth discourse[92] and completed the fifth chapter of grammar that deals with pronoun. These days I do not study with Sushilabehn. Even today I read twenty-five pages of the Ramayana. We have come

---

[89] Signed 'Bapu' with a note: 'Handwriting should improve. Spinning count has not been given. You should write whatever you have studied, so that one would know how much of that has been absorbed.'

[90] The measure is in pounds.

[91] Her father.

[92] Of the Gita.

to the part where Bharata meets king Guha.[93] I did not read much else today. I spun 120 threads. I slept at 10:30.

Date: 6.5.43

Today was like every other day. I stitched one petticoat. I would not need to tear off a saree to wear petticoat and *odhni*. Today we received a card from Vinodbehn. There was also a letter from Pujya Kashikakiba. There was a letter from Murabbi Narandas Bapuji, to which I wrote a reply. Today I studied verses 20 to 30 of the fourth discourse. Bapuji explained to me the chapter sixth of grammar dealing with adjectives. Since yesterday Ba does not permit me to press her legs. Today I had pain both in my eyes and head. I had some drops put in my eyes tonight. Pyarelalji has recommenced teaching me. He began to tell me a story, by the time he reached half way through the story, I recognized that this was the story of Androcles.[94] He did not continue with the story. It was time to sleep. I spun 110 threads.

Date: 7.5.43

Today the eyes were better. There was no headache either. There was a letter from Jayafoiba. Today I studied geometry with Bapuji. I also learnt verses 30 to 41 of the fourth discourse. Today I completed the fourth discourse. I read fifteen pages of the Ramayana. Today Pyarelalji did not teach. It was well past my bed time and therefore Bapuji said that I should sleep. I went to sleep. I spun 130 threads today.

Date: 8.5.43

Today I learnt about declinable (changing) and indeclinable (unchanging) adjectives and about predicative and sub-predicative

---

[93] MKG corrected 'છે' to 'છીએ'.

[94] The story of Androcles and the Lion from Aesop's fables.

adjectives, I also learnt verses 1 to 10 of the fifth discourse. I learnt the tenth chapter of the 'Reader' from Sushilabehn between 2 to 2:30. I learnt about 'complete sentence'[95] in the grammar[96] lesson. I studied grammar from 5 to 5:30. Pyarelalji taught me about atmospheric pressure, moreover I learnt about seasons, that is how cold and hot seasons happen and what factors contribute to it. Today I received some clothes: 4 sarees, 3 under-shorts, 4 blouses and 4 brassieres. I also received some books. Today I spun 120 threads.

Date: 9.5.43

Today Bapuji changed the time for the walk. Instead of 8, the time for walk has been decided from 7:45 to 8:30.

Today it so happened that Bapuji told me that I should sleep from 12 and after that I should apply ghee to his feet. But I had to write English. If I did not write English between 12 and 1, what would I show at 2? If I were to sleep from 12 to 1 and apply ghee on Ba's and Bapuji's feet from 1 to 2, instead I felt that instead of sleeping I should complete my English writing. Because when Sushilabehn asks for English homework I do not have any other writing to do and I write only English homework, I do not like to say that even that I have not completed. So then I went to apply ghee to Bapuji's feet, where I saw that Sushilabehn was already applying it. I was surprised and could not say anything. I just watched. What could I have said in response, tears flowed from my eyes. Even then I asked Bapuji: what is this? Bapuji replied that if you do not sleep I do not want ghee applied by you. If you change the rule I can also do likewise, isn't it? He said similar such things. And I walked away from there. I was pained, what if I had indeed gone to sleep? The day was such that I had to cry. Three–four incidents happened, but I could restrain myself, but I did not know that eventually even Bapuji would do such a thing and it would cause me pain. It has also so happened that on

---

[95] English term in the original.
[96] English term in the original.

some days when Ba is angry she does not allow me to press her legs or apply ghee to her feet. Today Bapuji did something similar. Why should I feel pain if Ba does not permit me to press her legs or apply ghee on her feet? But today even Bapuji expressed his displeasure by not allowing me to apply ghee. Therefore, if Bapuji could do such a thing, how are the others to be faulted? Bapuji should have warned me that if I did not sleep he would not allow me to apply ghee. Bapuji eventually admitted this. Today I spun 160 threads.

Date: 10.5.43

Today being Monday, it was Bapuji's day of silence, therefore I did not study with him. I studied the chapter 11th of the 'Reader' with Sushilabehn. I studied analysis of simple sentences[97] in grammar. I studied about volcanic mountain with Pyarelalji. There were letters from Murabbi Nimukaki and Manubehn. Today I spun 100 threads.

Date: 11.5.43

Tonight Ba's health had deteriorated; I sat with her from 3 to 5:30. She had severe headache and back pain. Her health remained weak through the day. Both Bapuji and Sushilabehn were busy and therefore did not teach me. Pyarelalji explained a little more about volcanic mountains. Tonight I had severe pain in my eyes and also had a headache. I applied castor oil in my eyes and slept early. Today I did not spin.

Date: 12.5.43

Today Ba's health was better. I had a slight headache. The eye is better. Bapuji was busy and he had given me a leave from studies. Today I spun 90 threads.

---

[97] English term in the original.

Date: 13.5.43

Today I was late in reaching for my lessons with Bapuji, therefore we did only 10 verses of the fifth discourse of the Gitaji. Even today I had no headache during the day but there was a slight headache at night. All other things go on in their routine manner. Today I wrote a letter to Murabbi Kakiba and another to Murabbi Nimukaki.

Date: 14.5.43

Today I studied the 11th chapter of the 'Reader' with Sushilabehn. Bapuji today started the sixth discourse. We did 10 verses. I did not study with Pyarelalji today.

Date: 15.5.43

Today I completed 11th chapter of the 'Reader' with Sushilabehn, we also did the 12th chapter. I studied verses 10 to 20 of the sixth discourse with Bapuji. I also learnt to draw directional maps and their measurements (scale).[98]

Date: 16.5.43

After many days, today received a letter from Samyukta behn. I was worried about her health. Her letter came as a relief.

Date: 17.5.43

Today was a day of silence for Bapuji. I did not study with Sushilabehn in the afternoon, but in the morning did the 11th chapter. Today I wrote a letter to Pujya Ramdaskaka. Pyarelalji taught me about the gramophone.

---

[98] English term in the original.

Date: 18.5.43

Today was the day of weighing. My weight was 102 lbs; I put on 2 lbs. Bapuji's weight was 110 lbs. Even Ba put on 2 lbs. This week all of us have put on weight. Today we did verses 20 to 30.[99] Bapuji explained about nouns in grammar lesson. Today I finished reading the Ayodhyakand of the Ramayana. This morning Ba said that all of you keep sitting with Bapuji all day long, no one comes to me. But I go only at the appointed time for my lessons, and at that time Ba is usually asleep. For past few days I sit in her room and write. Even after this Ba expressed the feeling that no one sits with her. Therefore, today I spent the entire afternoon with her, and for this reason I did not even go for my lessons. I sat with Ba the whole time. She liked it very much, that is my impression.

Date: 19.5.43

Today I studied English and completed the 13th chapter. Today Bapuji could teach only five verses of the sixth discourse. The reason was that Bapuji explicated on the meanings, which takes a lot of time. From tomorrow he will teach me pronunciations and will get to the meanings after we complete all the discourses. This evening there was rain with storm; we could not play.

Date: 20.5.43

Today we completed the sixth discourse. In grammar he taught me about nominative and accusatives. Today it was the turn to study English grammar,[100] which I studied. Bapuji taught me about nominative and accusatives.[101] Even today the rains continued and therefore we could not play the game. But, we played many new

---

[99] Of the sixth discourse of the Gita.

[100] English term in the original.

[101] This sentence is repeated in the original.

games. We skipped, played dhamaal gota and played with the ring. We got our exercise but we laughed so much that my stomach ached till the prayer time. Bapu, in the course of his talk, spoke about the victory of Tunisia,[102] he also spoke about his letter to Maxwell.[103] He spoke about Pujya Mahadevbhai as well. The rest of the activities follow their course. I sit with Ba during afternoons. She likes it when I sit with her. I also read to her.

Date: 21.5.43

Today we commenced the seventh discourse and did 10 verses. Bapuji explained about right angles in geometry. We began the 14th chapter of the 'Reader', and finished reading the Kishkindha-Kand in the Ramayana and commenced reading the Sunder-Kand. I made roti and khakhara this morning. For many days I have not shown this note to Bapuji so he remarked that I do not leave my diary with him. But, I do write the diary daily, but do not show it to him because I wrote about the day when he refused to allow me to apply ghee on his feet. I feel ashamed of showing it to him and hence I have stopped showing it to him. But, I will show it to him today. I have become lazy about spinning.

Date: 22.5.43

Today I gave the diary to Bapuji but my mind changed and Bapuji had not seen the diary due to other work. I did not remind him of it because I did not want him to read it.[104] Today, we completed 14 verses of the seventh discourse in ten minutes. We have decided that henceforth we will devote only 10 minutes to it and do as many verses as one can in that time.

---

[102] Written as 'Tunia' in the original.

[103] Sir Reginald Maxwell, Home Member, Government of India. For MKG's letter to him see, *CWMG*, vol. 77, pp. 85–98.

[104] She wrote in the margin 'And yet, I will show it to him'.

Date: 23.5.43

There was strong wind today. It was also clouded. Today was Ba's day of having a head bath, but she did not do so due to the weather. Today Ba was displeased with me because her petticoat was somewhat damp this morning. But these days I do not fold her clothes and I was not aware of it, the clothes come back ironed and if I were to open them out, the crease would get spoiled. It was my mistake that I did not check clothes before putting them out for her. But that does not imply that she would wear whatever I have kept out for her. If the petticoat was damp, she should have told me at that time, she should have asked for another one. She told me late at night, while we were talking about something else. All that I said was that it was my mistake and that I shall be careful henceforth. But after that I could not sleep for two–three hours and kept thinking. Does Ba feel distanced from me? Why does she not ask me to do things for her as she used to when I just came here? And, I have made a great error, what should be my repentance for it? I thought long, as to why I was not able to satisfy Ba. Most certainly, I am in error. Finally, I decided to be more careful. I do not share such things with Bapuji, and I do not intend on doing so.[105] Because, such small matters should not be taken to him. It is a form of telling tales. And Ba is innocent, she does get angry but there is nothing after that. What is there to tell him about? I have not felt bad in the least.[106]

Date: 25.5.43

Today I started the eighth discourse with Bapuji and studied about 90° angles in geometry.

---

[105] She wrote in the margin ' Bapuji asked, but I said nothing'.

[106] Note on top margin of pages 61 and 62 of her diary: 'But, I should be very careful in all the work assigned to me. I did not pay attention, and that was my mistake. But, I do try and be careful. And she is my elder. She has to say where I go wrong. She was not angry, she mildly warned me. I also wept, why did I make this mistake?'

Date: 26.5.43

Bapuji taught the Gitaji while on the morning walk. We completed the eighth discourse. Just then Sushilabehn came, so he began to narrate the story.[107] He told us the story up to the point where he reached Port Said. Today, the government replied to Bapuji regarding the letter he had written to Mr. Jinnah.[108] The government in reply wrote that till such time as you do not change your conduct, there will be no correspondence about political matters, the letter that you have written will not be delivered and we shall make this fact public. Mr. Jinnah says why does not Gandhi write to me? Now that a letter has been written but the authorities refuse to deliver it, we have to see what Mr. Jinnah does. Today I commenced the ninth discourse with Bapuji. Just as I sat down to study with Sushilabehn, Ba asked me to take down a letter addressed to Kashikaki. I took the dictation and hence could not study. This morning I got up after the prayers had commenced. Bapuji had woken me up but I fell asleep and did not hear the prayers. I woke up when the Bhajan was being sung. I had slept late, at 11:30. Bapuji told me that I sleep late and how long should he nag me that I sleep late. But the fact was that I had gone to play late in the evening and therefore I slept late. These days Ba

---

[107] The narration seems to be that of his life story and experiences.

[108] MA Jinnah on 24 April 1943 in his presidential address to the annual session of the Muslim League at Delhi had said: "Nobody would welcome it more than myself, if Mr. Gandhi is even now really willing to come to a settlement with the Muslim League on the basis of Pakistan... If he has made up his mind, what is there to prevent Mr. Gandhi from writing direct to me?... I cannot believe that they will have the daring to stop such a letter if it is sent to me." *CWMG*, vol. 77, p. 75, footnote 1. In response to this MKG wrote to him on May 4, 1924 (see, *CWMG*, vol. 77, pp. 75–6), and requested the Government to forward the letter to Mr. Jinnah. On May 24 Sir Richard Tottenham of the Home Department wrote to MK Gandhi: "I am to inform you that the Government of India have decided that your letter cannot be forwarded." See, *Gandhiji's Correspondence with the Government 1942-44*, (Ahmedabad: Navajivan, 1945), pp. 90–1.

sleeps in Bapu's room in the afternoon. For this reason I do not sit with her. I write my thoughts in this diary[109] and I do not wish to show it to Bapuji. Because I have written this for my knowledge and do not wish to show it. And yet, if Bapuji were to ask for it I would give it to him. It is not a matter of shame. I feel that if one has erred, one should seek forgiveness, why should that be a matter of shame? And hence, I would show the diary[110] to him.

Date: 27.5.43

Since morning I had this feeling that I would have to cry at least once during the day. And it came true. At 10:30 Pyarelalji came to make rotis for Bapuji, at that time I was cooking on two stoves, one big and the other small. On the smaller stove I was cooking vegetables for Ba, and was making rotis on the larger stove. He hurriedly walked in and picked up my pot of vegetables and placed it on an electric stove. He took the larger stove for himself and gave me the smaller one where the flame was low. At that point I said, Pyarelalji, if the vegetables are cooked on the electric stove, Ba would be angry, and I still have to make many rotis, when would I finish it? It was already 10:30. I was also late. I had just said this much and he became very angry. So, I told him that you come late and you want everything in a hurry. You should have told me that you would need a stove. He walked away leaving everything behind and warned me that he would tell Bapuji that he would not make rotis for Bapuji today. I felt very bad and I wept a great deal. Because of me Bapuji would have to go without rotis today. But I finished cooking my rotis and decided no matter what I would not eat today. Bapuji told me that I was not at all at fault, and that I should eat. But I had decided not to eat, probably even Bapuji would not eat. He told me that if I did not eat, he would also not eat. Therefore, I sat down to eat. But the same thought kept

---

[109] English term in the original.
[110] English term in the original.

coming back and it brought tears every time. Kanubhai had told me that I should be very careful and also have forbearance. I tread so carefully so as to not be faulted by anyone. How could this be? If I am not at fault, why should anyone be angry at me? I am not at fault and even then why should Pyarelalji be angry with me? All day passed, this idea did not leave me. At night I had severe headache. It pained even in the morning. Even now it pains. The eyes pain as well. My eyelids had gotten stuck at night. I had woken up at 3 o'clock, washed my eyes and tied a napkin around my head, which gave me some relief and I could sleep. Till then sleep had proved elusive. Bapuji must have come to wake me up at 5 o'clock. But I did not wake up. I did not even hear the prayers being recited. Today I sought leave of absence from Bapuji as I had some other work, but during the evening walk Bapuji taught me the 8th discourse, which we completed. Tonight, Ba had pain in her sides.

Date: 28.5.43

Today, while on the walk Bapuji taught me 18 verses of the ninth discourse.

Date: 29.5.43

Today I studied for 15 minutes with Bapuji but he taught me the Gitaji while on our walk. I wrote a letter to Murabbi Ramdaskaka.

Date: 30.5.43

Bapuji was busy today, so he gave me leave from studies but taught me Gitaji while on our walk together.

Date: 31.5.43

Today Samyuktabehn sent for me from Bombay four Andhra sarees, blouse and other clothes, one comb, etc. Now there is no shortage of clothes. Tonight everyone was heard laughing loudly. I went there. Dr Gilder[111] had received six letters, which he showed to Bapuji. In each letter the date 31st May was mentioned. The year was written as 19___?, which means that there was a question mark about the year. Doctor Sahib had said that we would be released on the 31st, so someone had played a prank with him. When I asked about it, others played a prank with me as well.

Date: 1.6.43

Today I wrote to Samyuktabehn acknowledging receipt of clothes. Bapuji gave me leave from studies, but after a while he called me again. I told him that he looked tired, and for that reason I did not wish to study. But, Bapuji insisted that he would feel at ease only if we did some verses of the Gita. But I declined. Even during the evening walk he asked me to go and fetch Gitaji, but his face and voice suggested fatigue, so I did not get the Gitaji. Then he spoke about Mahadevbhai's death. Before that I had asked him some questions about the Ramayana. Sushilabehn did not teach today. Dr Patwardhan[112] examined my eyes and put some medicines . He will come back tomorrow.

Date: 2.6.43

Dr Patwardhan examined my eyes again today. He said that I would need a new pair of spectacles. Even today Bapuji was busy and gave me leave from studies.

---

[111] Dr Manchersha Dhanjibhai Dorabji Gilder (1882-1979), cardiologist, Member, Bombay Legislative Council, Mayor of Bombay, Minister of Health, Bombay Government (1936-1939 and 1945-1952), Member, Rajya Sabha (1952-1960). First attended to MKG during the 1932 imprisonment at Yervada Jail.

[112] Dr Patwardhan of Amraoti, President of Hanuman Vyayam Prasarak Mandal, constructive worker.

Date: 3.6.43

Today I studied with Bapuji. We did 15 verses of the thirteenth discourse and did ten more verses during our walk together. The thirteenth discourse was completed today. This evening's post brought Pujyabhai's letter.

Date: 4.6.43

Ba did not allow me to apply ghee today because my finger was slightly burnt. I had not spoken about this to anyone. I did not wish to speak about it, as my fingers get burnt quite often and they also heal on their own. But Sushilabehn informed about it, so Ba said I need not apply the ghee. Today I dreamt that we had been released, when I spoke about this to Bapuji, Ba said we have to release Manu in a short time. We will find someone else. This set me thinking: do I not do my work properly? Have I made a grave error? Therefore Ba speaks of finding someone else. Does Ba still not consider me as one of her own? I like it here very much. I do not think that even once I have felt that I am in confinement or that I am forced to live in a jail. Nor have I wished for Bhai to be with us. On the contrary I thank god that I have such a wonderful opportunity to be of service. May that be, what is destined will happen. Today we completed that Valmiki Ramayana. From tomorrow I will read the Bhagavad to Ba. Bhandari[113] today informed Bapuji that I should purchase the new pair of spectacles with my own money. Bapu wrote in response that it is your responsibility to look after the prisoners. You have to provide her with spectacles or face the danger of her losing her eyesight. I asked if I should ask for money from home. Bapuji said no and also said that he would get them to give me new spectacles. And he received a positive response on this.

---

[113] Col. Madan Gopal Bhandari of the Indian Medical Services, Inspector General of Prisons, Bombay, was given Companion Order of the Indian Empire (CIE) in 1942.

Date: 5.6.43

Ba's health worsened tonight. She had palpitations and an attack of asthma. I did not go for the prayers and instead sat by Ba's side. After sometime I lay by her side. Through the day her health remained poor. I touched Ba's, Bapuji's and everyone else's feet today. In the evening Bapuji said that I ask all the children to take some vow on their birthday. 'If you wish I would administrate vow to you.' He told me that I should never speak a lie. I took that vow.

Date: 6.6.43

Today Dr Gilder was unwell. So I told him that I would give him castor oil. He replied that if I were to give him the castor oil at 4 a.m. he would take it, but if I were even late by five minutes he would not drink, I agreed. All wanted to see if I would wake up at 4 on my own. My sleep is sound; I do not wake up in the middle of the night. Once I sleep, I wake up only in the morning. It was difficult for me to get up at 4 a.m. But I had to keep my word so 'we'[114] slept having made all the preparations. I drank lots of water before going to sleep, so that I would be forced to wake up at night. Suddenly, I woke up but it was only 12:30. I went back to sleep and again woke up at 1 o'clock. I went back to sleep. At 2 o'clock I met Bapuji in the bathroom. He exclaimed, 'oh ho!' I was so frightened. I felt that Bapuji had got up for the prayers; and it was already 5 o'clock. I was scared that now everyone would tease me to no end. When I looked at the watch it was five minutes to two. I felt that if I were to fall asleep I would not wake up before the morning. So I decided to bathe. I washed my hair and even then when I come out it was only 2:30 a.m. I went to the couch used by Mahadevbhai and lay down there. And I gave castor oil to Doctor Sahib at exactly four o'clock. The day began with administrations of castor oil and during the day

---

[114] She has used the plural 'we' in the original for herself.

four others were also given the same. I slept for three hours during the day.

Date: 9.6.43

It is ten months to this day since Bapuji's arrest. The eleventh month begins from today. I completed the first reading of all eighteen discourses of the Gita under Bapuji's guidance.

Date: 10.6.43

Mirabehn has persistent back pain. Bapuji has asked her to fast. She began her fast today.

Date: 11.6.43

Tonight I did not feel well at all. I felt very uneasy. I had a headache. I felt better after I vomited. But I have not told anyone because everyone would keep saying 'I have fallen ill', 'I have fallen ill', and moreover, Ba wouldn't allow me to do anything else for her. I slept early today. I prayed to god: please take me away with you. Sometimes I envy Mahadevbhai, because he became one with Bapuji. What if god were to take me away while I am with Bapuji? But from where does one get such good fortune? This evening while at prayer I received a letter from Yuktibehn. I had been waiting for her letter since long. It came unexpected. It was a long and beautiful letter, full of news about everyone. I was overjoyed; but soon thereafter sadness once again enveloped me.

Date: 12.6.43

Now Bapuji has started to teach me the meaning of the Gita. Today Sushilabehn gave me only ten minutes. Mirabehn fasted for a day and a half and has started to drink orange juice. Her pain is less.

Date: 13.6.43

Today we had the inaugural game of ping pong. Bapuji began the game. We had great fun.

Date: 14.6.43

Today Ba dictated a letter of condolence to Vijyabehn, which she signed.

Date: 15.6.43

Since last three days I have failed to hand over the letter to Yuktibehn for it to be posted. I keep postponing it and I forget.

Date: 16.6.43

Today I hurt one of my ribs while playing. I hadn't pulled it but there was excruciating pain.[115] I made an attempt to sit for the prayers but could not. I got up at the time of the Ramayana recitations. I came and lay prostrate in the bed.[116] Sushilabehn offered to give me a massage, but I declined. She complained to Ba that I did not listen to her and would not allow her to examine me. I went to her, she examined me and gave me a hot pack. I fell asleep while she administered the hot pack. I felt much better. Initially, it pained me a great deal, I remembered my mother a great deal because whenever I pulled my ribs... [117]

---

[115] Syntax corrected by MKG: 'નિકળતી હતી' to 'નિકળતું હતું'

[116] Corrected by MKG: 'આવી સૂતી' to 'પડી'

[117] Incomplete entry in the original. End of Diary 1. There are no entries for the days between 16.4. 1943 and 26.6.1943.

Date: 27.6.43 Sunday[118]

SUSHILABEHN'S HAIR IS CUT!

Probably this new notebook was meant to begin with a note about Sushilabehn's hair being cut. Perhaps for this reason I had not begun a new notebook. Sushilabehn had severe dandruff therefore Bapuji cut her hair, and she is totally bald now. How lovely was her hair! Tears came to my eyes. Bapuji, please do not cut her hair, I pleaded. But Bapuji is not one to change his mind. They were cut off. Everyone joked and laughed about it all day long. Today I wrote letters to Kakiba, Kantibhai and Bhagwanjibhai. In the evening Bapuji made a count of the number of girls whose hair he has been responsible for cutting. He has cut hair of approximately thirteen girls. Sushilabehn's hair was curly and very pretty. I was envious of her hair. But she had her hair removed with enthusiasm and a smile on her face—that is a true mark of courage. Even if I were to have my hair cut of my own volition, I would not be able to restrain my tears. There was not a drop in her eyes. In any case, weeping is a general weakness of mine. So it wouldn't be such a big thing for me.

Date: 28.6.43

From today I have stopped taking bath with hot water. I have never washed my hair with cold water and therefore they wouldn't wash well. Still, let's see what happens. But I must give up the habit of using warm water. However, today I washed my hair with hot water, but I shall refrain from doing so in the future.

Date: 29.6.43

Ba had fever today. I sat by her side almost all day long. I did not study today.[119]

---

[118] Diary 2 begins with this entry.
[119] No diary entry for 30.6.43.

Date: 1.7.43

Sushilabehn had fever today. It measured 100.6°C. It was around 100°C in the evening. It is likely to be malaria. Today we received letters from Pujyabhai, Kanubhai and Ramdaskaka.

Date: 2.7.43

Today, I wrote a letter to Pujya Kakiba. Sushilabehn did not have fever today. But she was weak. Therefore, I did not study with her. Ba's health is steady. She generally plays carrom. Today, she played even ping pong. She remains joyful during games. [120]

Date: 4.7.43

Today I wrote letters to Pujyabhai, Ramdaskaka and Manubehn. Today being letter-writing day, I was busy all day long in it, therefore I lost track of time and did not study (with Bapuji).

Date: 5.7.43

There was a letter from Murabbi Sushilakaki today. These days I embroider a saree, almost all time goes in it. Since this morning I had a mild headache, which I presumed would go away. I applied ghee to Bapuji's feet and before that I cooked as well. I felt slightly cold when I applied ghee to Ba's feet. But I attributed it to a slight breeze. After that I covered myself with a blanket and lay down for about five minutes. I got up at 2 o'clock and studied. The cold persisted. After studies I read the newspaper but I felt very tired and was out of breath. I could not read the newspaper for long. I lay down in the bed. I was gripped by fever. It was accompanied by shivering. Today was Bapuji's day of silence. I had severe headache, which became even

[120] No diary entry for 3.7.43.

more acute in the evening. Sushilabehn asked after me two–three times and offered to press my head, but I did not feel the need for it. Bapuji put a mud pack on my forehead in the evening, which gave me relief.

Date: 6.7.43

I had fever today as well. Today Bapuji had a talk with me and said that sleep would be good for my eyes, and he would like that as well.[121] Hence, I would sleep from today. But he also said a sentence, which for me is a matter of great sadness. He said *I see that you give a promise but are unable to keep it*.[122] This is entirely true but at night I thought over this sentence. Why do I give such an impression? This line is a warning to me and it would be good if I could change this impression. Today I received letters from Yuktibehn, Kantabehn, Kapilabehn and others. These days Bapuji is translating the Ramayana. Today, Dr Gilder had fever.[123]

Date: 25.7.43

Today, Sushilabehn is displeased with me. I do not know for what reason. She has been somewhat displeased with me since yesterday, but today it was very pronounced. She grew angry once or twice. For some time things were very good between us. I am not perturbed by her irritation. She treats me like a younger sister. But I cannot fathom the reason for her displeasure. So be it! Ba becomes displeased all of a sudden and she is pleased soon thereafter, such things go on. I pray to god that while I am here, I should not cause harm to anyone. But some day I do make errors. Yesterday the vegetables were slightly

---

[121] This refers to afternoon sleep. Refer to the diary entry of 22.4.43 regarding resolution to refrain from afternoon sleep.

[122] Emphasis in the original.

[123] No diary entries from 7.7.43 to 24.7.43

burnt by me while cooking. Last night I had severe body pain for which I took quinine. I have written these notes after a gap of many days—pages are expensive, aren't they?[124]

Date: 27.7.43

Today I had fever once again. It was preceded by a sense of cold. I took quinine, which did not prevent the fever. I lay down without informing anyone. Later I informed Bapuji and thus everyone else came to know of it. The temperature was 103°C. Fever persisted all night. I felt very uneasy. In all these days I have not longed for home, but today I pined for home. I am worried about Yuktibehn. Her health is not good.

Date: 28.7.43

I had fever today as well.

Date: 29.7.43

Today I did not have any fever. I started wearing salwar-kurta[125] from today. Bapuji said that my dress of petticoat, etc. was dangerous. He said that I must keep warm. Sushilabehn has been saying this to me for long. But, I felt that I would need at least three pairs of salwar-kurta; what was she to do about this. I did not wish to get three pairs, but her insistence was such that I had to take three pairs. Now Mirabehn, Sushilabehn and I, all three of us wear salwar-kurta. We have become Punjabis. Even today I did not study.

---

[124] No diary entry for 26.7.43

[125] She has written સરવાલ (sarwal) instead of સલવાર (salwar), throughout the entry.

Date: 30.7.43

Bapuji has started to teach 'Margopodeshika' from today. I have recommenced giving a massage to Ba.

Date: 1.8.43

Today I wrote letters to Murabbi Sushilakaki, Kakiba and Mathuradas bhai. Now I am required to take a quinine tablet every Monday and Thursday. These days Bapuji has been translating the Ramayana. He spins a great deal. He teaches Sushilabehn and me. I had severe body ache today.

Date: 2.8.43

Last year on this day Bapuji had gone to Bombay for the AICC sessions. And today he is in the Aga Khan Palace. Last year I was really after him to take me to Delhi but he declined.[126] But it must be in my fate to be with him on this day today, and hence I came here. Who knew that I would have the opportunity to be here? The will of the god is known only to Him. Today I finished reading the Bhagavad to Ba. Ba wanted to hear it once again, hence I have started on it again.

Date: 8.8.43

Today it is one year since Bapuji's arrest. On this day last year the AICC resolution was passed. We saluted the flag and spun from 2:30 to 3:30. Pyarelalji recalled that last year on this day Bapuji's address began at 9 o'clock. Mahadevbhai and he wrote down each word that Bapuji said and today Mahadevbhai has reached in the presence of

---

[126] This should be Bombay and not Delhi as the AICC session was held in Bombay.

god. Who knew that Mahadevbhai would pass away! It's almost one year to his departure.

Date: 9.8.43

Bapuji was arrested on the morning of this date last year; he was brought to the Aga Khan Palace. It is one year to that date. Yesterday, Dr Sahib led us into saluting the flag. All of us sang 'Jhanda uncha rahe hamara', 'Sare Jahan se Accha' and 'Vande Mataram'. Even Ba came down to the grounds, which she did for the first time after I came here. Today I wrote letters to Kuvarjibhai, Pujyabhai, Ramdaskaka and Kakiba. We could hear shouts of 'Jay, Jay' from Yervada.

Date: 10.8.43 Tuesday

For quite sometime now I set curd, soak clothes, etc. I like this work. But from today this work has been stopped. Today was the day of measuring our weight. Mine was 103 lbs, Bapuji's was 112 lbs, Pyarelalji's 120 lbs, Sushilabehn's was 106 lbs and Ba weighed 90 lbs. No one has lost weight.

Date: 11.8.43

15th will be Mahadevbhai's death anniversary and we have decided to recite the complete Gita on that day. Sushilabehn, Pyarelalji and I study the Gita with Bapuji. Hence, from today my scheduled time of 4 to 4:30 with Bapuji has been changed. Today I received a letter from Vijyabehn from Porbandar. I also got a postcard from Pujyabhai, in which he writes about a flood in Upleta wherein about 15 khandis[127] of groundnuts were destroyed. This year there has been excessive rains all around. Bengal has floods, so do Kathiawad and Marwad. Some twenty to twenty-five thousand have died in Marwad

---

127 20 mound= 1 khandi = 746.48 kilos, approximately.

alone in the floods. Who knows how many cattle, etc. have perished? We came to know of this through the newspapers. On the one hand there is death by hunger and on the other this fury of the water! How unfortunate can Hindustan be? When we read about all this in the newspapers, shivers go down our spines. We have begun to lock the kitchen cupboard because there were some thefts. Today Ba's health was not good.[128]

Date: 14.8.43

Today Ba suffered a heart attack.[129] It began at 2 p.m., it subsided for a while and started again and continued till about 11 at night. Doctor Shah and others came. They examined her with a machine. Tonight I slept by Ba's side. Oh! What a beautiful feeling that was. Ba patted my head and adjusted my blanket. I caressed her as one caresses a child. At 12 o'clock she told me to go and sleep in my bed as she felt better. She has become very weak.

Date: 15.8.43

Today was Mahadevbhai's death anniversary. Last evening Sushilabehn had kept aside materials for making khichadi, vegetables and kadhi. It was distributed this morning. The room in which Mahadevbhai had lived was cleaned. Mirabehn and Sushilabehn decorated with flowers the platform where Mahadevbhai was cremated. I was with Ba and

---

[128] No diary entries for 12 & 13 August, 1943.

[129] It was most probably an attack of tachycardia. In a report to Col. Bhandari dated 12 March 1943, Dr Gilder and Dr Nayar described the medical condition of Kasturba thus: 'She has been suffering from chronic bronchitis with dilation of the bronchi. She has also complained latterly of pain of an angina character and has had attacks of tachycardia with a heart rate of 180 per minute.' *Gandhiji's Correspondence with the Government 1942-44*, (Ahmedabad: Navajivan, 1945), p. 275.

therefore reached there a little late. Today Bapuji went out again and reached the cremation spot at 7:45, I reached there when he was reciting verses. The place was exquisitely decorated. All furniture from his room was removed. The place where his body was laid was covered with a bed sheet from jail. The place where his head was laid was marked with ॐ and a cross (†) was made where his feet were placed. Flowers were placed all around, including on cupboards. All this was done by Mirabehn. At 10 o'clock the bell rang. I placed a lamp where his feet were placed. Doctor Sahib, Kateli Sahib, Pyarelalji, Mirabehn, Sushilabehn, Ba and I sat in prayers. We recited the 'Isa Vashya', which was followed by 'Vaishnava Jan', 'Ram Dhun', 'Mazda'. Mirabehn sang a hymn in English. Mirabehn, Doctor Sahib and Kateli Sahib left after that, the rest of us recited the entire Gitaji. The atmosphere was sublime and sombre. It took us approximately an hour and ten minutes to recite the Gita. After which Sushilabehn gave water to Bapuji and I to Ba. I soaked clothes and accompanied by Sushilabehn went to oversee the food being cooked for the prisoners. In the half an hour before the meals I studied Margopdeshika. Around 1 o'clock the food was brought up and the prisoners also came. Bapuji, Doctor Sahib and Mirabehn served them khichadi, kadhi and vegetables. Ba sat on a chair. Sushilabehn had slight nausea, I gave her some juice. Bapuji stayed their till everyone had eaten. I applied ghee to Bapuji's and Ba's feet. I slept at around 2:30. I was not able to sleep well last night. I woke up at 3:30. There was some spinning done. Everyone had kept a 24-hour fast. So Sushilabehn and I went to the kitchen to make halwa. Sushilabehn made a delicious halwa with almonds and cardamom. We served food to Bapuji at 5:45, after which we had our meals. I folded the washed clothes and made preparations for the prayers. I cut my hand during the evening. This has happened quite a few times, but today the cut was somewhat deeper and it pained. I went to Bapuji with the cut hand, although I had no intentions of doing so. Sushilabehn applied iodine and tied a bandage. We then went for a walk and did our prayers. Bapuji's silence began after the prayers. I applied ghee to his feet, and gave a massage to Ba and went to sleep. Tonight there was to be a moon eclipse, hence Sushilabehn woke me up at 2 a.m.. We watched the eclipse. One year has passed since Mahadevbhai's death. Years will just roll by. How fortunate of him to have died at Bapuji's feet. God may grant peace to his soul that would be the only prayer. Mahadevbhai was there one day and was gone the next! Today was Sunday, but could not write the letters. I will do so tomorrow.

Date: 16.8.43

Today I wrote to Kanubhai and Narandaskaka. Even today Ba's health was not good. Today I could not give her a massage because of the wound on my hand; could not even give her a head bath. These days I think that I should eat only boiled food. I will ask Bapuji and if he agrees I would adopt that. But I do not have the courage to ask him.[130]

Date: 18.8.43

A mouse came into my bed last night. I woke up to find the mouse. I told Sushilabehn who chased it away. Everyone teased me all day long that I must have gone to bed with a roti. Today I received letters from Pujyabhai and Yuktibehn.

Date: 19.8.43

I recommended giving a massage to Ba from today. Since yesterday we have stopped doing the meanings of terms in the Gita. Now we will concentrate upon pronunciations. We have started with the third discourse.

Date: 20.8.43

There wound on my hand has become septic. Sushilabehn said that I cannot give a massage to Ba because of it. Ba is somewhat displeased;

---

[130] No diary entry for 17.8.43.

she had told me yesterday that I should give her a massage today, but because of the septic I would not be able to give her massage. Doctor Sahib informed her of this. She became angry with me. Since last two days she has not had anything to eat. She only drinks milk. I have begun to spin again from today. Bapuji gave the permission to eat boiled vegetables and give up eating the pudding. I have begun with boiled vegetables, let's see how long I last. Bapuji told me that 'you do not recite the Gitaji during prayers and are not awake, instead you should sleep, because you do this only to please me; but this is not correct. You don't even sing the bhajans.' Therefore, I have decided that I shall wake up on my own and remain alert. Since the last three days or so I wake up on my own, and I am also alert. I wake up three-four times at night least it be the time for prayers! I go back to sleep but remain alert.[131]

Date: 22.8.43 Saturday

Ba is still displeased. She does not talk much with anyone. She has begun studying Gitaji with me. What am I going to teach her? We also read Gita Dhwani. Today I was with Ba till 5:30.

Date: 23.8.43 Sunday

We received a typewriter and books from Sevagram today. Many Gujarati books have come. Even today I felt feverish. Yesterday the temperature was 99.4ºC.

Date: 24.8.43 Monday

Today is Janmasthami. Mirabehn has decorated Bal-Krishna. This afternoon I had fever once again. Yesterday was the day of letter-writing. It took me an hour to finish writing the letters. At four o'clock I sat down to spin, hence I could not study. I studied for

---

[131] No entry for 21.8.43

about 15 minutes with Sushilabehn after which I spun for a while and went to play. But we made up for the lost half an hour today from 11 to 11:30. Bapuji said, 'you must keep to the scheduled time for all activities.' Today we kept to the half hour time which made Bapuji very happy. It would be good if this could continue. The hand has not healed so far. I have not begun giving the massage. Today after eight days Ba ate sweet potatoes, tomatoes and milk. Mirabehn joined in the evening prayers. The prayer was very beautiful.

Date: 25.8.43

Even today I had fever. The temperature was 99°C. I had severe headache and body fatigue.

Date: 26.8.43

These days I spin regularly. It would not have occurred to me but on 15.8.43, Mahadevbhai's death anniversary, I had decided to spin, but I could not spin. The matter ended there. On the following day Bapuji had a talk with Sushilabehn because even she had not kept her resolve to spin. He said, 'A true resolve of a person is always fulfilled. If you were unable to spin yesterday you should have spun this morning. And not just that, one must spin daily.' This talk applied to me as well. I therefore decided to make a resolution that I shall spin. Moreover he said, 'If all of us spin daily for half an hour the terrible hunger and slavery of 40 crore people would go away today.' I was convinced by this argument. The spinning continues till today.[132]

Date: 30.8.43

Today I wrote letters to Kakiba and Manubehn. I received two shawls today, hence wrote a response to Yuktibehn. Since last two days I

---

[132] No diary entries for 27, 28, 29 August 1943.

have resumed playing badminton. I played in the morning. I went because of the insistence of Dr Gilder and Bapuji. I really did not want to play, even after two days I am not fully into the game. They told me that I do not take enough exercise, and hence I go and play. Today Ba put me to a test. She had washed her hair. Every day I apply oil to her hair at 4 p.m. At 4 I asked her if I should apply oil. She replied, 'That would be my good fortune.' Tears came to my eyes at that very instance. Why did not Ba tell me to apply oil earlier at 3:30? I asked her. She replied, 'I wanted to check if you would ask, because till 4 you did not ask. Probably you thought that it would do if oil is applied tomorrow morning. But just then you asked. You passed the test.' I am constantly put through such tests. This has created a good impression about me, this I surmised from Ba's talk. She told me that I am punctual, but if I were to apply oil a bit earlier from tomorrow, we would have more time for reading the Bhagavad.[133]

Date: 2.9.43

We have stopped reading the Bhagavad from today. We have begun to read about the characters of the Mahabharata and the Ramayana. All of us spend half an hour daily with Bapuji studying the Gitaji. If our pronunciations improve, it would be a big task accomplished. We have completed four discourses. Bapuji says that it would take two months but our pronunciations would ultimately improve. It has been decided that we will take quinine twice a week.

Date: 3.9.43

These days I read history with Sushilabehn from 6 to 6:30 in the evening. Today I could not go to her because I finished all my other tasks only at 6:20. I had only ten minutes left for studies, I thought, why should I go for only ten minutes? I folded the washed clothes.

---

[133] No entries for 31.8.43 and 1.9.43.

At that time Bapuji came and said, 'One should not deviate from a time that has been agreed upon. If you cannot comply with it, it's better not to do it. It's not good to gulp down food in four minutes.' I told him that I would eat at 5:45. He asked me if I prayed before eating. I replied that I forget sometimes. Bapuji said, 'God gives us food for which we should be grateful to Him and we should pray that He give us the capacity to serve others.' Both these advices, one of punctuality and the other regarding prayers have come to be etched on my mind. Now, I sit down to eat at 5:45 and remember to say my prayer as well.

Date: 4.9.43

Ba's health is not good today. We finished the fifth discourse and began the 6th.

Date: 5.9.43

Today was the Parsi New Year. Sushilabehn woke up early and wrote 'Sal Mubarak' with flour at the door. Kateli Sahib came with a garland, a coconut, a pair of chappals for Bapuji and rose water for Doctor Sahib. Sushilabehn applied a 'tika' on their foreheads. A lot of sweets had been received from Surat. Therefore they said no sweets should be prepared at home. Both of them touched Bapuji's feet, after which all of us went to play badminton. Ba's health is not good even today.

Date: 6.9.43

Ba has a swelling on her nose and has excruciating back pain. After many days I gave her a massage at night. Today I did not play.

Date: 7.9.43

Even today, I gave her a massage at night.

Date: 8.9.43

Ba is somewhat better. Last night I ran a temperature of about 99°C.
I did not speak about this to anyone.

Date: 10.9.43 Wednesday

Everyone's weight was measured today. My weight has come down
from 104 lbs to 100 lbs. I lost 4 lbs. I do not know why the loss.
Everyone said that the loss was due to boiled vegetables and that
I had stopped eating pudding. But the fact is that before I came
here I never weighed 100 lbs. but I have lost what I had gained.
I had intermittent temperature, of which I had not spoken about
because I was cured after taking quinine. It causes trouble if I say it
and even if I do not say it. If I were to speak about it, I would earn
Ba's displeasure. She would say, 'She is bored and therefore she gets
fever.' If I do not speak about it then it causes me harm, but I am not
worried about that.

This evening I was forced to eat pudding, cream and vegetables
cooked in oil. I had to drink a bowl full of milk. I was given so much
to eat. Eventually, I vomited a bit. I did not want anyone to know
about it, as it would have caused greater displeasure to Ba. Sushilabehn
was seated beside me. She asked me as to what had happened. I told
her that I had vomited. She told me, 'Some people have this habit.
Even my sister-in-law had this habit. After her marriage, whenever
we insisted that she eat more, she would vomit. We teased her a great
deal and got her out of the habit.' She was teasing me, but I felt as if
I had vomited because I wanted to. The fact is that everyone has been
angry with me because I lost weight. This had left an impression on
me since the morning. My health was also not very good; and I over-
ate and hence the vomit. After this she went to Doctor Sahib and also
informed him. When I heard about this I could not contain myself. I
wept. I locked myself in the bathroom and wept. It was time for my
reading with her, so I went. I tried hard to restrain myself but I could
not and I wept. I just said that I did not vomit because I like doing

it. She clarified that it was not her intention to suggest that. She had merely spoken about her sister-in-law. I stopped crying. I went to play the game but I could not concentrate on the game. When she came there, I went away. I came up to my room. I did not want to go for the evening walk. But I went nevertheless. All that happened then was probably destined. Bapuji asked me, 'Why did you cry?' I gave no reply. He then told me, 'We have an agreement. You must tell me whatever happens'. I told him what had hurt me. I understand, I told him, that she had spoken to me out of love and that both brother and sister love me, but today I was hurt. I told him that I understand her intentions. Bapuji told me that I should not allow such things to hurt me. We spoke about Gitaji and how fast he had taught me the Gita.

Sushilabehn came there after the game and said, 'So Manu, you had ample opportunity to cry?' Bapuji asked her as to what she had told me. She was hurt and said that I will never say anything to this girl even in jest. Bapuji replied that he had not meant that. Sushilabehn asked me as to why I had spoken to Bapuji after the matter had been resolved between us. I told her that I had not complained but merely reported to him when asked. She was enraged. It pained me even more. I went to bed early but could not sleep till after 2 o'clock. I kept thinking as to why I had been brought here among others? Till 2 my eyes had tears. I was hurt that I am not to speak to Bapuji about anything. I remembered my life in Karachi. I have grown up with many sisters, but we never fought among ourselves. I am afraid of everyone[134] and pray to god that he should keep my relations with all[135] sweet. Why do such things happen? We got up in the morning; I did not feel like talking with anyone. I drank milk. She did not have her lunch at 11. She did not eat because she was angry. I felt bad that she should have to fast because of me. I decided that I too shall not eat. Finally I ate a

---

[134] She had originally written 'Su.Behn', i. e. Sushila Nayar, which she scratched and wrote 'everyone'.

[135] Originally 'her', changed to 'all'.

small portion of pea's rice on Ba's insistence. In the evening as I sat weeping, Pyarelalji came and explained the situation to me. I had half a khakhara and half bowl of milk for dinner. She also ate very little and said that she did not eat because she was angry. So be it, such is the will of god. I learnt a new lesson today that I should not take anyone's words to heart, and if one is hurt it should not be made apparent. I consider her to be like an elder sister and would continue to believe this. She is after all affectionate. Pyarelalji told me, 'You must let go of this hurt. You study Gitaji, but that is waste of Bapuji's time. One cannot be so hurt by everyone's words.' I told him that I was hurt because she did not eat, her words did not hurt me as much. I also felt that I make such mistakes repeatedly. My hurt was caused by my actions and not of the others.

Date: 10.9.43[136]

Today I received letters from Maneklal Bapuji and Pujyabhai. There were letters from Chandravali and Vijya, but they were returned as they were not from relatives. Pujya Anandlal Bapuji's health has become very frail. He has become a skeleton. Pujyabhai receives my letters irregularly and that causes him worry. He is also worried because Yuktibehn and Vinodbehn are not keeping good health. What is one to do?

Date: 11.9.43

Today is one year since the day that Pyarelalji came to Bapuji. He told me that he was about to begin a new year and I should not harbour any hurt and I should play and laugh like before. He also said that Sushilabehn's mind has also been purified. I told him that my heart has been cleansed. He promised to teach me English daily for ten minutes in the morning. Ba is unwell today, she has stomach

---

[136] There are two entries for 10.9.43.

ache. She ate late at around 2 p.m.. For the past three days or so I have headache. I went to sleep soon after lunch. I slept in my bed.

Date: 12.9.43

Ba is better. Sushilabehn is also well. Everything is all right.[137]

Date: 16.9.43

This afternoon, after sleep, as I sat applying ghee to Bapuji's feet, Kateli Sahib came with the news that orders of my release had been received. I took it as a joke, but he showed the order to Bapuji. I was scared. But Bapuji said that the order was for my release but it also gave me the option of staying here under the current restrictions and if I wished to be released at some later date, I would be free to go. Bapuji asked me for my views. All others said we should ask Bhai for his views. I said that Bhai would want me to stay and serve; moreover he has given total freedom to me to take my decisions. Bapuji said that 'I am responsible for Jaysukhlal, he would say nothing.' I said, 'I don't want to go. Even my studies are progressing so well.' Who would like to go away from someone like Bapuji? Would I get such an opportunity ever again in my life? I considered these issues and said that I did not want to go. Moreover, I am not a burden here, why should I go away? Momentarily, I was tempted to go out and meet Bhai and Yuktibehn, but that was for a moment only. I discarded that wrong thought in a moment. Bapuji wrote for me the reply soon after his rest.

'Maherban Kateli Sahib,

You have informed me that the government of the Central Provinces, whose prisoner I am, desires to release me. But, if I decide on my free will to stay here under the current restrictions, I would be free to do so. You have sought my response to this. I hereby give

---

[137] No entries for 13,14,15 September 1943.

you my reply. I came here to serve Kasturba. I desire to stay here so long as she wants me to. I hereby accept all the restrictions currently in force. I also understand that if in the future I were to seek release, I would be free to do so. I am therefore not required to seek the opinion of my father on this matter, I will however inform him of my wish to stay here by a letter.'[138] Bapuji wrote this draft. I wrote this in clear hand and gave it to Mr Kateli. I could not spin today.

Date: 17.9.43

Ba sent a telegram to Manilalkaka today. He has lost the case and she is very worried. The government sent the telegram, but afterwards came to Bapuji to ask for the money of the telegram. Bapuji said to Mr Kateli that you can inform the government that Ba has no money of her own, but she has some clothes which they can auction and recover three rupees from her. Everyone laughed out aloud.[139]

Date: 23.9.43

I wrote to Pujyabhai today. After giving a bath to Bapuji, Sushilabehn was taking her bath. She slipped in the bath,[140] there was a loud noise, which none of us heard. She became unconscious. But the shower[141] was on, from which the water poured on her and revived her. She bathed with cold water, wore her clothes and came out and lay down. She had hit her head hard. God saved her! At night I pressed her head for about half an hour. She did not eat lunch. I had a lot of work to do in the kitchen. I slept at 1 p.m. and got up at 3 p.m.; made juice and pudding. Today I had more work than usual.

---

[138] The letter is also reproduced in the *CWMG*, vol. 77, pp. 200-1, albeit there is a slight variation between the diary and the *CWMG*.

[139] No entries from 18.9.43 to 22.9.43.

[140] English term 'bath' in the original.

[141] English term 'shower' in the original.

I played ping pong—because of the rain we could not play with the ring outside. I had a leave of absence from studies today.

Date: 24.9.43

This morning after giving Ba a massage Sushilabehn and I went to the kitchen to prepare sweets and chevdo. Sushilabehn began work earlier than me. I could join her after the massage. We made chevdo, etc. Sweets have turned out very well. Even the chevdo is good. These have been made for distribution among the prisoners on Bapuji's birthday. We used jaggery to make sweets. We could not study today because Sushilabehn still has fainting spells. I applied ghee to Ba's and Bapuji's feet post afternoon sleep. The government's response about the expenses for the wire came today. Bapuji has been asked to pay for it out of his own account. Bapuji said, 'What was the need to inform me? If they could get water from rocks, they could get money out of me.' All of us laughed at this. Bapuji had responded to the charge of 'Congress Responsibility'. Tottenham has acknowledged the receipt and has said that Bapuji's response is under consideration.[142]

Date: 25.9.43

Today we discussed on tomorrow's programme. Mirabehn suggested that one of us should dress up as Roosevelt, another as Churchill; I should be dressed as a Sudhu, and Sushilabehn as Madam Chang-i-Shek. But this idea was later rejected. Pyarelalji declined to take

---

[142] On 15 July MKG made a detailed reply to the government charge of 'Congress Responsibility for the Disturbances, 1942-43' (see, *Gandhiji's Correspondence with the Government, 1942-44*, pp. 117-264), on 10 September he wrote to the Additional Secretary, Home Department, that he had not received the acknowledgment of the receipt of his reply to which Sir Richard Tottenham replied on 20 September 1943 that his reply had been received and was under consideration. See, *Gandhiji's Correspondence with the Government, 1942-44*, p. 265.

part in this saying that Bapuji does not like such enactments. But Mirabehn insisted that we must do something. Sushilabehn wore my frock; it looked very good on her. She looked much younger, she was to dress up as a Parsi girl. Eventually, I was made to dress up as a Parsi girl with a frock and embroidered cap. Doctor Sahib dressed up as Sardar Akbar Khan (person of the frontier province), Mirabehn dressed up as a Sikh, Pyarelalbhai as a Dakshini Brahmin, Sushilabehn wore a cross and Mirabehn's long coat. Mirabehn made a beard from Sushilabehn's hair and wore Doctor Sahib's coat and trousers over her kurta. She looked unmistakably like a Sardarji. Doctor Sahib wore Mirabehn's salwar[143] and white turban. Pyarelalbhai tied the turban for him. We laughed till we could no longer breathe. After the rehearsal, I read the newspapers to Ba and made gol-papdi for Bapuji because he does not eat sweets. It turned out to be more spicy because of the extra ginger that I put in it. At 4 o'clock Kateli Sahib came with a parcel of fruits and clothes received from Shantikumarbhai.[144] It contained two dhotis, four napkins, two handkerchieves, etc. of which two napkins were for Ba. The parcel contained a beautiful garland and a coconut with the swastika drawn over it. There were dry fruits as well, which seem to have been procured from Karachi. I studied from 4 to 4:30 and read to Ba. At around six, I read for a while with Sushilabehn. We had to make a garland for tomorrow so I sat down to spin. I spun for a while and after that went out to play. After the games I made a hank and soaked it a bit. After the prayers we got busy with decorations in the veranda and tied flowers to fruit baskets. Pyarelalji wrote, 'may we live for hundred autumns'. 'Truth alone wins not falsehood.' 'Lead us from darkness to light.' 'May we see hundred autumns.' 'May we listen to hundred autumns.' Mirabehn drew a lotus at the threshold and wrote ॐ. I worked with

---

[143] Even here she has written 'सरवाल' instead of 'salwar' (सलवार).

[144] Shanti Kumar Morarjee (1902-1982) was a noted industrialist and Chairman, Scindia Steamship Navigation Company. He and his wife Sumati Morarjee were close associates of MKG.

them for a while. Sushilabehn sent me to sleep at around 12 saying that Bapuji would be angry if I stayed up too late; they slept around 2:30. They made garlands and tied them to the door frames at night. Today and tomorrow remind me of the New Year celebrations we used to have in Porbandar. It was a new and different kind of joy. May god grant us this day for ages to come, with this prayer I counted the beads and went to sleep. We were required to get up early the next day.

Date: 26.9.43 Sunday

The auspicious moment! Not only the moment but the day itself was auspicious. Bapuji entered the 75th year of his life.[145] God, may you grant Bapuji a long life of several ages. Today Bapuji woke me up at 5. I brushed my teeth. I wanted to bathe but it was already time for prayers. Sushilabehn had already touched Bapuji's feet. I had not. I was under the impression that we were to touch his feet after having a bath and at the time of garlanding him. Sushilabehn reminded me at prayer time and said that she had already greeted Bapuji by touching his feet. I went to Bapuji. He was seated in the bed. I bowed to him and he patted firmly on my back. We did our prayers after that. Even Ba joined us for prayers today. We sang the following bhajan.

और नहि कछु कामके

में भरोसे अपने रामके...

After the bhajan we sang Raghupati Raghav. After the prayers Sushilabehn and I slept for a while and got up at 6. I went down to bathe. I touched Bapuji's feet and said may you live long and may god grant you your wishes. The garlands of flowers were delightful. Mirabehn almost danced at this beautiful sight. After this I went

---

[145] The birthday was observed according to the Vikram Samvat and marked as Rentiya Baras.

down to bathe.[146] I combed my hair. All of us wore sarees with red borders today. Ba had worn a saree spun by Bapuji. I once again touched Bapuji's feet and received two pats on the back. I prepared juice and gave it to Bapuji. I made tea. At 7:30 our short play was to begin hence I went to change the frock. Pyarelalji wore his dhoti like a lungi, Sushilabehn wore Mirabehn's coat and Doctor Sahib wore a turban and coat over Mirabehn's salwar,[147] he looked unmistakably like Sardar Samsher Singhji.[148] All of us dressed up and sat waiting in Mirabehn's room. Kateli Sahib went to Bapuji and told him that he had five visitors. Bapuji came into the room. Kateli Sahib introduced us. My given name was Jarbal Jariwala. All of us had names. I was the first to approach him and greeted him, 'Mahatmaji Sal Mubarak'. Bapuji laughed a great deal and gave me an affectionate pat on my cheeks. After me Sushilabehn went and greeted Bapuji, followed by Doctor Sahib. All of us were rolling with laughter. Sushilabehn and I had to sit down as we had laughed so much. It was great fun. Mirabehn was the last to enter. She said, 'Here is some halwa from our Punjab.'[149] Bapuji replied, 'Welcome Sardarji, I must accept your halwa.'[150] We joked for a while. Bapuji took us all for a walk in the garbs we had adopted. Ba also accompanied us. We were on our way to the Samadhi,[151] when Kateli Sahib said what fun it would be if the sergeant were to report that there were some strangers on the premises! As we went down the steps Kateli Sahib shouted, 'Jamadar'. Raghunath seemed frightened. He hadn't worn his coat. He came rushing. Kateli Sahib asked. 'Why were these outsiders allowed in?'[152] Poor man became senseless. We were laughing, but he was shaken and could give no response. After a while he realised and

---

[146] This sentence is repeated.
[147] Sarwal instead of salwar.
[148] In the earlier entries the name is Sardar Akbar Khan.
[149] These sentences are in Hindustani.
[150] These sentences are in Hindustani.
[151] Of Mahadev Desai.
[152] This sentence is in Hindustani.

said I could recognise Manubai and Sushilabai, but just could not place Doctor Sahib and Mirabai. Thus our play came to an end. We prayed at the Samadhi. Sushilabehn garlanded Bapuji and said that it was from Mahadevbhai. We returned. Bapuji said we must play. We went and played a game of badminton. We lost at 17 points. Sushilabehn and I were partners while Doctor Sahib and Kateli Sahib were partners. On our way back Bapuji read all the greetings we had written in the veranda. The first letter was ॐ. After which were

तमसो मा ज्योतिर्गमय।

मृत्योर्मामृत गमय।

सत्यमेव जयते नामृतम

जिवेन शरद: शतम

पश्चेत शरद: शतम

श्रुशुयाम शरद: शतम

आरिनारयम शरद: शतम

प्रनवाम शरद: शतम

भुयश्व शरद: शतम

Lead us from darkness to light

From death to deathlessness.

Truth alone wins not falsehood

May we live for hundred autumns

May we see hundred autumns

May we listen hundred autumns

May we thrive hundred autumns

May we salute you for hundred autumns

May we again and again live for hundred years.

A lotus was drawn after these lines. Bapu read all the lines. After this we got back to work. I gave him a massage. We put away the sweets and set aside oranges for the prisoners. Mirabehn had forgotten to drink milk. She decorated Bapu's room with asters and made ॐ with it. We made garlands and placed 75 dots on it. Bapuji's instructions are that garlands should be so made that spun yarn could be used. Doctor Sahib also made a small garland of the yarn that he had spun. We all changed our clothes and proceeded to garland Bapuji. I wrapped a cotton shawl made from the yarn I had spun around Bapuji's shoulders. Doctor Sahib garlanded both Ba and Bapuji, after which Pyarelalbhai, Sushilabehn and I applied tikas and garlanded both, we got affectionate pats in return. We had brought jaggery, sugar crystals and wheat in three new bowls. We gave these to them. We had got a pair of chappals each for Bapuji and Ba, as also ghee, oil and other things like gum and shikakai soap, which we had got from the market. We placed all these in a tray and brought it to them. The scene was obviously grand. Ba and Bapuji looked very grand amidst flowers and garlands around there. All of us prayed together. After the prayers we went to prepare meals. We had prepared bajri khichadi for all others. Bapuji said that he would eat what was cooked for others, he wanted bajri khichadi for himself. We steamed it separately. Ba and Bapuji sat down to eat together. He took gol papdi as sweet. That room, Ba and Bapuji eating seated amidst heaps of flowers! That scene was grand. After his lunch, the prisoners and warders came to garland Bapuji. Ba gave everyone two oranges each. We served them meals around one o'clock. The entire family was served vegetables, kadhi and khichadi and two oranges for lunch. After which we sat down to eat. Khichadi and kadhi were very spicy. I ate very little of it but my eyes and nose watered. After lunch I went down. Bapuji had said that he would allow ghee to be applied only if I were to sleep. I applied ghee to Ba somewhat hurriedly and sat down to spin from 2:30 to 3:30. Doctor Saheb, Sushilabehn, Pyarelalji and I spun together. After spinning I applied ghee to Bapuji's feet and studied Gitaji with him. Today being Sunday I wrote letters. At 4:30 Bapuji served everyone tea, sweets, chevdo, sev-ganthiya, we also ate it. From four o'clock Mirabehn started making a temple, a mosque and a church from clay, worked on it till 6. There were rains today so our game could not be played. We went out for a walk. I made 16 lamps from the clay dough. We placed them in Bapuji's room when he was out walking. Mirabehn placed the three clay shrines on a wooden platform and surrounded it with plants. The lamps were also placed around them. It seemed as if the temple was in a forest. This arrangement reminded me of the Girnar trail. We kept the room shut till prayer time when all the others were allowed in. We lit the lamps. The row of lamps looked beautiful in the night light. During prayers we sang 'Hari ne Bhajata'. Mirabehn also joined the prayers. The prayers were very moving. After the prayers we sat talking for a while and we recounted the fun we had all day long. Mirabehn and I did not tire of looking at the decorations of the temple, ॐ, etc. Our eyes were drawn to it often. I pressed Bapuji's feet, gave a massage to Ba and went to sleep. Thus, we passed the day in great joy.

Date: 27.9.43

Sushilabehn started painting the temple[153] today. Today Bapuji wrote a letter to the Viceroy. 'As you are about to leave, I wish to say a few words to you. You once considered me a friend hence this letter. No one has spread as many falsehoods and given me as much pain as you have. I pray to god that may He reside in your heart and that you realise what a serious and grave error you have done in understanding this Ramrajya.'[154] He wrote something to this effect.[155]

Date: 27.9.43[156]

Today I received a letter from Kaka, Bachi, Mota Babubhai, Vinodbehn, Bhagubhai, Anandji Bapuji, Indira, etc. After a long time

---

[153] English term in the original.

[154] She wrote in the margin, 'Murabbi Bhai (Pyarelal) explained to me in Gujarati the gist of the letter to the Viceroy, which I wrote down.'

[155] For the text of the letter to Lord Linlithgow, see, CWMG, vol. 77, p. 201.

[156] There are two entries for 27.09.43.

the whole family wrote to me. I felt good. Indira addressed me as 'Manu foi' now everyone calls me 'foiba' and teases me.

Date: 28.9.43

After many days I received a letter from Yuktibehn. She gave me the news that Pujya Motilal Bapuji died on 'Shravan Vad 7'. There is a letter from Kakiba that Shakri masi, Vasumatibehn, Sevantbhai, Manojnabhabhi have been released from Nagpur jail. None of us who were imprisoned together are still in prison.

Date: 29.9.43

Today I received a letter from Bhai, he has scolded me for writing a letter to Umiyabehn. I received a letter from Bombay Government that if I wish to be released, I would be released forthwith; I cannot decide to be released at a later date. It's not a matter of my will. I sent a reply that I came here to serve and nurse, and I remain here for that reason. Hence, I accept the condition.

Date: 30.9.43

Sushilabehn gave me an English test. I passed, but I did very poorly in sentence construction. She had given me three papers. It was a two-hour examination. I took it post the afternoon rest.[157]

Date: 2.10.43

Today being the 2nd it was Bapuji's birthday. I touched his feet. We did not do anything special.[158]

---

[157] No entry for 1.10.43.
[158] No entry for 3&4 October, 1943.

Date: 5.10.43

Since last three days I have slight fever. Today I felt very weak. I did not go out to play. Everyone wondered as to why I had not gone. I did not tell anyone as I was certain that if I were to tell them, they would not let me do any work. I said nothing, but Bapuji understood. He told me, 'You should tell me. These days you do not wake up in time for prayers.' Today our weights were measured. Once again I weighed 100 lbs, probably because yesterday I had taken laxatives. But the others teased me saying that I must be worried about something.

Date: 6.10.43

Today I completed a letter to Vinodbehn and gave it for posting. Even today I felt tired and weak while working. These days Ba studies Gitaji with Bapu for 45 minutes. She listens to the Ramayana at 12 noon. Each one is immersed in their own activities. Health is also good.[159]

Date: 8.10.43

Today I gave a letter to Mr Kateli.[160] There was a communication from the government that I cannot seek to be released at any future date. If I wanted to be free, I had to leave now. I declined the offer to be released. Ba had fever today. The temperature measured 102.5°c, which for Ba's

---

[159] No entry for 7.10.43.

[160] According to the *CWMG*, vol. 77, p. 203 this letter was drafted on 2nd October by MKG. The letter read: 'I understood the first letter of the Bombay Government according to my lights. But now I understand that, once I convey my intention to stay here, I cannot subsequently change my mind. This does not fully confirm to the complete idea of "one's free will". But I have come here and am staying here for the sake of service. That is why I accept the condition laid in reply to my letter, and it suits me well. Why should a *sevika* even entertain any wishes of her own? So long as revered Kasturba is here, I shall also be here.'

condition is high. She has a burning sensation in the urinary tract. She has become very weak. Last night she could not sleep at all. She would lie down, get up, and sit. I was with Ba in her bed. She clung to me like a child clings to her mother. She placed her head in my lap and tried to sleep. I slept by her side and then she did fall asleep. I went and slept in my bed. She woke up at 3 o'clock, I went to her side, pressed her head for a while. She held me in her embrace and lay down. I stayed by her side till 4 o'clock, I went and slept in my bed when she fell asleep. I could not sleep. I was worried that if I were to sleep I would not wake up when she needed me. Bapuji came at 5 for the prayers. He asked me about the night. I told him everything and that she had slept for about two hours at night. He asked me to go and sleep in Sushilabehn's bed. I lay down there till about eight o'clock. I got up, had milk, my head felt very heavy. I had an early meal and slept at 12:30 and got up at 3. I could not study today. I could apply ghee to Bapuji's feet only at 4:30. These days Bapuji spends a lot of time making 'cuttings'.[161] All other things happen according to schedule. These days we get a storm and rains around 5 p.m. Today the rains came after our games. We had a good game. For past two days or so, I have not been able to sleep. Today I wrote a letter to Yuktibehn.

Date: 9.10.43

Ba's health is not good even today. The burning sensation in the urinary tract persists. Her body seems aflame. She has become very irritable. The storm came before we could play. Today we had a funny incident. During the rain and storm Ba went out and sat on a bench. Sushilabehn told her, 'Ba come inside otherwise you would fall ill.' Ba replied that she was fine. Bapuji had taken a mud pack, he removed it and went where Ba was, and said, 'Come inside, you will fall ill.' Ba became irritated. 'So you care for me at all? You don't ask me how I am. I nearly died last night but you did not even come to my side.' She was

---

[161] English term in the original, probably refers to newspaper cuttings.

very angry. Bapuji replied, 'I sent Sushila to be by your side. I also came but you were asleep and did not want to wake you up. Come inside and we shall talk.' Ba said, 'I don't want to.' She eventually did not come inside. She was angry and gave no one a proper answer. I was afraid that she was angry because I had slept outside her room. I asked Bapuji who said that there was no such thing. She was angry with Bapuji. I was relieved that I had not caused her anger. We played our game in the veranda. These days about a hundred persons die in Bengal every day. Gujarat too has famine. Prices have increased unrestrained. A tin of vegetable oil (dalda) which was for 2 rupees how costs 10 rupees.[162]

Date: 14.10.43

It is after eight days that I write this diary. How lazy. I have completed two recitation of Gitaji. Bapuji said that now every seven days we will complete the recitation of all 18 discourses. I recite all the discourses which are recited in daily prayers once again. I study the Margopadeshika for fifteen minutes. Bapuji says that if I were to do the Margopadeshika well, my studies would progress well. It would match my studies of the Gitaji. Therefore, I study every morning for half an hour. 22nd October will be Doctor Sahib's birthday. We decided to make chocolates in the shape of cigarettes and wrap golden foil over it. We made condensed milk by boiling it and made three types of chocolates, one with cocoa, the other with cocoa and groundnuts and one with groundnuts. The chocolates have turned out well. Pyarelalbhai wrapped golden foil over them and packed them in a tin. Today being 'Sharad Purnima' Ba had asked us to make dudh-poha and bhajiya. These days we play our game in the veranda. Because of the heavy rain the court[163] has become wet, they are laying a new layer of dirt and pulling a roller[164] on it. Because of heavy rain today we had to sleep inside our rooms.

---

[162]   No diary entries for 10 to 13 October, 1943.

[163]   English terms in the original.

[164]   English terms in the original.

Date: 15.10.43 Saturday

I wrote a letter to Umiyabehn after a long time. It pains me that I have made a grave error in not writing to her in all these days. I wrote four letters for Ba this week, to Mama, Kakiba, Manubehn and Mathurdasbhai. I wrote only one personal letter this week. Today it is one and a quarter years since Mahadevbhai's death. We placed many flowers. Sushilabehn and I reached the Samadhi early and arranged the flowers. While we were still arranging the flowers Bapuji arrived there at 8:30. We arranged all the other flowers and walked with Bapuji. During the walk he told us how he taught mathematics to Ramdaskaka. He said, 'That boy was very dull. I used to teach him mathematics while walking from Durban to Phoenix. The boy developed into a bright person.' I did not wake up in time for prayers.

Date: 16.10.43 Sunday

Today Bhai sent sweet melons for us. It has come through Shantikumarbhai from Bombay. Probably he had travelled to Mumbai. Everything is well with me these days. I had got up in time for the prayers.[165] As it disappears the poisonous snake spews venom. I wrote letters to Kakiba and Nimukaki. I have still not given the letter to Umiyabehn for posting. Ba's health is not good.

Date: 17.10.43 Monday

Sushilabehn is making a tablecloth[166] for gifting Doctor Sahib on his birthday. She taught me a new kind of crochet stitch.[167] She spent all day doing this work. Today was Bapuji's day of silence but he took my class, otherwise we cannot complete the recitation of the Gitaji

---

[165] Three lines have been scratched out and blackened. Hence the context of the following sentence remains opaque.

[166] English term in the original.

[167] She has used a Gujarati term 'crochia' for crochet.

in seven days. If I made an error he would signal. I got a tight slap from Bapuji today. Bapuji has decided that he would give me a slap if I do not wake up for prayers. He hits hard, but is also very sweet. I spun today.[168]

Date: 18.10.43

The tablecloth[169] was completed today. Today I went to Bhai to understand the letter. He read the first paragraph and kept it aside. He asked me, 'Why do you want to read such a dirty letter?'[170] Even I felt the same. We did not read it any further. I went to sleep at 11:30. Ba's health was not good, and I sat there gently pressing her body. Bapuji had given permission to complete work on the tablecloth[171] and I did that for half an hour.

Date: 19.10.43

The newspapers reported that the new Viceroy Wavell[172] has arrived. Ba's health continues to be poor.

Date: 20.10.43

I received a letter from Bhai today. He does not seem to have received my earlier letters, hence he did not know that the government of Central Provinces had issued my release order. The new Viceroy was sworn in today. Linlithgow has gone. Let's see, how this one turns out to be. May god grant him good sense.

---

[168] Seven lines have been scratched out and blackened there on.
[169] English term in the original.
[170] One sentence has been scratched out here on.
[171] English term in the original.
[172] Field Marshall Archibald Percival Wavell served as the Viceroy of India from 1943 to 1947.

Date: 21.10.43

Today's newspaper reports that Bhansalikaka and Mohan Sahasi were arrested; Bhansalikaka was taken to Wardha and released. Today Ba had a severe burning sensation therefore Bapuji gave her hot and cold bath.[173] She was given hot and cold bath[174] alternatively for five minutes each. These days I study English grammar[175] with Pyarelalji after my walks. Today I completed one recitation of Gitaji and did the eighteenth discourse once more. Bapuji says that I should not think of doing anything else till I know discourses 10 to 18 faultlessly. These days I read Kaka Saheb's *Smarn Yatra*[176] to Ba. Today we received a parcel of dry fruits from Karachi, including cashew nuts, almonds, dry figs, apricots and magas. I stored them properly this afternoon. By mistake I placed cream of buffalo milk in the cream of goat's milk. Last night I forgot to set the milk to curdle. This morning when I went to set the milk there was a bowl of cream which Ram Naresh had set aside. I used it believing it to be curd. It tasted strange when I had it during breakfast; I was surprised that cream had turned rancid. Doctor Sahib asked me not to eat it, but I still did. Later I realized that Ram Naresh had cleverly taken out the cream of goat's milk and placed it on the table.[177] I felt very bad that I did not realise that it was cream. I did not realise it in my haste. It was good that we had some butter from yesterday, otherwise we would have had to give ghee to Bapuji. All day long I kept thinking about this. Even this morning I could not get up for the prayers. Two dogs had somehow come in at night and were on Bapuji's seat; I shooed them away. This morning I got my slap. These days I read the Margopadeshika in the morning. Bapuji weighed 111 lbs. He lost 1 lbs. Ba reduced from 89

---

[173] English term in the original.

[174] English term in the original.

[175] English term in the original.

[176] *Smaran Yatra*, an autobiographical account of his childhood was published in 1934.

[177] English term in the original.

lbs to 85 lbs. I came down from 100 lbs to 99 lbs. Bhai lost 7 lbs and
came down to 119 lbs from 125 lbs. All of us lost weight this week,
though there is no reason for this loss. These days I take a hot water
bath[178] in Bapuji's bathroom.[179] I bathe at 11 a.m.. I spun for some
time. I spin in the evenings these days.

Date: 22.10.43 Friday

Today was Dr Guilder's birthday. There was much activity. I did wake
up in time for prayers, and bathed soon after that. At 7:30 all of us went
to Doctor Sahib's room with garlands and flowers. Ba applied a tika to
him, put a garland around his neck and gave him her blessings. After her
Bapuji garlanded him with a hank of 62 threads that he had spun, after
him I, Sushilabehn and Pyarelalji greeted him with a hank each. We
placed a tika on his forehead, gave him a garland of flowers and crystal
sugar and sweets. Ba distributed sugar to everyone. We brought him
to the dining room[180] and we had arranged as if he had received many
parcels.[181] There was a box of 'smokeless' cigars[182] chocolate wrapped
in golden foil. Another basket contained other sweets. One bundle[183]
consisted of a cotton tablecloth[184] made from cotton that I had spun.
Sushilabehn and I had embroidered the edges and corners on which
Bapuji, Mirabehn and Pyarelalji had embroidered 'G' in Gujarati,
Hindi, Tamil and Urdu. Bapuji had embroidered the Tamil letter,
while Pyarelalji had done it in Urdu and Mirabehn had embroidered
Hindi and Gujarati letters. We had typed 'smokeless cigarette'[185] on a
label.[186] We gave each of these items separately. We teased each other

---

[178] English term in the original.
[179] English term in the original.
[180] English term in the original.
[181] English term in the original.
[182] English term in the original.
[183] English term in the original.
[184] English term in the original.
[185] English term in the original.
[186] English term in the original.

and laughed a great deal. All of us went for a walk after which we had breakfast. We had prepared many varieties of items for breakfast. The game of badminton has started again from today. The entire day passed joyously. The prisoners were served kadhi, khichadi and vegetables for lunch and tea, chevdo and jalebi in the afternoon. Even Mirabehn joined our evening game. We had great fun. Ba came out to play after three days today.

Date: 23.10.43 Saturday

I did not wake up for the prayers today. Today being *ekadashi* I was not required to give a massage.

Date: 24.10.43

Ba has severe burning in the urinary tract hence Bapuji gives her hot and cold hip bath.[187] Ba feels much relieved.

Date: 25.10.43 Monday

These days my study of the Margopadeshika is progressing well. I study English with Pyarelalji for about 15 minutes. I like it. He is teaching 'tenses'[188] in which I am very weak. I study regularly with Sushilabehn. A new programme has been made for me today, which stipulates that I should not study for more than three hours. I am forbidden to read in electronic light in the morning. I bathe early and play badminton. Studies are progressing well. It feels good. Today being Monday I went to Dr Guilder. For sometime now I go to him on Mondays to study. He taught me about wireless, change of seasons, causes of cancer and how a chick grows inside an egg. He explains very well. Ba dictated letters for Bhai and Manubehn. Kakiba's letter has come from Delhi. There is a letter from Pujyabhai. He sent his

---

[187] English term in the original.
[188] English term in the original.

blessings on my decision to stay back here. He is very happy. I went to Dr Guilder and neglected cleaning Bapu's utensils. Bapuji began to clean them when Mirabehn came and took the task upon herself. Bapuji told me, 'The task that one has accepted should be done at its scheduled time. You work very hard. Girls of your age tend to be very irresponsible, you are not and hence one cannot pressurise you about work. You should have gone after cleaning the utensils.' What Bapuji said was absolutely correct, but the fact is that on some days I clean them at a later time. Bapuji said, 'That you remembered the task is good. There is no harm that Mirabehn cleaned them, but you should remember to do the accepted task at appointed time.'

Date: 26.10.43 Tuesday

The bath[189] has helped Ba a great deal. She said that she no longer has the burning sensation. Dry fruits including almonds, cashew nuts, dry figs and apricots have come from Karachi.

Date: 27.10.43 Wednesday

Today I woke up in time for the prayers. I had gone to sleep late last night around 12. After counting the beads I started to think about the circumstances under which I came to be here, the opportunity that came my way. I also remembered that after I came here I even lied once. Memories of Pujyabhai and the sisters flood my mind. God will protect them all. The condition of Bengal too worried my thoughts. I had some headache as well. I took a quinine.

Date: 28.10.43

I could not wake up for the prayers. I got my slap soon after I squeezed juice this morning. These days I bathe early in the morning. Cold

---

[189] English term in the original.

weather is upon us. I feel very cold during early mornings. Today I cleaned Pyarelalji's room. I took out all the books, separate lists for Gujarati, English, Marathi and Hindi books had to be made. I spent all my time in this after I gave massage to Ba. I did not study, as even after the rest I went back to work, which lasted till evening. We have begun to read the Bhagavad once again, now I read while explicating the meanings of terms.

Date: 29.10.43

Today is Diwali. I bathed early. I have to make puran-poli today. Even Bapuji will eat them. Initially he declined, but then he told me to ask Ba. If she would refrain from eating them, Bapuji would eat. Ba said she would not eat it. It's after eating such things that Ba falls ill. I made separate ones for Bapuji's with ghee made from goat's milk. I also made them separately for the others. It took up to 11:30 to prepare them. I could not read at all this morning. We gave bhajiya, tea and dates to the prisoners in the evening. Today we received letters from Kuvarjibhai, Kanubhai, Umiyabehn, Pratap, Shankarlalji and Yuktibehn. I received a letter from Umiyabehn after a gap of five to six months. It gave me great joy; I stitched one side of the border of Bapuji's dhoti, the other side remains to be done. After our evening walk we went to the samadhi after dark. Doctor Sahib, Kateli Sahib and Pyarelalji were arranging incense sticks around the ॐ, we also helped them. They were also placed around the star shape. The wind was strong and it took a while for the incense sticks to be lit. We also placed lamps. It looked very beautiful, like stars in a dark night. Some lamps were placed around the pool also. After the prayers I went down to see the beautiful decorations. After many years Bapuji ate puran-polis and that too made by me. We passed the day joyously. At night Ba touched Bapuji's feet.

Date: 30.10.43

It is the New Year today. May god grant peace and happiness to all in the world and bestow health upon all on this auspicious

day—that is the only prayer I have. The New Year is not new in
fact. Let alone the world, over 2000 persons die every day in India,
Bapuji is imprisoned, Diwali cannot be celebrated. It has been a
customary festival of the Hindus and so we have no choice but to
observe the festivities. I touched Bapuji's feet as soon as I woke up
for the prayers. I bowed to Bhai and other elders in my heart and
received their heartfelt blessings. I touched the feet of all the others
and received their blessings. May this be the last ever black Diwali,
may god never give us such a Diwali. Dr Guilder came and greeted
Bapuji and said 'Sal Mubarak'. Bapuji replied, 'Is this at all a new
year! I am totally devoid of enthusiasm. Our new year will be on
the day of India's independence. Till then we have no new years.
Many new years such as this have passed, but I have faith that what
is happening and what was happened, is for the good of India. You
must have read Behramji Malabari's poem "That I saw the relatives
of Shah Alem begging in the streets." Our condition is akin to their
condition. What place enthusiasm and festivities could there be!' All
of us played badminton. It is particularly cold today. These days I
delay washing my clothes. So be it. God knows what he wants this
year to be like. We can only pray for peace in the world. The day
passed in such thoughts. I remembered the new years in Porbandar,
Mumbai and the one spent in Nagpur jail. Usually, there would be
a lot of running around today. Newspapers reported the death of
Porbandar's queen Rupali Ba. I felt sad. She was good. They must be
in mourning at this time.[190]

Date: 1.11.43

Today I wrote letters to Lakshmikaki, Ramdaskaka and Yuktibehn.
I wrote to Kanubhai also. Today I had severe headache. I slept early.
There was slight fever at night. I had backache as well. I have begun
menstruating.

---

[190] No entry for 31.10.1943.

Date: 2.11.43 Monday

Today was the day of silence but Bapuji taught me. He would write terms from Margopadeshika to which I would give answers. He taught me Gitaji in the same way. Ba's health was somewhat weak today. I studied with Doctor Sahib. He taught me about lunar eclipse, day and night, light and darkness. It is very interesting.

Date: 3.11.43

From today Bapuji has started to write a memoire of Mahadevbhai.[191] Letters were received from Lakshmikaki and Manubehn.

Date: 4.11.43

My health is all right today. Menstruation has stopped. Kateli Sahib gave me two notebooks and told me not to announce it otherwise he would not be able to give them. Notebooks are not available in the market.

Date: 5.11.43

Today there are letters from Ramdaskaka and Bhai, who has sent my watch. Today I read Bapu's memoir of Mahadevbhai, wherein he described Mahadevbhai's death and the rituals which were performed for the cremation. Reading it makes me envious of Mahadevbhai. How wonderful it would be if I were to meet a death like Mahadevbhai's? Where does one get such good fortune from? He did extraordinary service, paid all his debts and went away. But my debts will still have to be paid. If they are all paid up quickly and I met his end: how joyous that would be! It is a death that makes one envious. I did not go for a walk today because Ba's health was not good and I spent time with her.

---

[191] This document is not available.

Date: 6.11.43

Today I wrote letters to Manubehn and Sushilakaki. Sushilabehn has caught a cold.

Date: 7.11.43

I did not go back to sleep after morning prayers. Today is Mirabehn's birthday and Bapuji had asked me to make for her a garland of eighteen threads, which took quite some time to make. Today Mirabehn completed eighteen years of her life with Bapuji. She came in 1925. She counts her birthday as the day of her arrival to be with Bapu. All of us woke up early in the morning. We had packed all the things to be given to her in separate parcels[192] with distinct addresses on them. In one box we had placed images of calf and kid made from clay. They are very dear to Mirabehn. On the box was written 'Government of Home Department'.[193] It was packed like a radio set. Another parcel[194] consisted of jaggery, honey, ink, clips, saree, soap, oil. These were given to her in the morning as she touched Bapuji's feet. It was very beautiful. There is a handmade photograph wherein god Krishna has placed his hand over Bapuji's head. The photo is very good. By the time we opened all the parcels[195] it was already 8:15. After which we played a game of badminton.[196]

Date: 8.11.43

Bapuji has caught a cold today. Ba came out for a walk in the garden. I did not go out for the evening walk. We played with the ring[197] because Doctor Sahib had some pain in his arm.

---

192   English term in the original.
193   English term in the original.
194   English term in the original.
195   English term in the original.
196   English term in the original.
197   English term in the original.

Date: 9.11.43 Monday

Bapuji's cold worsened today. He had fever last night. He is to take castor oil tomorrow. I studied the Gitaji and Margopdeshika today. It being the day of silence, an eerie silence paraded through the day. Today is Dev Diwali. Ba is to conduct the ritual Tulsi Vivah. I had to make all the arrangements. We made a canopy with four sugar canes, drew a flower at the centre on which was placed a potted plant. Sushilabehn drew a beautiful ॐ in front of it. I brought a lot of flowers. Thus we decorated the place. All these preparations were done after dinner. I cooked the *prasad*. At the time of evening prayers Ba performed the puja, sang the aarti and recited verses. She told me, 'Last time I was alone, this time you are with me—it feels good.' The decorations were abundant. She also got me to perform the puja. After the death of my mother, I witnessed Tulsi Vivah for the first time. When Ba was alive we used to do all festivals, after her death it seemed that everything had gone with her. It all came back and tears filled my eyes. Memories of my mother came back. Because of all this work I could not study with Doctor Sahib, nor could I go for my evening walk. We celebrated the day with a lot of enthusiasm. It was my turn to sing the prayers today. It felt very good after Bapuji's silence got over.

Date: 10.11.43 Tuesday

Today I went to study with Doctor Sahib. He has begun to teach me physiology. He has asked me to take detailed notes. Pyarelalji is very happy with this and said that I could become a nurse while being here. He tried to persuade me that he would prepare me for matriculation examination while I am here and later on I could train to be a doctor. These days I wake up for the morning prayers. An incident occurred today. Bapuji took castor oil. He took one teaspoon[198] full of it. He had two or three bowel movements in the morning. Bapuji went for his bath, as he was wiping his body dry he felt the need to use the latrine. Bapuji felt that he could wait till he had dried his body. Just

---

[198] English term in the original.

then Bapuji felt very giddy. Sushilabehn was in the bathroom and she had removed her clothes to take her bath. She caught hold of Bapuji. She asked him if she should call for Pyarelalji and the doctor. Bapuji kept refusing. She held on to Bapuji with one hand and wore her clothes with the other. She called Bhai. He rushed in and called the doctor. They gave him a chamber-pot. After which he was made to lie down in the bathroom on a mattress that was brought in. He lay in the bathroom for half an hour and kept lying down even after he came out. If Sushilabehn had not been attentive Bapuji would certainly have fallen. All day long he lied down. He did eat khakhara, milk and vegetables. We could not study today. In the evening Dr Shah and Dr Bhandari came for a visit. They took away the bottle of castor oil. Dr Shah said that it should be thrown away as it comes mixed with Nepalo.[199] Usually Bapuji takes the same amount of castor oil and he passes stool twice or thrice. But what happened today has not happened ever before. Therefore everyone said that there was something in the castor oil. We could not play for long this evening. Our time was spent with the visitors. This afternoon Bapuji lay down in the sunny veranda. We also slept there. Everything was delayed today. God protects all. Today I received a letter from Pujya Foiba and Vinodbehn. Vinodbehn's letter was delivered very late. Today news was also received regarding Sushilabehn's sister-in-law, Shakuntalabhabhi, that she has delivered a baby girl. She had to be operated upon. Her condition is very fragile. Sushilabehn has been worried. Her face turned ashen when she read the news and that is quite natural. On one side is Bapuji and on the other are the relatives, one does not knew what is to be done.

Date: 11.11.43

I have caught cold. There was slight fever last night. I could not study English even today. Bapuji's health is better.

---

[199] A kind of laxative.

Date: 12.11.43

The cold persists. I had severe headache also. This evening we washed the shells which were used to make ॐ on Mahadevbhai's samadhi. We made ॐ with flowers instead. But Bapuji said let's make the ॐ with shells, so we together set to work. I asked Bapuji if I should give him support to which Bapuji replied, 'I see that I receive support from Mahadev otherwise I do not have the strength to bend down and work.' We spent the walking time in doing the ॐ. After which we walked till prayer time. Bapuji stopped reading today.

Date: 13.11.43

I have been gripped by severe cold. I was given some drops. I had a strange sensation in my throat. I did not allow those to be put again. I slept early and did not give massage to Bapuji. I had some fever.

Date: 14.11.43

Today I wrote letters to Lakshmikaki and Ramdaskaka. There is some improvement in the cold. There was no fever. Sushilabehn has fever.

Date: 15.11.43

I am totally free of cold. This afternoon we received news that Sushilabehn's sister-in-law Shakuntalabhabhi passed away. There was a telegram. I came to learn of it when I woke up. I was saddened. Our friendship was based on one meeting and that too we barely met for three days. What would be Mataji's condition? I kept thinking about her. Sushilabehn has been crying a great deal. Let us see if they would release her on parole? If she were to be released she would be able to provide some solace. The newspaper reports that Shri Jay Prakash Narayan[200]

---

[200] Jay Prakash Narayan (1902–1979), freedom fighter, socialist, political leader, led the 'Total Revolution' movement against the Emergency.

has been made to sit in an alcove of ice and in order to prevent him from sleeping he is forced to sit on an armless chair, moreover he is not given food. This evening Sushilabehn sang 'Mangal Mandir'. She could not sing, even I choked. We, with great difficulty, sang the first stanza. Today Ba received a letter from Pujyabhai. The atmosphere has become mournful because of Shakuntalabhabhi's death. I applied oil to Sushilabehn's hair. She placed her head in my lap and wept.

Date: 16.11.43[201]

Bapuji has asked me to write Gitaji.[202]

Date: 27.11.43

I write this diary after nine days. I will write some things about these nine days in this itself. The mood today, that is these days, is somewhat all right. We have to forget what happened, don't we? Something that happened yesterday. I did not know some parts of the Margopadeshika. I had read those parts, and still did not know them. I did not know *Rupa*. I gathered the impression that Bapuji did not like this. My day was spoilt. Why did I not know? Moreover, my right eye flickered a great deal. I was worried that something is the matter. For past several days there are no letters. It is said that flickering of the right eye is not a good sign. Although I do not believe in it I felt somewhat uneasy in my heart. These days I have severe constipation and that also makes me uneasy. All these reasons came together and I wept. I did not go out for a walk with Bapuji and instead studied the Margopadeshika. Bapuji asked me, 'Why are you so melancholic? Ba has not said anything.' These days Ba's health is not good and something or the other happens. But I am quite

---

[201]　No diary entries from 17.11.43 to 26.11.43.

[202]　Diary no. 11a, 11b, and 11c contain her transcription of the Gita.

habituated to it. Bapuji told me, 'You should not be sad. There must always be laughter and play. Someday such things happen. But, even such things, I do not like. You must retain capacity for laughter and play.' Despite this, I did not feel better. I slept for a while, placed the mosquito net over the bed, gave Ba her massage and slept early. All this happened yesterday. In the interim period Mirabehn had fever. That evening she was given her enema. I spent one afternoon with her. Today the right eye has stopped flickering.

Today at 11 o'clock I received a telegram from Pujyabhai that Anandlal Bapuji had passed away. That means he passed away yesterday. I was saddened by this. I could not sleep even for a moment this afternoon. I kept thinking of Vijayabehn. That poor girl had the solace of having a father. I could see him before my eyes. Bapuji said that he was fortunate to pass away. It is a fact that he was in great pain. Now he is gone. Moreover, who was there to care for him? His son and daughter must have grown weary of providing service. Because looking after even a healthy person could be tiresome, what then of a sick person? The situation in Porbandar also causes pain. What relatives? So many of them but they are relatives only in name. It is good that we are away from them. I also felt that could Bapuji's relatives be of this kind? But when his own son is the way he is, what can one say about relatives? Does any of the relatives care about Bapuji? These and other such useless thoughts churned in my mind. I got up at 1:30. Ba's health is not good. Her breathing is laboured with asthma. Ba and Bapuji wrote a letter to Vijayabehn. I could not go out for the evening walk. I was with Ba. My fruits were delivered this evening. A tin full of cashew nuts have come. Almonds, walnuts, black grapes. Dry figs and other things have been brought from Karachi. Bapuji had written a letter to the Government, reply to which has been received stating that since the members[203] of the working committee[204] have not taken back the August Resolution

---

[203] English terms in the original.
[204] English terms in the original.

they cannot be allowed to meet for consultations.[205] Bapuji had also written a letter about the late receipt, by ten days, of the telegram for Sushilabehn.[206] That too has been responded to with regret and assurance that such an incident would not be repeated. A letter had been sent about permission for Dr Guilder to meet with his daughter. This request has been sent to the Home Department[207] in Delhi. All these are notes for the intervening period. I shall make the effort to adhere to the rule of daily notes.

Date: 28.11.43 Sunday

Bhandari came today with the news that Doctor Sahib's meeting is scheduled for tomorrow. Doctor Sahib is delighted. Ba's health is frail today. I wrote for her—letters to Kakiba and Nimukaki. I wrote to Vijyabehn, Radhabehn and Ma-Bapuji letters of condolence.

Date: 29.11.43 Monday

Today was the day of Doctor Sahib's meeting. He got ready early in the morning. He was driven in a motor[208] to IG Bhandari's office

---

[205] MKG wrote to the Additional Secretary, Home Department, on 26 October 1943 that he had no power to alter the Congress Resolution of 8 August 1942, which could only be done by its Working Committee and offered to meet and discuss the situation with the Congress Working Committee (see, *CWMG*, vol. 77, pp. 202–4). The Government in its reply of 18 November stated that '…since there is no change in your attitude towards the Congress Resolution of August 8th, 1942, and the Government have received no indication that the views of any of the members of the Working Committee differ from your own, a meeting between you appear to serve no useful purpose.' *Gandhiji's Correspondence with the Government, 1942–4*.

[206] See, *CWMG*, vol. 77, pp. 205–6.

[207] English terms in the original.

[208] English terms in the original.

at 12:30 and returned at 4 after the meeting. I studied the Gitaji with Bapuji. Ba's health has worsened. She takes her enema[209] in the bathroom,[210] after which she sits in the bath.[211] She feels uneasy so I give her a bath these days. I also wash her clothes. Today I washed them quite late. I slept and woke up late and did not study much.

Date: 30.11.43

Today Ba's health worsened further. Her asthma has become acute. She is unable to sleep at night. Colonel Shah came at night. Oxygen[212] has been called for. The need might arise any time, hence it has been kept. I left Ba's side at 11:30 and went to sleep.

Date: 31.11.43 Tuesday[213]

Today Bapu wrote a letter to the government that it should either release Sushilabehn on parole or permit the baby to be brought here.[214] Even today Ba's health is very weak; she can neither sit up nor stand.

Date: 1.12.43 Wednesday

Ba's health remains unchanged. She felt slightly better in the evening. We have reached the third part of the reader, I hope that my English would improve further. We have decided to play badminton little earlier than usual. Bapuji says that we must play a lot during winters.

---

[209] English terms in the original.

[210] English terms in the original.

[211] English terms in the original.

[212] English term in the original.

[213] It should be Wednesday. Also November does not have 31 days.

[214] This letters bear the date 1.12.43. *CWMG*, vol.77, p.208. This entry is probably of 1.12.43.

For quite some time now there is no letter from Bhai. I am worried. Even Yuktibehn has not written.

Date: 2.12.43

Even today Ba's health is weak. I did not go for a game of badminton this morning. I was with Ba. After many days I went for the evening walk. I took some rounds and came up. Her day passed well. Doctor Sahib has sought permission for visitors to meet Ba so that her mental disquiet could be reduced.[215] If the visits are permitted, Ramdaskaka and others could come, she would feel better.

Date: 2.12.43 Thursday[216]

Today I wrote letters to Shamaldaskaka and Kanubhai. Ba had to be given oxygen gas.[217] She felt slightly better in the evening. But she had headache in the morning, her breathing was laboured. I stayed with Ba till about 11 p.m., after which I slept. I got up again during the night.

Date: 3.12.43 Friday

For the past two or three days I have been waiting for a letter from Bhai, but there are no letters from anyone. I spent the day waiting for letters. During the day Ba's health was better. Her bathing has been stopped, we give her a sponge[218] bath these days. Tonight at 2:30 her health worsened. She had a heart attack. She had severe headache. I woke up. I went to her side. I placed her head in my lap and pressed it. She could not sleep. She was breathless, had cough and chest pain. I sat with her

---

215 Three lines have been crossed out from here on.
216 There are two entries for 2.12.43.
217 English term in the original.
218 English term in the original.

till 6 in the morning. I slept from 6 to 8 in the morning. I slept a great deal in the afternoon, despite this I felt tired today. I felt cold and had feverish sensations. I took quinine and drank warm water, after which I felt better. I went to play as well and that felt good. Kateli Sahib came and noted the names of all the relatives who could be given visiting nights to meet Ba. The list[219] was quite long. Ba felt weak all day long.

Date: 4.12.43

Bhandari came today with the news that a telegram had been sent to Ramdas Gandhi, just than Ramdaskaka called from Nagpur that Nimukaki has been sent for a visit. If she were to reach today, the visit would take place today itself. Ba and Bapuji would be allowed to remain present during visits, no one else would be allowed to remain present. Ba's condition is somewhat better today. Nimukaki came for a visit. I touched her feet but did not speak with her at all. This seems to have helped Ba a great deal. She smiled all the time. Devadaskaka is to come tomorrow.

Date: 5.12.43 Monday

Today is Bapuji's day of silence. I studied Gitaji with him. I made a list[220] of books. Devadaskaka came in the evening. He spoke about Shakuntalabhabhi and other happenings in Delhi. Initially, Ba said that he should come tomorrow. Bapuji wrote in a note that who knows what would happen during the night. Devadas would have to return from the gate, which is not a good thing. Therefore he was allowed in.

Date: 6.12.43 Tuesday

I waited for the post, which did not come. I am worried about Bhai. Today both Nimukaki and Devadaskaka came for a visit. They were

---

[219] English term in the original.
[220] English term in the original.

allowed in one after another. If both were to come together Kateli
Sahib would have to take a note of that, hence this arrangement. I
gave my watch to Devadaskaka. Ba's health remained all right during
the day but deteriorated quite a lot at night. I went to sleep at 11, but
did get up intermittently. These days I sleep inside.

Date: 7.12.43 Wednesday

Even today Nimukaki and Devadaskaka came for a visit at 3 o'clock.
Bapuji taught me this morning, all other studies have stopped as of
now. Ba's health was all right during the day. Albeit, she is very weak.
Today is the last day of Nimukaki's visit but Devadaskaka would be
permitted to come for two more days. For the past three days or so
our evening games have stopped due to the visits. We went out for a
walk but Ba felt suddenly uneasy and we were called in. The prayers
were conducted outside. The cold was severe and Ba was requested to
go back inside. She did not have the strength to walk hence Pyarelalji
carried her inside. I was with her till about 10 o'clock, after which
Bapuji asked me to rest as Pyarelalji was with her. Bapuji told me, 'If
you wish to preserve your health, you should do as I ask you to, and
it will see you through.' I went to sleep at 10:30 and Bhai sat by her
side. Ba insisted that he too should sleep and hence he went to rest.
She had not slept till about 11:30, so I went and sat by her side till
about 3:30. She had severe cough, breathlessness and pain. I gave her
a hot water bottle and pressed her body. With great difficulty she fell
asleep. I wanted to sleep by her side. The cold was severe. She was
well covered under blankets. I tried to lay by her side, but I shivered
with cold, I moved to my bed. She slept well till morning. I woke
up at 8. Sushilabehn squeezed the juice and did other things. I drank
milk and went for a walk.

Date: 8.12.43 Thursday

Today, Manubehn, Ramibehn, Urmibehn and Ramibehn's daughter
were all permitted to visit Bapuji together. Mama (Ba's brother) was
not permitted to come with them. Manubehn and the children

brought the house alive with joy. Urmi danced, she dances very well. Manubehn sang 'Kahan ke Pathik'. She sang two more songs on which the baby danced. After they left Mama came, we gave him tea and other things. Nimukaki had brought methi pak, which we gave him and served him almonds and cashews. He was very happy. Devadaskaka came at 3, and was with us for two hours. There was some time for the evening games, which we played. I could not study with Bapuji. We have heard that Kishorelalbhai, who is in the Nagpur Jail, is in frail health. He weighs only 75 lbs. He has acute asthma and fever. Devadaskaka brought up the possibility of either seeking his release or getting him parole. Bapuji declined. He said, 'I have accepted that I have lost Kishorelal. I would not be surprised if he were to attain, like Mahadev, eternal sleep in Nagpur Jail. Who knows, maybe the key to swaraj lies in the sacrifice of such persons while they are imprisoned.' Devadaskaka also spoke about Prabhudasbhai's illness. He, along with Kashikakiba and Chhaganlal Bapuji, has one-time permission to visit Bapuji.

Date: 9.12.43 Saturday[221]

Manubehn was allowed in with great difficulty. She and Ramibehn came and stayed for one and a quarter hour. Today was the last day of Devadaskaka's visit, he sat a little longer. My health also worsened at night. I had severe stomach cramps and wondered if I would be able to get up in the morning. Somehow I managed to complete night chores. But, by the grace of god, I woke up with great resolve.

Date: 10.12.43 Saturday

Today I waited for letters from Bhai and sister just like I used to during the initial period in Nagpur Jail. I was worried as to why there were no letters. Is someone unwell? The entire week passed in waiting. Today

---

[221] Two days 9th and 10th are mentioned as Saturday, in fact 11 December was a Saturday in year 1943.

I completed the first part of the Margopadeshika. These days Bapuji is deeply worried. He is worried about Ba. Last night he did not sleep well. My health is also not good. I am mentally tired and have physical fatigue as well. All of us sat out in the veranda in the sunlight. Bapuji and all of us stayed there till evening. A bed, whose height can be lowered and raised has been sent for Ba. We take her out in that bed.

Date: 12.12.43 Sunday[222]

There was no point in waiting for the post it being Sunday today. My health is better. Even Ba felt better though she felt weak at noon. I played today. Bhai had fever and could not come out to play. Advani came in lieu of Bhandari today. He had come at the time of Mahadevbhai's death. Bhandari has gone on leave, hence Advani would come in his place.

Date: 13.12.43

I could not sleep waiting for the post to arrive. When would Kateli Sahib come with the post? Eventually I was disappointed. It should not be termed as disappointment because there was a letter from the Government and another for Sushilabehn from her home. Sushilabehn has been worried and the letter bought news for her, which made me feel good. Bapuji had written to the Government to either release Sushilabehn on parole[223] or have the infant baby[224] sent here under her care. The Government replied that neither were possible. Sushilabehn's brother wrote that when her sister-in-law was critically ill he had met with Maxwell[225] and tried very hard to secure her release. At that time Maxwell told him that Gandhiji's

---

222 No entry for 11.12.43.
223 English terms in the original.
224 English terms in the original.
225 Sir Reginald Maxwell, Home Member, Government of India.

associates can be released only after they have been kept in a dark cell for three months. Bapuji felt bad and said, 'I was hopeful that they would accept one of the requests, but they did no such thing. Because, they do not want the outside world to know what is going on here. Therefore, they are not prepared to release anyone but me. Now, they are unwilling to release even me.' We had some fresh news and the day passed quite all right. At night all those thoughts came to me. I was angry on the one hand that why do not they write letters. On the other I felt that what can they do? What hardships do those on the outside face? Ba's health remained stable. She slept well at night. Today I did the eighteenth discourse of the Gitaji. Bapuji has decided to write to the Government seeking a reason for its decision to not release Sushilabehn on parole.[226] Bapuji said that if he were to decide to obtain parole for her, he would fight till he secured it. Sushilabehn told him to do no such thing. 'No one can say what step you would take. Hence, I do not want you to fight.' Bapuji said that he wouldn't do that, but would write to the Government that they had not communicated any reason for the refusal.

Date: 14.12.43

Ba could not sleep at night. I stayed awake with her from 2 to 5 in the morning. I was about to join the prayers but Sushilabehn persuaded me not to. I had slept for a few moments between 2 and 5, but I had slept by Ba's side. I woke up at 8:30, drank milk and went out to play badminton. I slept well in the afternoon.

Date: 15.12.43

Today I waited for the post, but nothing came. Ba's health remained uneven. This evening she had palpitations. We were shocked, but the

---

[226] This letter was written on December 14, 1943. See *CWMG*, vol. 77, p. 212.

palpitations came under control in a while. She was very tired and did not sleep at night.

Date: 16.12.43

Today I received Bhai's letter. I felt very good. He wrote after a long time. Usha and Anupama have also written. Ba's health remained poor. She did not sleep at night. We stayed awake by turns. My health was not good either. I had to take quinine.

Date: 17.12.43 Sunday

We got the news that Devadaskaka would come on Tuesday, soon thereafter we were told that he would come today. Lakshmikaki and the children also came. They came at 3. We made ice-cream for the children. Ramu and Mohan liked it very much. Bapuji made a comment on their bodies. They are very thin. Bapuji said that Dr Dinshaw Mehta should be consulted and they should get exercise. Ba gave a saree to Tara. They would come again tomorrow. Ba's health was poor.

Date: 18.12.43 Monday

Ba's health was average. Devadaskaka, Lakshmikaki and the children came. The house felt so much better. The children made friends with me. I told them many stories. After which Tara, Mohan and Ramu told one story each. I spent all my time with the children. Ba's health worsened at night. All of us stayed awake by turns.

Date: 19.12.43 Tuesday

They came even today. This was to be their last day of visit. They have gone back to Bombay and they would try to get permission for more visits. Devadaskaka will try and seek permission for others also; he has taken the names of all other relatives. We were informed today that a nurse would be arranged for Ba. Ba has given the names of Prabhavati (Jayaprakash's wife) and Kanubhai. We have to see if they would be allowed.

Date: 20.12.43

The day passed all right, but the night was bad. These days Bapuji's BP[227] remains high—therefore his bed was placed in front of Mirabehn's room. Bhai was also with him. They were sending me to sleep there. But Ba said that I should sleep with her, therefore I slept in her room. She could not sleep till 1 o'clock. Sushilabehn also played the gramophone so that Ba could sleep, but she could not. Finally she was given a sleeping pill, after which she slept. She slept through the day as well.

Date: 21.12.43

Both day and night passed well today. There was no major difficulty. She came out to watch a game of carrom, hence she slept at ten. She slept well through the night.

Date: 22.12.43

Both day and night passed well today as well. I had fever. During the game, I got angry over a minor thing. I had fever and all the others were discussing this insignificant thing, hence I got angry. Moreover, some old things which I had shoved inside my head were revived. Vinodbehn's letter brought news that Fulkorkaki's son Devadaskaka has passed away. How many have died like nine pins? All of us have to take that path. I thought about Mahadevbhai. My English studies have stopped completely, which also made me feel bad. All such things went on and spoiled my night. I slept little. I fell asleep after 2:30.

---

[227] English term in the original.

Date: 23.12.43

Today a letter from Vinodbehn brought the news of one more death! Fulkorkaki's son Devadaskaka has died. It made me sad. In the past three months so many persons passed away: Prabhudasbhai, Anandlal Bapuji, Motilal Bapuji and Devadaskaka. I had a slight fever this evening.

Date: 24.12.43

Sushilabehn and I take turns to play badminton, one day she plays and on the next day I play. Today was my turn to play, I went. After a long time I went to the samadhi of Mahadevbhai. I specifically desired to visit it. All of us played in the evening as well. Late evening we got the news that Jamnadaskaka, Shamaldaskaka, his family and Devadaskaka and his family would come for a visit tomorrow. All the relatives have been given permission for a visit. I did not feel too well tonight. I slept early at 9 and at 11 went and slept in my bed. Sushilabehn gave the massage to Ba.

Date: 25.12.43

Christmas days have begun. All days are equal here. Mirabehn came at night and sang two hymns. Ba's day passed well; but she had to get up four–five times at night.

Date: 26.12.43

Devadaskaka and his family were the first to arrive today. The visits commenced from 3 o'clock. Devadaskaka has arranged for all relatives to come for a visit. What if Bhai also comes! After them Jamnadaskaka came, followed by Shamaldaskaka and his family. After them came Ramdaskaka and Kanho. Ba had no complaints all day long today. The day was good.

Date: 27.12.43 Monday

Even today Jamnadaskaka, Devadaskaka and his family came for a visit. I was with the children through the entire duration of the visit.

Date: 28.12.43 Tuesday

Today was the last day of Devadaskaka's visit. Tomorrow Kanu would arrive. Devadaskaka told me that he had informed Bhai regarding the permission for a visit. Let's see when he comes now.

Date: 29.12.43 Wednesday

Today Kateli Sahib came with the information that my family would come. Bhai, Kanubhai, Yuktibehn, Aruna, the young baby,[228] Hansa faiba, Vijayabehn, Dhirubhai, Kanubhai. All of them came in the afternoon. I felt good meeting Yuktibehn. She has become very weak. Both babies[229] are doing well. Yuktibehn had pleurisy and was very unwell, she has been well only since the last eight days. Perhaps she became well only so that she could meet me. They gave me the news of Gangakaki's death. In recent past many from our family have gone! Bapuji said that if Yukti were to stay here her health would improve speedily. But how can that be? Vinodbehn is the same; Yuktibehn told me that. I slept at 12 O'clock remembering Amerli and Porbandar of my childhood.

Date: 8.1.44[230]

I write this diary after 29.12.43. During this week Shamaldaskaka, his family, Santokkakiba, Keshubhai, Radhabehn, Kuvarjibhai, his

---

[228] English term 'baby', in original.

[229] English term 'baby', in original.

[230] No diary entries from 30.12.43 to 7.1.44.

daughter, etc., came for a visit. Devadaskaka came yesterday and even day before yesterday. Even Kantibhai came. Kashikakiba, Ambabhabhi and her daughters came yesterday. It has been decided that Kanubhai would come every alternate day. The government agreed with great difficulty on the condition that he would be allowed every alternate day if Devadaskaka were to be here, in his absence Kanubhai would not be permitted every alternate day.

I asked Bapuji the reason for his taking goat's milk because he says that one should take a vow not to take cow's milk in order to protect the cow. Bapuji said that such a thing was right but, 'I had gone to Bengal where I saw them putting a tube through the cow's vagina and pump air to fill her udders with milk. What pain it must cause her? Imagine if such a thing were to be done to a woman, how would she scream? But this meek creature is silent and for this reason I gave up milk in every form. Later Dr Mehta suggested goat's milk saying that no such thing is done in this case. From then on I started to take goat's milk. Why do the animals give milk? For their young ones. Mothers give milk for her young ones. We should keep the extra for us. But, those people torture meek animals in order to earn money.' This he explained to me. Ba's health remains precarious. She watches the game of carrom till 10 o'clock. She listens to the gramophone when Bapuji goes for his evening walk. My eye has worsened, I was prohibited from reading and writing for eight days. A nurse did come. She stayed for two days. How can she like being here? She had to stay without her children and there was no one like her with whom she could talk. On the third day she said that she would not be able to work and went away. She was required to look after Ba but she could not do that. How can they like being imprisoned in a jail?

Kanubhai came today. He sang three or four bhajans. The poor man faces great difficulty regarding his meals. He eats at Dinshaw Mehta's house. They eat in the European manner, and he has not become accustomed to it.

Bapuji has been prohibited from taking his walks outside the wire fencing. He used to take his walk there because that area gets sunlight. Bapuji said that this makes him angry. 'What would they lose if I were to stand in that thirty-foot area? But there is animosity between affirmation and negation. They have no choice but to allow visitors to meet Ba, hence they gave the permission. They do not want to release Ba.' I asked him as to why do they not release Ba, what could Ba do? Bapuji said, 'Suppose Ba were to die, they would have to send me out to perform her last rites. Something would happen even if I were to be out just for one day. Such are their calculations and hence they do not release her. Maulana Sahib was not released even at the death of his wife. Their policy these days has become very cruel!'

Date: 9.1.44 Sunday

Ba did not feel well tonight. She could not sleep. I stayed awake for about three hours. In the first part I stayed with her from 1:30 to 2:30, after which Pyarelalji stayed awake from 2:30 to 4. I woke up at 4 and till 6 stayed by her side. I went to sleep at 6 and woke up at 9.

This afternoon Chandubehn, Bindubehn, her sister-in-law, Dhirubhai, Vasantbhai and Kanubhai came for a visit—this was unscheduled and sudden. Bindubehn and her sister-in-law danced.[231] Chandubehn and the other two women sang bhajans. Ba felt very good. We gave food to Kanubhai. He ate vegetables, roti, milk, dates etc.; to the others we gave dry fruits. Dhirubhai had imaginatively drawn pictures of Bapu's fasts, which he had brought. They were quite good. Chandubehn had got for me a set of salwar and kurta made to my measure. I kept the salwar. Bhai is still at Parla. Yuktibehn is well. Bapuji has begun to observe day-long silences. He would speak only to teach Sushilabehn and me, would converse with visitors, the sick and the officials only about Ba's illness. He would remain silent during his walks, bath and massage. He would speak only when necessary during the prayers. It is not decided as to how long the silence would last. He would observe silence so long as he can.

---

[231] 'Dance', English term in the original.

Date: 11.1.44[232]

Today we were informed that Prabhavatibehn would be transferred here. She would reach either today or tomorrow. Kanubhai came today, he read the Bhagavad to Ba, sang bhajans and ate with us.

Date: 12.1.44

Today Mathurdasbhai's family came. His daughter Jyotsana performed a dance.[233] By evening Prabhavatibehn reached here from Bihar's Bhagalpur prison. She spoke about life therein. She also narrated the episode of Jayprakashbhai's escape. Ba felt better.

Date: 13.1.44

Our work was divided and allotted to us. I would stay with Ba till 1. During this time Prabhavatibehn would be free to do whatever she likes. I would be free after 1, so I could resume my studies, etc. after I take some sleep. Today Harilalkaka sent a wire that he would reach by Thursday morning. We kept waiting all day long but no one came. We had no visitors today, which felt good. We have had visitors almost daily and all our time passed with them. Today we got some rest.

Today the government replied to Bapu's letter[234] regarding treatment of Mirabehn's arm. The doctor from Karachi, whose treatment she liked, has been permitted to visit her.

Date: 14.1.44

Manubehn, Kakiba, etc. came for a visit. Surendrabhai was with them.

---

232 There is no entry for 10.1.44.
233 'Dance', English term in the original.
234 Neither this letter nor government's reply are in the *CWMG*.

Date: 15.1.44

Today was Makarsankranti.[235] Hence, Ba asked us to make til ladoos and had them distributed to the prisoners. Her health remains unchanged. She cannot sleep at night. After Mirabehn, it's been my turn to catch the cold. I sat by Ba's side from 2 to 5:30 am. I slept from 5:30 to 8:30.

Date: 16.1.44

Now that Prabhavatibehn is here she is with Ba during the day and night. My cold has become more severe. I was woken up at night but lest I should give my cold to Ba, I did not go by her side.

Date: 17.1.44

My cold has become even more severe. I am not woken up for the prayers, nor do I make any attempt to wake up for prayers. These days in the mornings I squeeze juice, do some other work and read the Margopadeshika for half an hour and then go for a walk. These days I walk regularly, because Prabhavatibehn takes her walk early and stays with Ba. The enema takes about half an hour. I work in the kitchen thereafter and if there is no work to be done in the kitchen, I read the Margopadeshika for half an hour more. During this time Sushilabehn gives a massage to Ba, after which I give her a bath, administer her medicines. Perhaps, on some days I do waste some time, but not very much. I take my bath around 11 or 11:30, wash my clothes and have lunch around 12 noon. By the time I put away food and clean the kitchen, it is usually around 12:30. I sleep till 1, when I am woken up by Bapuji after his lunch, I clean the utensils and go to Ba's side. I stay with her till about 3; if time permits I

---

[235] Makarsankranti or Uttarayan is observed on 14 January and not on the 15th.

study a little with Bapuji. These days we have visitors, and as a result studies have become rather irregular. I study geometry with Pyarelalji from 3 to 5. At 5 we play for an hour till 6. From 6 to 7:15 we have our meals; I work in the kitchen and complete all pending tasks. I take Ba out in a wheelchair and play the gramophone till 8 o'clock when Bapuji returns from his walk. After the prayers, I make beds, finish all other tasks, give a massage to Bapuji and go to sleep. Ever since Prabhavatibehn came here I do not give massage to Ba at night. Sushilabehn and I stay awake one night, while Prabhavatibehn and Pyarelalji stay awake the following night. I stay awake from 2 a.m. to 6:30 a.m.. I sleep after the prayers till about 9. I also sleep early at night. Days pass in this manner.

Today, Yuktibehn, Aruna, Harjivandas, Bhupat and Kanubhai came to visit. Yuktibehn brought clothes, adadiya sweets and photographs of Sharda Mandir. There were six pairs of salwar-kurta. They were large for my size and hence I sent them back. She sang the bhajan 'kelibhare payal'. She will go to Sevagram. Pujyabhai is still in Mumbai. I had given my watch to Devadaskaka, it has come back repaired.

Date: 28.1.44[236]

I write this diary after a gap of nine days. I have become rather irregular in the recent past. Today Pujyabhai, Chhaganlal Bapuji, Devadaskaka, Ramdaskaka and Sumitra came for a visit. Bhai brought a pair of salwar-kurta, which fitted me well. He has kept other clothes with Kanubhai who would bring them tomorrow. Bhai's visit made me feel very good. He looked somewhat weaker. He has been in Mumbai for quite some time, who knows who cares for his food and drink. When he came here from Karachi, he looked all right. He told me that I had become very irregular in my letter writing. 'Today you must write to Karachi. You must write to everyone regularly.' We

---

[236] There are no diary entries for the period of 18.1.44 to 27.1.44.

spoke about Karachi in general terms. Today being the 26th and hence Independence Day, Bapuji, Sushilabehn, Pyarelalji, Prabhavatibehn, Doctor Sahib and I had observed a twenty-four hour fast. We had decided to give bhajiyas, tea and groundnuts to the prisoners in the evening. We had to make the bhajiyas. Sushilabehn and I got down to the task from 2 o'clock, for this reason I could not sit for long with Bhai. I had a lot of work.

We had organized community spinning to mark the Independence Day. Sushilabehn, Pyarelalji, Bapuji, Prabhavatibehn, Doctor Sahib and I spun from 11:30 to 12:30. We had visitors in the afternoon.

We saluted the flag in the evening and sang three songs. 'Vande Mataram', 'Sare Jahan se Achha' and 'Jhanda Uncha Rahe Hamara'.

'The purpose of my life is to ensure that India obtains her freedom, complete in every respect, through the path of truth and non-violence. And it has been so for long years. To fulfil this purpose, on this 14th anniversary of Independence, I resolve that till India obtains freedom I shall not pause and would not allow all those on whom I may have any vestige of influence. I pray to the One, whom none has seen through their eyes but one whom we call through God, Allah and Paramatma, that He may give me the strength to fulfil this purpose.'[237] Bapuji had written this message, which Doctor Sahib read out.

It was my duty tonight. I kept awake from 2 to 6, and slept from 6 to 9 in the morning.

Date: 29.1.44

Today Venilal Bapuji, Nipunbhai, Kantibhai-bhabhi, Pushpabehn and others came for a visit. Ba's health was poor. She told me in the evening that she did not enjoy this afternoon's visit. No one sang a bhajan or performed something else; all the visitors were also new to this and for this reason Ba did not enjoy the visit.

---

[237] The original is in Hindustani.

Date: 30.1.44 Monday

Ba's health was very poor today. She had an attack of asthma. Bhandari came at 1 o'clock to check on her. Her breathing was very laboured at that point. Moreover, it was Bapuji's day of silence. Ba wept this afternoon. Kanubhai came to visit and stayed till 7 o'clock. A 'heart bed'[238] has been sent for Ba. I had the night duty. I stayed by Ba's side from 2 to 5 o'clock. I woke up at 2 on my own. The night was difficult. We sang ten to twelve bhajans, Sushilabehn also sang. Ba said, 'Now, I am a guest of two or four days. God should call me to him. I can no longer bear this pain.' She often says such words. It is quite tragic. God only knows what is to happen. I pray daily that she be cured. Even Bapuji's BP was high today.

Date: 1.2.44[239]

Today Kanubhai received permission to be with us. He came this very evening. All his things were brought over from Dinshaw's house. All of us felt good. I felt very good at this development. All our duties and hours were decided. I have been assigned duty every morning from 5 o'clock to 9. If enema has to be administered I have to do that between 9 and 11 o'clock. I have afternoon duty from 1 to 3 o'clock. I do not have night duty anymore. One day Pyarelalji and Prabhabehn are to be with Ba from 11 to 2 and 2 to 5 respectively, the next day Kanubhai and Sushilabehn are to do the duty. I was taken off the night duty on account of my eye problem. I pleaded but failed to convince them. There is no improvement in her health. She is very weak and uneasy. Wrote a letter to Abhabehn today.[240]

---

[238] As in the original.

[239] No entry for the date 31.1.1944.

[240] Note on the top of the page: 'Bhandari brought Dr. Jivraj Mehta from Yervada, but was not allowed to meet Bapuji.'

Date: 2.2.44

I wrote a letter to Pujyabhai today. I could not go for the 3 to 5 class. Ba had a burning sensation and I applied cold presses on her. I went to study at 4 o'clock. Bapuji teaches from 6 to 6:30.

Date: 3.2.44

The enema had no effect on Ba today. She insisted on taking castor oil. There was no pressing need for it but she wanted to take it. Her health remains unchanged. She has become extremely weak. I could go to the class from 3 to 5. I also studied with Bapuji from 6 to 6:30. I was with Ba from 5 in the morning till 7 o'clock, again from 1 to 3 in the afternoon and from 7:15 to 8 in the evening. I was with her at night as well. The night was not bad, she slept better than most other days.

Date: 4.2.44

Ba had taken laxatives during the day today but she had no bowel movement. She passed the day in unease. The night too was bad. At 2:30 in the night Ba asked Kanubhai to wake me up, which he did. She had a coughing bout every few minutes. She had severe body ache. She told me, 'Daughter, press it hard. I will not be alive for too long.' Tears filled my eyes. What is my fate? I came here to nurse Ba and God is not willing to keep her well. Bapuji came to her side at 3 o'clock. Kanubhai had brought her bed to the veranda and he and I gently stroked her body. When she saw Bapuji, she told him, 'Bapuji, these are my last breaths. I am in a great deal of pain.' Bapuji replied, 'Go. But go with peace, won't you?' He asked us to recite verses from the Gita. Kanubhai and I recited the twelfth discourse. We took her bed inside the room. We read the eleventh and the ninth discourse of the Gita. Pyarelalji was also awake. Ba asked us to sing bhajan 'Rama charan', after which we sang 'Janiye Raghunath Kuvar', prayers of the Vidyamandir and other prayers and hymns. We sang for about

40 minutes. Prayers gave her some sense of peace and quietude. Ba asked me to be near her. I stayed with her till 5:15, after which I slept. Bapuji had told me that he would wake me up at 6:30, but he did not. I woke up at 7:30.

The theft from the kitchen has increased lately. Therefore Bapuji said that we should not get work done by the soldiers and do everything ourselves. Pyarelalji, Kanubhai and I would do the kitchen work. Bapuji said that it would be good not to bother Sushilabehn with kitchen work these days. Kanubhai and Pyarelalji made rotis and boiled vegetables. We ate that with curd. I made the rotis for the evening meal; during the morning cooking time I was busy serving Ba.

Date: 5.2.44

We cooked and cleaned utensils and did all other work ourselves. The atmosphere has become grave and quiet. Kateli Sahib does not come down for tea, nor does he eat with us. Sushilabehn eats raw vegetables. Ba's health was poor, her pulse was very slow. Sushilabehn made a plan of staying awake the night, but Ba would know that something was amiss, so she gave up the idea. We feared that something untoward would happen tonight. Bhandari and Dr Shah came for a visit at night. But the night passed with god's grace. Ba is going through a phase that is bad for her. I do not know what god has willed for her. Who can hurt the one protected by Rama? God would have willed for her what is good for her.

Date: 6.2.44

Dr Dinshaw Mehta has been permitted to visit Ba. He came. I gave her a massage, sponge bath and enema. She liked it. It takes about one to two and a half hours. These days everything has become irregular, hence I neither study geometry nor do I read or write other subjects. I did not feel too well today. I had headache and body pain. I drank one dose of quinine. I woke up at five today. The day and night passed; her condition was neither good, nor bad.

Date: 7.2.44

Today, even after the morning enema, Ba did not have any regular bowel movement. She had to use the latrine repeatedly and also soiled her clothes. Kanubhai carries her to the commode and still she feels very tired in the process. I remember a different Ba. I was at Sevagram. It was a rainy day. Ba was taking out her chamber pot to clean. I pleaded with her to let me do it for her. But Ba would just not give it to me. In what condition has the same Ba been placed today? Even here, during high fever, she would walk to the bathroom and would ask me to wait outside. Even though weak, she would not permit me to wait inside the bathroom. But such is Nature; who can know what one would be made to endure? Today I wrote letters to N. Kaka and H. Kaka.[241]

Date: 8.2.44

Her health continues to worsen. She could not sleep at night; hence the day did not pass well. She is unable to lie down to sleep. She sits with support and takes short naps. She cannot be left unattended even for a minute because her condition is fragile. Today, after the evening prayers Bapuji said to Doctor Sahib, 'We should administer enema on alternative days because Ba has become extremely fragile. It would be good if god takes her away. Her going away is preferable to agony of pain.' My heart melted. I prayed that god should cure her and transfer her illness to me. It did happen in the lineage of the Mughals, Babar took upon himself Humayun's pain. Why then, can I not take upon myself Ba's illness? Each night, I count the beads twice for Ba's health. God alone knows that he intends.

Date: 8.2.44[242]

Tonight she could sleep for a while, though not for very long.

---

[241] As in the original. Probably Narandas Gandhi and Harilal Gandhi.
[242] Two entries for the same date. This is probably the entry for 9.2.1944.

Date: 21.2.44[243]

After a gap of many days, I have sat down to write. It's been a long break. I am unable to write regularly. I do not like this at all, but I am so occupied with various tasks during the day that I have neither the time nor the solitude to write this diary. Bapuji has forbidden me to write at night.

Between the 8th and the 21st many new and strange incidents took place. Ba's health has taken a critical turn. Vaidyaraj (Sharma) came for four days.[244] His medications were tried out, but it had no effect and therefore yesterday he left. Some of those days, Vaidyaraj slept outside in the motor car. He was called in whenever necessary. Every time he was needed Kateli Sahib's presence would become necessary. This went on for three days. On the third day Bapuji learnt that Kateli Sahib has to stay awake at night to let the Vaidya in. This was tantamount to torture for him. Bapuji wrote a letter to Bhandari at 2 o'clock in the morning that either the Vaidya should be permitted to stay inside the prison or he would be forced to discontinue the medication.[245] Bhandari gave the permission after this. This is an example of how deeply Bapuji cares for others even during such illness.

Vaidyaraj tried his best for four–five days but finally saw that his medication had no effect, hence yesterday he sought Bapuji's permission to leave. He was overcome with emotion that he had been of no help whatsoever. Bapuji consoled him that, 'You tried all that you had, but to not avail. What can we do?'

During this period Bhai came. Bindubehn, Chandubehn, Nimubehn, her two children, Navinbhai, Dhirubhai and others

---

[243] No diary entries for 9.2.1944 to 20.2.1944.

[244] MKG wrote to the Additional Secretary, Home Department on January 27, 1944 seeking permission to engage services of 'some Ayurvedic Physician.' See, *CWMG*, Vol. 77, p. 219. On 31 January he wrote seeking specific permission for 'Vaidyaraj Sharma' of Lahore. See, *CWMG*, Vol. 77, p. 223.

[245] See, *CWMG* Vol. 77, pp. 229–30.

came. On the day of their visit Ba's health had worsened and had to be given injections. They dispersed soon. Someone performed a dance.

I also got new experiences in life; some incidents took place which makes my mind agitated. I had some talk with Bapuji, before that I had the same conversation with some others. I narrated the same incident to Bapuji. Lack of attention to careful speech and improper choice of words can create misunderstanding and can have grave consequences. I learnt that. I prefer to believe that such experiences would teach me to change my bad habit of saying whatever comes to my mind. It also taught me that how the others perceive what appears to be innocent conduct to me. This incident took place between the 8th and the 10th but I cannot get rid of it even now. When I hear of the same story from different persons in a tone of mockery, I laugh along with them, but it causes a great deal of pain. Bapuji spoke to me very nicely and that gave me some consolation, but when I hear others speak of it, I do feel hurt. I do not wish to cause any further anxiety to Bapuji while there is a serious illness in our family.

Since Yesterday Ba's illness has taken a critical turn. Bapuji spent all the time with Ba. He refused to teach me. He was very worried. He kept repeating 'Hey Ram' all the time. The atmosphere was imbued with devotion and continues to be so. She was given an enema in the evening. Bapuji asked us to finish with massage and other things quickly. Bapuji did not eat either roti or fruits. He did not take milk with his evening meal. I slept at 8 o'clock and woke up at 12—midnight. I stayed awake till 1:30, and slept again after that. These days two persons are required to attend to her day and night. She is unable to pass urine at all. Her body is swelling up. Bapuji said that we should stop all medication now. He said, 'Now it's up to god to release her. If she needs anything give her honey in warm water and chant Ramanama.' Doctor Sahib also said that we can no longer do anything. 'After all we are not god.'[246]

---

[246] This phrase is in English in the original.

Her condition remains unchanged even this morning. Bhai came at around 10:30. Shantikumarbhai has asked him to stay back, hence he would be here for some days. Devadaskaka, Manubehn, Ramibehn, Keshubhai and Santok Kakiba came this evening. Before their visit Harilalkaka came. He had come having drunk alcohol. Ba became very upset with this, and spoke as if delirious. She grew even more upset when Manubehn came at 6:30 in the evening. All of us wept. Her pulse was very fast and irregular. It measured 122 beats. Manubehn sang some bhajans, which made Ba somewhat less upset. She slept at 8. She has had one glass of Horlicks during the day; apart from this she has had warm water and honey. Bapuji does not want to give her anything anymore. It is ten o'clock and she is still asleep. I do not stay awake the nights because if I stay awake the routine tasks of the next day suffer. Sushilabehn is required to stay awake. All others stay awake as well. Bapuji does not like my staying awake. He says that I would fall ill. Tonight Devadaskaka will sleep here. He was suddenly informed of Ba's condition. He passed the journey in great anxiety. He had assumed that Ba was no more. He read the newspapers at Bombay station, which had not reported any such thing. He was quite happy at the lack of news. Dr Dinshaw Mehta has also been permitted to stay the night.

Date: 22.2.44 Shivaratri, Tuesday

Last night at approximately 11:30 Devadaskaka, accompanied by Dr Dinshaw Mehta, came to spend the night. I was awake when they came. How could one sleep when someone is so critically ill in the house? The night was particularly bad. If she spoke up in pain or showed other signs of disquiet we would sing, 'Sriram bhajo sukh me dukh me'[247] or some other bhajan or the 'Rama dhun'. She also would speak in extremely heart-rending voice, 'Hey Rama! Take me away. During this life time I have toiled away for everyone. I cooked

---

[247] Literally, 'Worship Sri Rama in pleasure and pain'.

and fed all. But, I have done nothing for you. I was engrossed in Bapuji. Hey Rama! Cleanse my sins. I will commit no more sins.' She would say to the one sitting by her side. 'How much have you cared for me, how you have served me! What more am I fated to demand of you?' She kept on like this. The morning prayers were conducted late around six o'clock. Even I had woken up for it. Devadaskaka left after the prayers, at the time of breakfast. At that time Bapuji was noting down the daily intake of calories.[248] Bapuji commented about the attitude of the Government, pointing out the time it had taken to obtain permission for Kanubhai. He said, 'Churchill is convinced that I am his biggest enemy. What is one to do? He believes that he would not be able to suppress and control the country if I were to be kept out of prison. But even otherwise, they will not be able to supress the country. Once people acquire confidence, they will not forget it. I consider my work to have been over. There are certain shortcomings in me, which I desire to overcome. And for this reason I make an attempt to keep alive. This 'calorie' counting is part of the daily practice to remain alive.' After this Bapuji got ready for his walk. He washed his feet and came to meet Ba. At that time Ba was lying in my lap. Bapu said, 'Can I go for my walk?' Ba said no. Never before Ba had declined his request to go for a walk however poor her health might have been. She declined today. Probably because this was to be her last day. Ba sat with her head in Bapu's lap. I sang the 'Rama dhun'. Ba sat with perfectly calm but sad face with her head touching Bapu's. Bapu asked her twice or thrice if he could go and take his walk. But he did not get her consent. She spoke up, 'Where shall I go? Hey Ram!' Bapuji replied, 'Where else do you have to go? Now, you must go wherever Rama takes you. Go to his lap. You can go with Rama if you break the shackles of worldly attachments. Imagine, if you were to go after me, I would have constantly worried as to what would become of you. But you will go away with your head in in my lap.' Ba said, 'I feel very sleepy today.' She asked for

---

[248] English term 'calories' in the original.

some tea. We gave her 2 ½ ounces of tea. At 9:30 Bapuji and I went out for a walk. We walked for fifteen minutes. During this time Sushilabehn was with Ba. Every five minutes Doctor Sahib checked on her. That is, one doctor and one nurse were always in attendance. After the walk Bapuji finished with his massage and bath in a hurry. And he asked me to get his food. I asked, 'Will you not have almonds and cashew nuts even today?' Bapuji replied, 'I can have them only after Ba goes away or after she gets well again. It just takes far too much time.' I brought to him mashed vegetables and some milk and butter. Bapuji finished his meal in 10–15 minutes and came to Ba's side. Meanwhile, all of us also had our meals one after the other. I went to sleep at around 1 o'clock. By then Devadaskaka had come and was reciting the Gita. Pujyabhai was with Ba. Her condition was very fragile. Her pulse had become very slow. It was not possible to tell as to at which moment Ba would leave us and go away. I came back to her at 1:30, as I could not sleep. At 2 o'clock Manubehn, Santok kakiba and Devadaskaka[249] and others came. She told Devadaskaka as if to thank him, 'Son, you have served me so well. You came here so often. Be happy and enjoy what is in your destiny.' It was as if this was her last blessings. In the afternoon the Government gave permission to take photographs. Kanubhai took photographs. He did not take even a single photograph of me along with Ba. I said as much to Bapuji to which he replied, 'You should have no desire for a photograph. You have served Ba for so long. Keep her image in your heart. What else there is to it? If someone does not take our photograph,[250] can we get one taken by force?' I understood and went away to prepare jaggery for Bapuji. Meanwhile, Doctor Sahib and Sushilabehn spoke to Bapuji regarding giving an injection[251] to Ba. Bapu's first response was no. But Devadaskaka related one opinion

---

[249] There is a contradiction, as earlier she has written that he had come in around 1 o'clock.

[250] English terms in the original.

[251] English terms in the original.

of an American doctor who had said that treatment could be beneficial even at this stage and so Bapu said yes. But later he realised that it would involve so many more injections[252] and medication, considering this he declined. Bapu was about to set out for a walk. Ba was in Bhai's lap; she had trouble breathing. Suddenly she spoke up, 'Bapu!' Bapu was called in, he took Ba in his lap and asked, 'What is happening to you?' Ba replied, 'I do not know, something is happening.' Her words were tragic and sad. Her eyes seem to roll up. Every one began to chant the 'Rama dhun'—'Raja Rama Rama Rama, Sita Rama, Rama, Rama.' I also rushed in. Bapuji closed his eyes and placed his forehead on hers as if he were blessing her. They had spent their lives together, now he was seeking final forgiveness and bidding her farewell. The scene was heart-wrenching and tragic. Her pulse stopped and she breathed her last. All the unbearable pain ceased. All of us were present. All our eyes had tears. Devadaskaka wept with his face at Ba's feet. He called out to her, 'Ba, Ba' as if to wake her up. But Ba had already reached her final home. She breathed her last at 7:45 p.m. Lord Shankar took her to His Kailasha at a time when in temples the auspicious day of Shivaratri was being observed through special worship. Bapuji trembled for a while, but Bapuji gained control over himself. He comforted Devadaskaka. He asked us to vacate the room. We removed all the belongings to the veranda. He closed Ba's mouth and lay her on the cot. The mosquito net was removed from the cot. Meanwhile, Bhandari came and asked, 'What is your wish regarding the cremation?' Bapuji said, 'If the sons want, the body could be handed over to them, or else permit friends who are like relatives to come in. We could have the cremation here. If you cannot allow friends to come in, I do not want the relatives who are already present here to remain.' Bhandari promised to consult the Government over telephone[253] and left. Meanwhile Bapuji carried Ba to the bathroom.[254] Kanubhai and I washed the room and

---

[252] English terms in the original.

[253] English terms in the original.

[254] English terms in the original.

sprinkled some cow urine. I also brought a ghee lamp. Bapuji permitted all the women to go in and bathe Ba. All of us went in. During this period Mathurdasbhai was at the gates. He was allowed in only after Ba's passing. Bapuji, Sushilabehn, Manubehn and I bathed Ba's body. Some urine passed from her body. Some of us thought that she was still alive, but these were horses galloping away in our imagination. We applied vermilion on her forehead. While I was at Sevagram, Ba had placed in my care a saree with red border which was made for her by Bapuji. I had sent for this saree when I came here. She had told me, 'If there were to be search and seizure at the Ashram, you have to protect this saree somehow. Because I wish to be cremated in this saree. We wrapped this saree around her. We brought her to Bapuji's room. We placed her head in the northern direction. We had demarcated the area with lime. We placed a prison-issued bed sheet and over that Ba's body wrapped in the red bordered saree soaked in the water of the Ganges. We had kept her hair open and parted it in the centre. We placed flowers around her. Her visage had never before seen peace about it. It also glowed with light. We arranged flowers and applied vermilion on her forehead. We removed her bangles and wrapped a hank of Bapu's spinning on her each wrist and also placed a hank around her neck. We placed a lot of flowers around her; she looked like Jagadamba incarnate. Since this morning she had been saying, 'Let me sleep.' She met eternal sleep with ease, much ease and peace just as we go to sleep every day. I placed incense around her. Gradually, one by one every one came. At 9 o'clock we did our daily prayers after which Manubehn sang, 'Vaishnava jan to', we did a dhun of 'Raghupati Raghav' and recited the Gita. There were eighteen of us who recited the Gita. Initially, Bapuji said that each of us should recite a discourse each, but there was a danger that our rhythm would be interrupted. Sushilabehn pointed this out. All eighteen of us recited the Gita together. Bapuji was deeply immersed in the recitation. Among those who recited the Gita were Radhabehn, Sushilabehn, Pyarelalji, Kanubhai, Devadaskaka, Jamnadaskaka, Swami Anand, Prabhavatibehn and I. The recitation took one and quarter hours to complete. Shantikumarbhai reached after we completed the recitation. Meanwhile, the Government also sent a message that hundred or even more friends could join the cremation. Shantikumarbhai and Lady Thackersey[255] made a list[256] of persons to be informed by phone.[257] Swamikaka went with the list, but Bapuji said that only Shamaldaskaka should be phoned.[258] How were the others to reach? It was decided that we shall not wait for those who cannot reach. They went away around 12 midnight. Bapuji took me to the bathroom[259] and gave me a thread that Ba wore in her hair, which he had washed, along with Ba's bangle and beads she wore around her neck. He said, 'The things that Ba used should go to you.' Eventually, all of us went to sleep. Bapuji forbade me from keeping awake all night. I lay down in the bed at 1 o'clock. But how could I sleep? These days I have not been able to sleep much, but how was I to sleep tonight? Hitherto I was preoccupied, which allowed me to do my tasks with courage. My mother passed away when I was twelve and again at fifteen I had someone I could call 'Ba'. But, if one is fated to be motherless, how is one to get a mother? Yesterday, i.e. on 21st, it is eleven months since I came here. Ba is gone. Many wrote to me that I am very fortunate. But if I were really fortunate, why would Ba go away? I could not be of service to her even for twelve months. 'Motiba! I would weep even if you were to say a few words to me. This caused you a lot of pain. I have committed many mistakes, some I know of and of others I am unaware. Would you please forgive me! My nature is such that tears flow even at a few words said to me. Please do not take this to heart. You have reached the house of god, leaving us children behind. No amount of gratitude

---

[255] Lady Premlila Vithaldas Thackersey (1894-1977), committed to the cause of women's education, Chairperson, Kasturba Gandhi National Memorial Trust (1956-72), Vice-Chancellor, SNDT University.

[256] English terms in the original.

[257] English terms in the original.

[258] English terms in the original.

[259] English terms in the original.

can express how grateful I am to god for giving me this opportunity to be of little service to you.' At 3 o'clock Sushilabehn drew me close to her, as affectionately as Yuktibehn does. She embraced me. I wept. She explained to me that our tears cause pain to Ba's soul. The soul cannot decide on its onward journey. When we weep, the soul is drawn towards us, the soul cannot decide whether to come to us or go on the onward journey. The soul's destination is someplace else. For this reason we should not weep. This consoled me. But images and memories came flooding in. How very tragic was my mother's death! The images came back.

Date: 23.2.44

Finally, the morning came. All of us came together for the prayers. The prayers were held at 6 o'clock. I squeezed some juice. Bapuji had some juice and jaggery and immediately sat beside Ba's body. All of us went in there after completing our assigned tasks. By 7:30 people from the outside began to come in. The first one to arrive was Khurshedbehn. After which, one after the other people kept coming in. Among the persons I knew were Sumatibehn (Shantikumarbhai's wife), Savitribhabhi, Kamal Nayanji, Kamlabehn, Krishna Hutheesingh and others. Many of them offered flowers and garlands to Ba's body. Ba was laid in a bed of fragrant flowers. There was unprecedented light about her forehead. Kanubhai took many photos.[260] Leelavatibehn came and wept with her head in Bapu's lap. Manubehn did aarti at 9:30. 'Vaishanava jana' was sung. Even Bhai was present; he did a lot of work. It is his good fortune, his destiny otherwise how could he be in Aga Khan Palace, given its distance from Karachi?

We brought Ba's body out in the veranda. We placed it on a bamboo carriage. Her face was uncovered. All of us chanted 'Raja Rama Rama, Sita Rama Rama' and brought her to where Mahadevbhai's samadhi is. She used to say, 'I want to be cremated

---

[260] English term in the original.

by Mahadev's side.' Her words proved correct today; her time to be by Mahadevbhai's side had come. I sprinkled vermilion and haldi. Bapu and all others stood at one side. Devadaskaka performed all the rituals. Bapu told Devadaskaka, 'I performed Mahadev's last rites. You should perform Ba's.' Harilalkaka was also present. Shantikumarbhai, Kanubhai and others arranged the funeral pyre. Ba was laid on a pile of wood, and some were placed on her as well! Kateli Sahib had a sandalwood tree from the garden cut and dried; those were also placed on the pyre. This was the first time I had witnessed death and cremation. When Ba was alive she cared for all of us, worked all day long and she left all that and submitted herself to eternal sleep. After all the preparations were over, Bapuji led us in prayers. We began the prayers with Isa Vasyam, followed by Asato ma sad gamaya, Mazda, Mirabehn sang an English hymn, it was followed by Mangal Mandir Kholo, the twelfth discourse of the Gita and we sang the Ramadhun to end the prayers. The funeral pyre was lit thereafter. For some time we stood and sat around the pyre after which we went some distance away under an ambli tree. Some sat on chairs while others on the ground. Mridulabehn spoke to me about Bapu's activities in the prison. The body had a lot of water retention hence it took about six and half hours for the body to be entirely burnt. At one point the body fell from the pyre. The half-burnt body was a dreadful sight. The body was lifted with sticks and placed on the pyre again. At 4:40 p.m. the pyre was fully burnt. We went in with withered faces. Bapuji bid farewell to the visitors after which he bathed. All of us bathed and had some lime water. I drank something at 5 p.m. that day. I had not even had a sip of water since the time of Ba's death because I was told that it was not permissible to drink even water before the cremation. All of us were very tired. Bapuji had roti, vegetables and milk. All of us also had our meals. As we were about to complete our meals Bhandari came. Bapu told him, 'If Manu and Prabha could continue to be prisoners here, both of them and I would like it. Prabha could continue to be a prisoner here, but if that were not possible she would prefer to go back to the jail that came from. And I want to teach Manu.

There is no other reason. Hitherto, she was preoccupied with her work and was unable to make much progress with her studies. But, now she is free from these responsibilities. It is both our wish that it would be good for her to continue to be here. Kanu must go back as he has been doing significant work outside. Moreover, his father also feels that he should not stay here without any work.' Bhandari went away after this conversation. Around that time Ramdaskaka reached. He touched Bapuji's feet. Tears flowed from his eyes. He felt pained that he could not see Ba while she was still alive. Bapuji consoled him that if he had come while Ba was alive, he would have seen her in agony. He took his bath. I served him food. He conversed with me. Both the brothers must have talked late into the night with Pyarelalji and Sushilabehn. I went to my bed. I could not sleep. I fell asleep for a while around midnight to wake up again. I kept thinking about Ba, the agony of death and the onward journey of her soul.

Date: 24.2.44

Devadaskaka sang, 'Atma tatva chintyo nahi' during the morning prayers. Everyone was present for the morning prayers. No one went back to sleep after the prayers. I took up spinning. Bapuji also did not lie down, so I squeezed some juice for him. I did some regular chores, bathed, washed clothes and cooked breakfast; by then it was time for the morning walk. Who would keep us in the house today? All of us walked together. All of us spoke of our memories of Ba. Bapuji does not allow the shock of Ba's death to show but it is apparent that his heart cries out for Ba. Outwardly he jokes and talks normally. We collected flowers to offer at the pyre. I also collected many flowers. We also collected the funeral ash. We had placed five green bangles in the funeral pyre. All these five bangles were found whole and unbroken despite having been in fire and placed among logs of wood. Everyone remarked that this was a sign of eternal saubhagya. It was miraculous! Or else, how could all five bangles emerge whole and unbroken? Prabhavatibehn has all these five bangles.

Date: 25.2.44

Today was the last day on which the three brothers were permitted to be here. A priest came this morning and he got some rituals performed. Ash and bones were collected. A part of them would be taken to Allahabad. Malaviyaji has sent a telegram to this effect. The rest would be immersed in river Anandi tomorrow morning. Many telegrams and letters have been received. And why not? The mother of India is no more, and which child of hers would not have been pained. Prabhabehn, Sushilabehn and I kept some ash. We kept the ash in the same bottles which earlier held Ba's medicines. We placed chits on it with Ba's name, the dates of her death and cremation. We also cleaned the cupboards.

Date: 5.5.44[261] Parna Kutir[262]

The diary came to a halt. Because it was not certain as to when I would be ordered to leave and the diary would get left behind or I may not be permitted to take it out. But destiny had ordained something else.

Today we came back from our game when Kateli Sahib received orders that we should all be sent to the superintendent. We could not fathom the reason for this order. But we realised that something was the matter. At around 6:30 or 6:45 Bhandari came and said that all of us were to be released the next day morning at 8 o'clock. Government had decided to release Bapuji on grounds of his ill health.[263]

---

[261] There are no diary entries from 26.2.44 to 4.5.44.

[262] Lady Premilia Thackersey's home in Pune.

[263] On 28.4.44 the Government had released a medical bulletin on MKG's ill health. In a cable dated 4 May 1944 to the Secretary of State for India, the Viceroy reported, 'Latest reports show progressive deterioration in Gandhi's anaemia, blood-pressure and kidney functions, all of which in the opinion of Dr. B.C. Roy shared by the Surgeon-General Candy, have tendency to produce coronary or cerebral thrombosis…This is a case in

Kanubhai was permitted to the prison to nurse Bapuji on the 4th. Therefore, none of us were prepared for this order of release. The subject of release and transfer was a daily topic of conversation. They used to tell me that I would be the first to be sent away. But my faith in god was complete, I did not feel that I would be separated from Bapu; and that came to be true. I went into the kitchen to prepare jaggery for Bapuji. For some time now we do not take any work from the soldiers. Ramnaresh was overcome with emotion. He said, 'Mother allow me to prepare the jaggery today.' I also felt that he should be allowed to do so, even Sushilabehn said, 'Let him do it.' He made the jaggery, while we got busy with other tasks. Bapuji went out for a walk; all of us also went to the samadhi. Our overwhelming feeling was that if the release orders were issued a few months before, Ba would have survived and gotten better. But god's will was done. Today was our last day to place lamps at the samadhi. Each day I would pray for Ba and Mahadevbhai's blessings that I should be able to serve Bapuji to the fullest, and I did receive the blessings and I was not separated from him.

We did our evening prayers after the walk where we sang 'Hari ne bhajata'. Mirabehn also joined the prayers. The prayers were sombre.

I gave Bapuji his massage. During the walk and the massage Bapuji said, 'I am afraid. There is a pressure on my mind. I do not know what I would be able to do once outside. I feel no enthusiasm.' None of us were enthused by the news—how could we be? We had bid farewell to two of our near and dear ones in a span of twenty-one months.

---

which I consider we should be guided by medical opinion. Deterioration in Gandhi's health appears such that his further participation in active politics is impossible and I have no doubt that death in custody would intensify feelings against Government … I am accordingly instructing Bombay Government to release Gandhi unconditionally at 8 a.m., on Sunday, 6th May, with announcement that release is entirely on medical grounds and am informing all Governors accordingly." *The Transfer of Power*, vol. IV, pp. 948–9.

After the massage we got busy with packing.[264] Sushilabehn and I got to work in one room, while Pyarelalbhai had to pack his belongings, books and stationery[265] collected over five years. Therefore, none of us slept much at night. Sushilabehn and I lay down in the cot at 4:15 a.m.. For the last one and half years we have grown close like sisters. But now we are to be freed. She has treated me like a younger sister. She affectionately caressed me to sleep, but her affection overwhelmed me and I wept. Neither of us could sleep. Doctor Sahib packed[266] up by 2:30 a.m.. Mirabehn had packed[267] her belongings a month ago, and yet she worked away till 1 o'clock. She also helped Sushilabehn pack her things. I went to bathe at 3:45 a.m. and finished rest of the work after that. All of us were very tired. Bapuji also could not sleep, he felt some sort of burden.

Date: 6.5.44

Bapuji got up at 5 o'clock. A health bulletin was issued. Dr Guilder, Sushilabehn, Bapuji, Kanubhai, Kateli Sahib and I joined the prayers. After the prayers Kateli Sahib offered a purse of seventy-five rupees to Bapuji and did a sastang dandvat pranam. He is an affectionate devotee. It is rare to find a superintendent[268] such as him. After the prayers I squeezed juice and helped Pyarelalbhai pack things. At 7 o'clock we went to the samadhi. It was our final goodbye. Who knows when again Bapuji would be able to come here? I lit many incense sticks at the samadhi. There were many flowers as well. We offered prayers in this order. (1) Isa Vasyam; (2) Aasto ma sadgamaya; (3) Azaubila; (4) Mazda; (5) Mukam Karoti vachalam; and finally (6) the twelfth discourse. We bowed before

---

264 English term in the original.
265 English term in the original.
266 English term in the original.
267 English term in the original.
268 English term in the original.

the samadhi for one last time and sought forgiveness. I could hardly speak during the prayers. The scene was sombre. We turned back. As the clock struck 8, Bhandari Sahib came. Bapu, Sushilabehn and Bhandari travelled by the first car. Bapu had instructed us to be ready before 8 as he did not want even a minute's delay. Doctor Sahib, Mirabehn and I were taken by the second car. Pyarelalbhai and Kanubhai were in the third car. After reaching here[269] I checked all the belongings and went down to the kitchen to prepare vegetables and other things. Bapuji had fruits, raw vegetables and ghee. There is work to be done all day long. Sushilabehn does not have even a free moment.

Date: 11.5.44[270]

Today we reached Mumbai. Bapuji is Shantikumarbhai's guest.

Date: 18.5.44[271]

Today we went to see the place where the blast[272] had taken place. Bapuji was with us.

Date: 20.5.44[273]

Bapu wrote some letters today. He called me at 6:30 and wrote about my going back to Rajkot and asked me to send a copy of that to Bhai, which I did. The first letter that Bapuji wrote was to Durgabehn.

---

[269] Lady Thackersey's house, 'Parna kutir' in Poona, MKG stayed there till 11 May 1944.

[270] No entries for 7.5.44 to 10.5.44.

[271] No entries for 12.5.44 to 17.5.44

[272] There was a blast and fire on the Bombay docks on 14.4.44.

[273] No entry for 19.5.44.

CHI. DURGA   May 20, 1944[274]

I may be regarded as crippled for the present. God does not allow even a Mahatma's pride to last. These lines are for all. Once I start writing letters everyone expects one from me, but before I can satisfy their wish, maybe I will be there. Write to me in detail. Let all those who wish to write do so.

Blessings from Bapu[275]

Bapu wrote a letter about me.

Juhu, May 20, 1944

CHI. NARANDAS

I drafted an article for you while laying in bed. I was afraid that there would be some errors[276] in it, but that did not happen. I didn't feel like making a fair copy with ink. If you want any changes to be made in the draft, send it back to me. I will think over your revisions and will make a fair draft and send it over to you. We have enough time still.

Secondly, you know Manu (Jaisukhlal's daughter); she has created a very good impression on me. I have not seen any other girl in our family with the same spontaneous spirit of service that she has. The devotion with which she looked after Ba has captured my heart. She would like to remain with me, but I do not wish it. I am a broken vessel[277] just now, and therefore, can give her nothing. The others are busy with their work. And what can they give her now? Her education

---

[274] Manubehn has written the date as 12.5.1944.

[275] Also see, *CWMG*, vol. 77, p. 276.

[276] There is a difference between the diary and the letter published in *Akshar Deha*, Vol. 77, p. 266. In the diary the word is 'Bhul' – 'errors', while in the Akshar Deha it is 'check –bhus', 'છઠ-ભૂસ' corrections, hence the translation here differs from the one in *CWMG* vol. 77, p. 278.

[277] In the diary the term is पात्र (vessel), in Akshar Deha it is भाजन (vessel), while *CWMG* has translated it as 'reed', the term 'vessel' is closer to the original than 'reed'.

must go on regularly. That can be done only if she is with you. She is not the type of girl whose presence would irritate you. She is simple-hearted. She is all right[278] in her studies, has a good voice, and her health is fairly good. She does not know how to take care of her health. She forgets everything concerning herself while serving.[279] I do wish that her knowledge of Sanskrit and Gujarati should improve. I myself taught her the Gita. Her pronunciations[280] are fairly good. Purushottam[281] or you can help her to improve her pronunciation still further. Jaishukhlal will pay whatever expenses on her account you think reasonable to ask her to send me a wire whether or not you can receive her. I intend to send her with the first available escort. If you are inclined to refuse, do not hesitate to say so.[282]

Blessings from
BAPU

'Not revised.'

May 20, 1944

BHAI SHRI GAGAN[283],

I read your article on Mahadev. May I entrust you with a job for Mahadev as long as you are here? Narayan[284] does not like to attend

---

[278] In the diary the term is ठीक, literally 'all right', while in *Akshar Deha*, the term is 'ठोठ', 'dull', the *CWMG* has translated it as 'dull', while here the sense closer to the diary has been retained.

[279] In the *Akshar Deha* there are two sentences which are not in the diary. These have been rendered as follows in the *CWMG*. 'She is obedient. She will do whatever work you give her.'

[280] In the diary as also the *Akshar Deha* the term is 'उच्चार', literally pronunciations. In the *CWMG* it has been rendered thus, 'she can recite it fairly well.'

[281] Addressee's son.

[282] Also see, 'silence-Day Note to Manu Gandhi", CWMG vol.77, p. 240.

[283] Gagan Vihari Lallubhai Mehta.

[284] Mahadev Desai's son Narayan Desai.

school or college and whatever he has acquired has been through Mahadev. I cannot, in my present condition, do anything for him. After I get well, I do not[285] think, I will be free. As long as I am out (of jail) he wishes to stay with me. It would be nice if you can spare some time for him. You can teach him economics, Sanskrit, Bengali etc. if, on reflection, you think it would overtax you, then please do not take it up. I have made this request because I saw in your article your overflowing love for Mahadev.

Secondly, Smt. Saudamini[286] also kindly offered whatever help I might need. If Chi. Uma[287] does not care anymore to be nursed like an invalid, by all means let her give some time to me. I will think over what she can give. How much time and when, that also I will have to think over. May be you two will not be able to spare time. I am only hungry for the company of the good and, therefore, I accept whatever is offered or is available from any source.

Blessings from
Bapu.

CHI. VIJAYA[288]

JUHU
May 20, 1944

From today I am exercising the liberty of a few letters.[289] I am in Juhu till the 29th [290] at any rate. Then, may be three weeks, in Poona. The silence will end on the 29th [291]. But do come over

---

[285] In the *CWMG* vol. 77, p. 279, 'I do think, this closer to the original, as also *Akshar Deha*.

[286] Addressee's wife.

[287] Addressee' daughter, Uma Randeria.

[288] Vijaya M. Pancholi.

[289] In the *Akshar Deha* and *CWMG*, liberty of.

[290] In the *Akshar Deha* vol.77, p. 264 and *CWMG* vol. 77 p. 276, the date is 29th.

[291] MKG observed silence from 14 May 1944 for 15 days, while in Mumbai.

here...[292] I am glad that Nanabhai[293] has been released. About me it is as you say.

Blessings from[294]

Bapu

CHI. NARANDAS,[295]

I went carefully through your Annual Report. I have not yet started writing anything.[296] I have written only three letters to invalids. But Daridranarayana is the greatest invalid in the world. You are His materials devotee.[297] You celebrate the Rentia Baras on the occasion of my birthday and every year you make your plan of service more rigorous. This year the test will be the hardest so far. May you succeed in it. This time, while in Jail, I read about Marx and Engles[298] and whatever literature I would get about the great experiment in Russia. What a great difference between that experiment and our spinning wheel? There also, as with us,[299] the whole nation is invited to join the Yajna. But the experiments there and here are as different from each other as East from West or North from South.

What a difference between our spinning-wheel and their machines driven by steam or electricity? But all the same I prefer

---

[292] The following lines from *CWMG* are not in the diary. She indicated it by putting three dots.

[293] Narsimhaprasad Kalidas Bhatt, Principal, Lok Bharati, Sanosara.

[294] In the *Akshar Deha* and *CWMG*, 'Blessings to all of you from.'

[295] Undated in the diary, the date is 20 May, 1944.

[296] This letter is clearly written before the letter of the same day addressed to Narandas Gandhi. As in that letter MKG mentions sending a draft of an article.

[297] In the *Akshar Deha* vol.77, p. 265, and *CWMG* vol. 77, p. 277. 'You are one of His matchless devotees.' The English rendering adds, dedicated exclusively to His Service. Which is not in either *Akshar Deha* or the diary.

[298] And Engles, not either in *Akshar Deha* or the *CWMG*.

[299] In the *CWMG*, it reads 'as in India', this rendering faithful to that at the diary and the *Akshar Deha*.

the snail-like speed of the spinning wheel. The spinning wheel is a symbol of ahimsa, and ultimately it is ahimsa that will triumph. If, however, we who claim to be rotaries are weak, we shall dishonour ourselves and discredit ahimsa. Your activity is excellent indeed. But you should now introduce some new changes in it. There is a science of the spinning wheel, as there is one of the machines. We have still not fully evolved the 'technique'[300] of the spinning wheel. It requires deep study.

Just as knowledge without faith is useless, even so faith without knowledge is blind.[301]

May 21, 1944

CHI. KRISHNA CHANDRA

I would just read your letter. At present I am not able to write much. Please, therefore, be content with the little I write. What I write to one of you should be regarded as addressed to all. I do not know anything about the quarrel between Balvant Sinha and Amtussalaam. I think it is good that Manulal is leaving. It is desirable that he should settle down somewhere. But he is a restless soul and will not do that. God protects him because his intentions are good. What is Parnekar[302] doing?

Even if I don't write, those who wish to write to me may do so.

I will not be in a hurry to go there. My heart is there of course. Now I will come[303] over only after it cools down. The silence will end on the 29th. After that I am eager to spend a couple of weeks at Dr Mehta's Sanatorium. Blessings to all. Why is Shankaran displeased?

Blessings from
Bapu

---

[300] English term in the original.

[301] In the *Akshar Deha* and *CWMG*, 'blessings from Bapu' missing in the diary.

[302] Yashwant Mahadev Parnekar of Sevagram Ashram Dairy.

[303] It is 'go' over in *CWMG* vol. 77 p. 281, 'come' is more faithful to the original.

Letter to Pandit Madan Mohan Malaviyaji.

Pujya BHAI SAHEB[304]

The doctor has permitted me to write such letters. I don't deserve your love. I know that I am unable to fulfil your wishes.[305]

The doctors don't permit my travelling long distances. The fact is I don't feel as if I am out of jail. Is being released on grounds of health any release at all? Let us see what way God shows me after I am all right.

Your Younger Brother

CHI. GOMTI,

Today I feel like writing to you. The letter is for all of you. Vijayabehn and others came and saw me. Manju too came.

I do not worry about Kishorelal. He has come into the world to endure joy and sorrow silently.

I get news about you, too. I feel satisfied.

Tell Durga that she may accept Shantikumar's invitation and come. Lilavati tells me that she is unhappy there. We should not be unhappy. This is only philosophizing. That she is unhappy there. We should not be unhappy. This is only philosophizing. That she is unhappy is, however, a poet, so let her come here. She will get some peace of mind at any rate. Bablo is here, and that is also one reason why she should come. I am, of course, here too. Let her do what she thinks best...[306] ask her to write to me in detail about her activities.

Blessings from
Bapu

---

[304] Originally in Hindi, undated in diary, it is of 21.5.1944.

[305] Pandit Malaviya had sent a telegram to MKG on May 20, 1944: 'If doctors permit, suggest your staying Allahabad two months, consultations necessary important matter. Wish meet you when your health permits. MKG had sent a reply via telegram the same day. Your kind wire. Doctors won't countenance such journey. Suggest talking through messenger after end month. Till then complete silence.' See, *CWMG*, vol.77, p.280

[306] Omission as in the source, also in *CWMG*, vol.77, p. 283 and *Akshar Deha* vol.77 p. 271.

The following notes and entries are not in chronological order; they have been translated here in the order in which they appear in the diary.[307]

Date: 20.5.1944

Today 'Mission to Moscow' film was screened at Shantikumarbhai's house. Bapuji sat through it for two hours. He did not like it.

Date: 22.5.1944

We offered prayers in memory of Ba today. We recited the entire Gita, as always. Mirabehn sang the 'Ram dhun' and 'Wondrous cross'.

I went with Shantikumarbhai to see his office in Mumbai. I also saw Elphinstone College, where Mahadevbhai studied, and the university. I came back home with Shantikumarbhai at 6:15 after the day-long excursion.

Date: 23.5.1944

A long letter from Pujyabhai came today. He has resigned from his job as he is dissatisfied with it. He has left my decision to me.

Date: 12.4.1944

Today Prabhavatibehn was transferred; she was escorted by four sergeants, five policemen and one matron.

Date: 4.5.1944

Kanubhai came today.

---

[307] Editor/Translator's note.

Date: 5.5.1944

The release orders came at 6:30 p.m.

Date: 6.5.1944

All policemen left at 8 o'clock as we were released.

Date: 11.5.1944

We reached Mumbai.

Date: 18.5.1944

Meghanibhai came and sang to Bapuji, which he liked. Bapu's letter to Quid-e-Azam Jinnah, which was proscribed by the Government was published today.

Date: 15.5.1944

Bapuji has taken silence for fifteen days so that he can rest and recuperate.

Date: 22.2.1944 Tuesday

Ba's death at 7:35 p.m.. Pujyabhai was present.

Date: 23.2.1944 Wednesday

Ba's cremations. 10:40 to 4:40. Bapuji was present throughout. Ramdaskaka came in the evening.

Date: 24.2.1944 Thursday

Devadaskaka stayed. We saw all of Ba's belongings. He spoke with Bapuji till midnight.

Date: 25.2.1944 Friday

Devadaskaka, Harilalkaka and Ramdaskaka collected ash from Ba's pyre. They took the ashes with them. Pujyabhai was with them.

Date: 29.2.1944 Tuesday

We recommenced twenty-four hours of unbroken spinning at 7:35 p.m..

Date: 1.3.1944

The spinning stopped at 7:35 p.m.. Bapuji commenced and ended the spinning.

Date: 2.3.1944

The recitation of Gita commenced after the prayers at 5:30 a.m. and at 7 we completed the recitation of all 18 discourses.

Date: 9.4.1944

Orders were received to transfer Prabhavatibehn to the Bhagalpur jail.

Date: 16.8.1942[308]

This entry was written at Sevagram. It was written in a rough[309] notebook, hence felt advisable to copy the same in this notebook.

---

[308] Parts of diary no 12 deal with the Aga khan period, hence taken here.

[309] English term in the original.

Today was the last day of the AICC meeting. I expected Bapuji and Ba to return tomorrow. I cleaned Ba's room and rearranged her belongings. Who knew that all of that would be turned upside down?

The clock struck 8:30. A bell, calling us to the kitchen to make rotis rang out. I had to go and clean the toilets. No one had forced this sanitation work on me. I felt that in Ba's absence I must do that work. I must gather all types of experiences. I called Pujya Shakri Masi. Just then Gomtikaki came and said, 'Manu! The AICC resolution has been turned down.' I was stunned. While we spoke about it Dhirenbhai came and said, 'There was a telephone call and Bapuji has been arrested at 6 o'clock. All members of the Working Committee have also been arrested.' Today was the last day of my cleaning duty hence I went to complete the cleaning work. But my heart was left behind in that telephone call and the conversations of all others regarding it. I quickly completed the cleaning work and went where the phone was. The names of the arrested persons were conveyed to us. Bapu has been held captive in a bungalow in Poona. Mirabehn, Mahadevbhai and Mrs. Sarojini Naidu have been held along with him. We were afraid that Bapu would commence a fast. What would be the outcome if that were to happen? We made a telephone call to inquire about this. We were told that Shri Birlaji had taken a promise from Bapu that he would not commence fast immediately upon his arrest. His last call was 'Do or Die'.[310] This is his last message. The telephone connection was severed mid-conversation hence Murabbi Kishorelalbhai could not speak at length. Just then, a call came from the bungalow at Wardha that Vinobaji has also been arrested. All of us decided to pray. I rang the bell. We also called people from the village. We gathered at Murabbi Kishorelalbhai's house to pray. All the faces wore a withered look. There were tears in the eyes. It was as if all the trees, fruits and flowers of Sevagram, Nature herself seemed to be in tears. The sun hid behind the clouds. Bapuji's cottage appeared

---

[310] She has used both the Hindustani call 'Karenge ya Marenge' and 'Do or Die'.

bereft of light like never before. We prayed and sang Bapuji's favourite hymn 'Vaishnava Jana To', we sang the Ram dhun almost weeping. Kishorelalbhai said that we should observe a twenty-four hour fast. It was not a compulsion. It should be observed by those who want to. Children were not to observe it. But I observed the fast. Everyone rushed around. Some were making precautionary arrangements lest their belongings were confiscated. I went into Ba's room. Ba was not arrested. After a lot of trying we were told on the phone that if they were not arrested Murabbi Pyarelalji, Ba and Sushilabehn would leave this evening and reach here tomorrow.

But by afternoon we came to know that Ba was to attend the evening meeting and also address the people. But they were arrested before the meeting! I had arranged her belongings, filled water in her pitcher, cleaned and cooked vegetables and made rotis in the hope that Ba was due to arrive today. Who knows at what inauspicious hour I did all that she left us forever!

Ba was arrested and Sushilabehn and Pyarelalji were arrested with her. I stayed in the office waiting for the telephone to ring. We received secret information that Sushilabehn has been kept with Ba. We were very worried because Ba's health at the time of her arrest was rather frail. Ba and Bapu had made the jail their dwelling, therefore I too became eager for going to the prison. All the ashramites were also eager to go to the prison. I wanted to be arrested the very next day. But Bapuji had given my charge to the manager of the Ashram, Pujya Chimanlalkaka and he wouldn't let me court arrest without the consent of Pujyabhai. He told me that it would be a long struggle and I was the youngest member of the Ashram. How was he to let me go to prison unaccompanied? He said that I should go if the elder women went to prison. I accepted his decision.

Ba had told me before she left that, 'Manu, this sari has been made from cotton spun by Bapuji's hand. I do not know when I would get another one. Therefore, take as much care as possible. Because, I would like to be cremated in this sari.' I kept all the things that she had pointed out, including Bapu's letters to Ba, carefully. When will she come back? I gathered together all that I possibly could. But for now we spent days without Ba and Bapu in a disinterested fashion. All of us prepared our minds to join the battle.

We came to know that Ba and Bapu are in the bungalow[311] of the Aga Khan. We were somewhat relieved that Ba was with Bapu and we had nothing to be worried about.

Date: 15.8.1942[312]

Today was a cruel day for the entire country. How sad would Mother India be to lose a son? Or did the sacrifice bring a smile to her? But none of her people would have courage enough to laugh at the passing of a brother. No one had imagined if in their dreams that one with such a handsome visage, golden complexion would fall so suddenly! We heard it on the radio[313] at 10 p.m. that Pujya Mahadevkaka had passed away in the Aga Khan Palace, but the Government's morality was such that who would believe this news! We made a phone call, but the phone wires were cut! How to ascertain the truth? All of us wondered about it, just then a wire sent by Col. Bhandari reached us that Shri Mahadev Desai had died that morning at 8:30. We had no choice but to believe it. We spent the night with Durgabehn. That day Narayanbhai had fever. Kishorelalkaka came and said, 'He was a mahayogi.' He was required to take the place of Bapu and perform the duties. Albeit he was in deep sorrow because the two of them had a bond closer than that between brothers during twenty-five years of close relationship. He was required to give solace to all of us who wept. His eyes did turn moist while pacifying Durgabehn. The next morning we came together for prayers, wherein we recited the entire Bhagavad Gita. The Ashram was gripped by deep sorrow.

[The rest, I heard from Bapu at Aga Khan.] Bapu said that on Friday Mahadev wrote the letter to Lord Linlithgow[314] and gave it to

---

[311] Bungalow English word in the original.

[312] This entry follows the entry of 10.8.1942.

[313] 'Radio', English term in the original.

[314] For the text of the letter, see, *CWMG*, vol.76, pp. 406–10. 'Wrote' here indicates transcribed to make a fair copy.

Kateli in the morning. That morning he joined me for a walk and said, 'Bapu, now I should be all right. I even slept well last night. I intend to start writing something.' Bapu was glad to hear this. After the walk he made a toast[315] for Bapu and said with great delight, 'Look here Bapu! What a fine toast I have made. Now, we shall make something new every day.' Bapu went to get his massage. Just at that time Col. Bhandari came. He and Mahadevkaka chatted with each other. Suddenly he said that, 'I feel dizzy, my head feels giddy.' Ba asked him to lie down. Mahadevkaka lay down on a bed in that room. Ba called out, 'Sushila, Sushila, come soon, something has happened to Mahadev.' Sushilabehn rushed in at Ba's call and felt his pulse. Every day he used to sing, 'My pulse is in your hand, lord protects me.' He gave up his pulse to the lord. How was Sushilabehn to feel it? She called out, 'Bapu, Mahadevbhai is dying, come soon.' Bapu replied, 'Mahadev cannot die. He has to write my biography.' Sushilabehn called out, 'Bapu, come soon.' Bapu went in and placed his hand over Mahadevbhai's forehead and said, 'Mahadev, Mahadev.' He tried to open his eyes. That was his last act. He did manage to have one last darshan of Bapu. Bapu took Mahadevbhai to the bathroom[316] and gave him a bath. Bapu remarked, 'Mahadev desired to die in my arms and he also wanted to write my biography. God heard his first prayer.' After the bath Mirabehn placed flowers over the dead body and wrote 'Om' where the head was placed. She and Sushilabehn recited the Gita. Bhandari asked Bapu about the arrangements for cremation. Bapu replied, 'Mahadev was a true son of mine. I will light the funeral pyre.' He was cremated in the compound of Aga Khan Palace. This place has been marked by a platform now.

We knew nothing of this on the outside. Many rumours took wings. Someone said Bhandari gave him poison and Mahadevbhai died. But that proved to be a total lie. Mahadevkaka was under tremendous strain due to the impending fast of Bapuji. God took him away either to relieve him forever from that strain or He did

---

[315] 'Toast', English word in the original.

[316] 'Bathroom', English term in the original.

not want Mahadevbhai to bear witness to this scene. Mahadevkaka desired a death in Bapu's arms, god fulfilled this desire. Such auspicious death is available only to a true devotee. Leave us out, but a child of five who had only a day-long friendship with Mahadevkaka said, 'Who took away Mahadevkaka? Will he never meet me again?' Thus, Mahadevbhai had become Mahadevkaka not only to the likes of us, but also to that of a five-year-old child. It was as if god had determined a weekly event for the Ashram. On the 8th, Bapu went to the Aga Khan Palace. On the 15th Mahadevkaka entered god's palace and on 22.8.42 Kishorelalkaka went to the governmental palace.

During the night of 22.8.42 at around 1 a.m. some 30 policemen accompanied by a seargent[317] and an inspector[318] came. After the commencement of the struggle the Ashram had instituted a practice that whenever the police van came, bells should be rung—one, two, three and one, two, three. Shakari Masi woke me up suddenly and said 'Manu! Come, you're very enthused about jail going, aren't you? The police have gone to Kishorelalbhai's home.' My heart beat faster. I was initially afraid at the sight of loaded guns. There were some 30 stout policemen and the sergeant and inspector. But somehow I gathered courage. I asked Murabbi Kishorelalkaka whether I should ring the bell. The police said, 'We have not come to arrest anyone, we have come merely to search.' They searched extensively; we gave them all the keys, but they could find nothing. I said, 'Kishorelalkaka, allow me to ring the bell.' He consented and I rang the bell. The police superior asked me, 'Are you intent on mischief? We have come with our guns loaded, but we hope that we would be required do no such thing here.' Kishorelalkaka pleaded for patience and said, 'There is no cause for alarm, there will be no trouble. This is our rule hence, this girl came and asked.' This conversation took place in Hindi. They searched for three long hours, at 4 a.m. they asked Kishorelalkaka to sign a paper, which he declined; these people

---

[317] English term in the original.
[318] English term in the original.

produced a warrant[319] and told him to get ready within half an hour to quarter of an hour. He was ready in five minutes. We said the prayers I was made to sing 'Vaishnava Jana to' and 'Thake na thake chanta e'. He told me, 'Oh! You wanted to go, but in your place I am going. Follow after me. Do not lose courage.' Hitherto I had not witnessed search and arrest, this arrest of Kishorelalkaka was the first instance. He took Gitaji, some other religious books, one packet of slivers and the spinning-wheel with him. He had no other luggage. His health is frail, he has severe asthma and in spite of that he did not take even a woollen jacket with him. We were worried about his food, his clothing. We insisted a great deal that he should carry some warm clothing with him. He replied, 'if god wants to save me he will, but I will wear only jail issued khadi clothes, otherwise I shall go about naked.' That was his firm resolve. There was a light drizzle, we placed garlands around him. Gomtibehn put a kumkum tilak on his forehead, placed a garland around his neck and touched his feet. That brave woman sent her husband off to the prison joyously. That scene was wonderful. If we read about it in history we would wonder if such a brave woman actually lived! But the progeny of such brave women live on and such scenes are a testimony to it. We had in our midst Durgabehn who surrendered her husband forever and bore the tremendous blow of the immortal death of her husband, and I witnessed this other scene. There would be many other such brave women, and now I can believe that there were such women in the past.

Date: 31.8.1942[320]

This was the third week. This day of this week was for me a day of festivities. On the night of the 30th it was decided that we, the women, were to join the struggle. I jumped with joy. There were three-four other girls of my age—they were elder to me by three or

---

[319] English term in the original.
[320] There are no entries for 17th to 30th August, 1942.

four years who were also very eager to go to the prison. We asked whoever we could find to narrate their jail experiences to us. Since all the women were about to proceed to prison, men realized that they would have to roll rotis and for this reason they took over the kitchen work. They did not know how to roll the rotis and the bajra rotla got burnt, they boiled some vegetables. We offered to teach them, but why should the proud men learn from us? They ate their rotis they had made with great relish and said that the wheat rotis had a special taste that day. Thus, we passed time in fun. At 3 o'clock we got ready and offered prayers. Many told me that I looked much younger in a frock and hence would not be arrested. That day I wore a saree for the first time. I was of fourteen years of age. After the prayers we bowed to all the elders and seven of us including a Muslim woman set out for Wardha. On the way we stopped at Kakaji's (Jamnalalji) bunglow[321] and put our luggage there. I went to touch Mataji's (Janaki Devi) feet. We reached Gandhi chowk around 5:30, where we made speeches and shouted slogans. A motor van came. There were about 40 policemen in it. They made loud noises of the petrol motor, the louder the noise the greater our energy. They made the noise so that people would not be able to hear our speeches. To harass them people would enter narrow lanes, they would be forced to come out of the police van and follow after us. Meanwhile, there was a wedding precession going on, accompanied by a band. The police made the band walk ahead of us. If they were to refuse, they would face the prospects of a beating. The poor groom's party had to proceed to the wedding without the band, as mid-way the band had to lead us. We were flanked by the band and the police in front and behind us. This had an advantage. If we were to shout slogans and people were to gather, they would have faced the sticks of the police. So, people would come out stealthily. But because of the band people could claim that they had come out to see a wedding procession; this allowed us to do our work. This went on till 7 o'clock in the evening.

---

[321] English term in the original.

We were about to return home when the police superintendent came to arrest us and took us to Wardha prison. At that time there were thirty-five women lodged in the Wardha prison and seven of us were added to them. The authorities kept us in the open yard, but it started to rain and all forty-two us were put inside a tiny cell. A person who has not been inside can hardly imagine how we managed. We somehow spread mattress using every nook and cranny and slept huddled over one another. We chanted slogans all night so loudly that people on the outside could hear us. Somehow the night passed. In the morning we got some coal dust to clean our teeth after which we said the prayers. How were we to bathe? There was a trough of water akin to the one made for cattle. We were to use that water for all the necessities. Because I was the youngest, I was somehow given three-four pitchers of water. Moreover, I had worn a saree. How was I to wash my clothes? I was taken to the superintendent. The elder women said that this girl is only fourteen and she can barely wash her clothes. Let that be, they said, this girl is Mahatmaji's niece. You cannot arrest someone as young as her and once arrested you cannot heap hardships over her. She will bear whatever hardships you give her because she has read the jail regulations before she came here. But, that does not imply that her clothes should remain dirty, and especially when we, her elders are around her. Kindly give water enough for her needs at least. The superintendent immediately took me by my hand and said, 'Come daughter! I will have your clothes washed for you. The water will be released immediately.' In a short time the tap flowed with abundant water. Everyone, including those who had not bathed in eight days, bathed that day. We were given rab for breakfast. I did not like its taste. But once in jail what is like and dislike? I ate it just to get the taste of jail food, but I soon vomited. It made me unhappy that our bodies should not be able stomach jail rab. I was deeply ashamed. At 12 noon we were served jowar rotla, udad dal and leafy vegetables cooked with lots of garlic and onion. I could with great effort eat two morsels. This happened because it was my first day. As a result I had fever that night, but I lay without telling anyone about it. It had disappeared by morning. We spent the afternoon playing antakshari. I spun 1280 threads. In the evening all the women did raas and played games. There were women as old as forty years and some were twenty-five to thirty years old. Even those found time for games in the prison. They experienced the joys of childhood spent in parental home once again in the prison. In this way jail for them is a celebration also. Thus we passed the day. It did not rain today hence we slept in the open yard. At 5 o'clock in the morning the bell of our barrack rang and we got up startled. We were told that we were to be shifted to Nagpur prison on that day that is 2 September 1942. We were asked to prepare for departure. Everyone got ready hurriedly and we set out for Nagpur by a bus at 9 o'clock. We reached Nagpur by four. On the way we asked the policemen accompanying us about food. What arrangements other than way side hotels could be made for food? They bought some groundnut and jaggery and gave them to us, which we ate. We also sang national songs.

We reached Nagpur. Our matron[322] Radhabai was at the prison gates to escort us inside. The iron gates of the prison were so large as if a demon stood facing us. Each one of us was accounted for and taken inside. We were forty women. At a distance of about sixty feet from the first gate were another set of gates. The intervening space of 60 feet was taken by offices[323] of the superintendents,[324] the jailer[325] and other clerks. We crossed the second gate. The prison proper begins from that gate. On one side were the barracks[326] for male convicts and opposite to them were lodged the male political prisoners. They were permitted to step out into a large compound. We were shouting slogans, the men came out. Vinobaji was among them. We, from a distance, did pranams to him and Kishorelalkaka.

---

322 English term in the original.
323 English term in the original.
324 English term in the original.
325 English term in the original.
326 English term in the original.

At a distance of about five-minutes'[327] walk were barracks[328] for women. The area between the second gate and the gates of our barracks[329] resembled a small village because prisoners could be seen driving carts, there were granaries from which provisions for the kitchen were supplied; there were wells and a bakery[330] where bread was baked; storages for grains and many such other things. The area was enclosed by fort-like tall walls with shreds of glass fixed on them. One has to cross this area to enter out barracks. Once a person enters it, she is imprisoned. The large gates of our barracks opened to allow us entry and immediately closed behind us. This was a large prison. The female criminal convicts had made a beautiful garden in there. However large a prison might be, large numbers lodged there in makes it small. It could accommodate at the most 100 to 125 women. There were 75 women convicts and 125 of us, political prisoners. This made the space cramped. But they made adequate arrangements for us. The seventy-five women who had hitherto lived in two barracks were now shifted into one. We had experienced cramped spaces in Wardha hence we spoke on their behalf, but why would the authorities do anything for them? But when we plainly refused the living arrangement some of us were accommodated in the hospital meant for women prisoners. There was one trough of water for bathing and washing. Later we erected bathrooms[331] made of bamboo. All two hundred of us bathed from the water in that trough. The water was plentiful. Our activity consisted of spinning and little else. From morning to meal time we would spin. If we got an opportunity to bathe we would take a break. Otherwise we would bathe in the afternoon or the evening and at times during the night. We were allocated 'B'[332] class, since the day we reached

---

[327] English term in the original.
[328] English term in the original.
[329] English term in the original.
[330] English term in the original.
[331] English term in the original.
[332] English letters in the original.

there. The food was good even in 'C'[333] class. These days people on the outside do not get wheat to eat. But ever since Jamnalalji went to that jail during the time of individual satyagraha, wheat was provided by him to even criminal convicts; this practice has continued ever since. Therefore in 'C'[334] class wheat rotis and jaggery or hot khichadi along with mango pickle were given as breakfast, dal, rice, vegetables and roti were given for lunch and the same for dinner. To us, in the 'B'[335] class quarter pint milk, two 'tea spoon'[336] that is small spoonful of sugar and half a piece of bread were given as breakfast. Lunch consisted of dal, rice, vegetables, roti, khichadi, wheat porridge and 1 ounce of packaged butter; the dinner was also that. The breakfast was at 7:30 in the morning, lunch at 12 noon and dinner at 7 in the evening. Till 5 o'clock we would spin from 1200 to 2000 and sometimes even 3000 threads. At 5 o'clock our matron would visit us. She would bring our post with her. Only those who have experienced it would know as to how eager we were for the post and the news from the outside that letters brought. Our matron[337] was Radhabai. She was very good, kind, honest, straightforward and simple. She had worked in the prison for the past 10 years. She was widowed at the age of 15 or 16; she had two children, a son and a daughter. She later studied and after passing her matriculations she joined the Nagpur central prison as a jamadarni at a salary of Rs 25. At present, because of her qualities, she draws a salary of Rs 150. She has won over not only us but also the criminal convicts. She educated many illiterate convicts and she received letters in their hand after their release. She would counsel the convicts and many who were sentenced for twenty long years would be released because of the efforts of this good woman in ten or seven years. She was a devotee of Bapuji but that poor woman had to do a government job for the

---

[333] English letters in the original.
[334] English letters in the original.
[335] English letters in the original.
[336] English term in the original.
[337] English term in the original.

sake of livelihood. I used to read out the autobiography in Hindi, which she heard with great interest. She also listened to the stories of Motiba with deep interest. She became a mother to me and a sister to other women. She dealt with all the women with immense affection.

Thus we passed our days. One morning we heard about Pujya Bhansalikaka's fast all of a sudden. We got no further news of it, either from the newspapers or from the letters. Parts of letters that contained this news were made unreadable as they were blackened out with tar. I shiver whenever the memories of those tragic days or the days of Bapuji's fast come to mind. The whites had molested the women in Chimur and unleashed all-round terror. How was that sage like Bhansalikaka to remain unmoved by this plight! He is unable to walk long distances and does not use either horses or bullock carts. He set out with a fellow ashramite (Balvantsinha) for Chimur and ascertained the facts for himself. He went to Delhi and met Aney[338] who did not give a straight answer. Bhansalikaka began his fast from Aney's doorstep. The fast commenced on 10.11.1944,[339] we also organized community fasts inside the prison. He fasted for 62 days and broke his fast on 12.1.1943[340] after Aney gave an undertaking that he would visit Chimur and intervene in the matter. The day he broke fast he consumed separate[341] milk. His normal diet consists of jaggery, onion, til and milk. He eats all these things together but his body has become that of iron, hence nothing happens to him. He sleeps only for three hours.

He used to teach all of us. One day I had placed a rose in my hair. I went to Bhansalikaka for my class. 'Behn! Does this flower belong to the bush or your hair?' he asked. I replied, 'But Bhansalikaka that flower would wither away and fall, what about that?' 'Even our children die, are we for that reason to pluck away what belongs

---

[338] M.S. Aney.
[339] The date should be 10.11.1943.
[340] The date should be 12.1.1944.
[341] English term in the original.

to the tree? You have deprived the honey bee of its food. What if someone were to snatch away your food?' Bhansalikaka explained. I was convinced and I stopped putting flowers in my hair from that day. This is one example of the minute things he would explain. In two months of the conclusion of that fast, one evening unexpectedly a thunderbolt hit us. It was our matron who gave us the news. Bapu had commenced a fast on 10.2.43. What now? He would get the newspaper only after the night passed. I passed the night gasping. Somehow the night passed and morning came. The jail officials were frightened as to what we would do. Therefore, they opened the gates early and came in. At 7 the superintendent[342] came and I was the first one to ask him, 'Has Bapu commenced a fast?' 'Yes, but the Government would release him, careful, don't you go on a fast of your own, and there would be "force of feeding."'[343] I told him that I would fast and kept fast on the first three days. Rehanabehn[344] was with us. During our prayers she would see through her inner eye. She would narrate that to us and the newspaper the following day would corroborate her narration. We came to have faith in her. For all twenty-one days, we organized communal spinning and relay fast; each day two women kept a fast, thus making a chain. During those 21 days 42 women kept a fast. During this fast of 21 days Bapu had allowed himself water squeezed with lime. We would spin and keep silence from six in the morning to twelve noon or would do prayers and sing devotional songs and prayed to God for a new life for Bapu. I observe twenty-four hour silence on Mondays. Johrabehn and Kantabehn would also keep twenty-four hours of silence. On 3.3.43 those fasts concluded. But the Government had kept sandalwood in readiness and also decided the path from which his dead body would be carried because the Government wanted that Bapu should pass away. And for this reason Bapu—who wanted to live decided to take

---

[342] English term in the original
[343] English phrase in the original
[344] Rehana Tayabji (1900-1975).

lime water on 22.3.43. He was on the verge of death. The way of the god is unique. Bapu wanted to continue his work and god wanted to work for him; for this reason he was saved.

Thus the 21 days passed. After that each day we prayed to god that nothing new should come upon us. During this fast those on the outside, including relatives, were allowed to meet Bapu. Pujyabhai and Umiyabehn were among those who had gone to see Bapu.

On 19.2.43 I had a dream that I was in Aga Khan Palace and I was transferred there by the Government to serve Ba. I recounted my dream to the others the next morning and prayed to god to make my dream come true! And it came true. On 18.3.43 the jailor came in three or four times and took my name. All the others said that I was being released being the youngest. But to myself I kept saying how wonderful it would be if they were to take me to Motiba. The superintendent came in the evening. I asked, 'Where are you taking me?' Pramila Masi asked, 'Is she to be transferred or released?' The superintendent replied, 'Only those who have earned great merit can be taken to Poona, where do you think you are being transferred to?' I said almost involuntarily, 'Poona'. He said, 'Yes, we are taking you to Poona.'

19.3.43

Today at 4 a.m. I set out of the gates on the way to Poona. Many of the women wept. I touched their feet and sought blessings. I was to set out of the jail after nine months. The matron took me to the superintendent to settle my accounts. The jailors were like elders to me and treated me like a daughter. I touched their feet and a jail motor took me to the station. I was accompanied by two elderly policemen. An entertaining incident took place at the station. Usually 'B' class prisoners are made to travel by inter-class.[345] I was also to travel by inter-class. But the poor policeman had no idea as to which was inter-class and which was IInd [346] class. The poor man made me sit in

---

[345] English term in the original.
[346] English term in the original

an unoccupied IInd class. The guard came. He asked for my warrant from the policemen, which they gave. The warrant had specified inter-class. He chided me, 'Behn! Even you couldn't ascertain this?' 'These people did not show the warrant to me. Therefore, I know nothing about it.' The blame came on the poor policemen. They said that they did not know how to read, which had caused this to happen. I told him that I would go to the inter-class provided my seat was reserved. I would move only after the arrangements were made. I spoke a bit firmly, hence the guard told me to stay where I was. He signed the warrant.

We reached Kalyan. A funny incident took place there as well. Those elderly policemen had stayed awake the previous night to keep a watch over me. We were to wait at Kalyan station for two hours after which our next train was due. They lay down to sleep. The waiting room was for men only. They reasoned among themselves as to no one is going to take me away or help me escape. I thought that I should go over to the women's waiting room, bathe, and comb my hair. I went out to bathe. After a leisurely bath I came back and found the two policemen sound asleep. I met an acquaintance of mine. He asked me everything and I told him that I was on way to Aga Khan Palace. I was not at fault; the two policemen were asleep and I did not know enough about jail regulations whether I was permitted to speak to others about jail matters. I told him everything. That man gave me a cover[347] and urged me to write a letter to my father. I declined to do so, as I was a prisoner and I knew that I was not entitled to write letters. I had spoken to him frankly but later I got worried that if he were to inform the newspaper what would happen to these two poor policemen. I urged that person not to leak this news to either the papers or anywhere else. He promised that he would not to do so. On the way I had a chance to read the newspaper, wherein the Government had made it known that Kasturba had suffered a massive heart attack and the Government had arranged to send

---

[347] English term in the original.

Manu Gandhi from C.P.[348] as a nurse.[349] I was relieved that there would not be a problem now. On 20.3.43 around 4 o'clock I changed train. The *Mumbai Samachar* had detailed news about Ba's condition. Tears came to my eyes. I wondered if I would be able to meet her or not. I somehow passed two hours and at 6 o'clock we reached the Poona city station. The police superintendent searched for me and I for him. We were not acquainted with each other. I had to travel in his car. What was I to do now? All the other passengers went their own way. There was a lot of military presence, the whites walked up and down; I was a bit scared as well. Ultimately I got very angry on the elderly policemen. I told them to follow me, as I would somehow find the office. I went straight to the station master. I asked him and reached the office, a little while later the police superintendent came there. He took me to the Aga Khan Palace in his motor car. It took us 25 minutes to reach Aga Khan Palace from the station. It was 7 o'clock when I reached home. Bapuji was still on his bed. He had not resumed his walks after the fast. He ate his dinner of vegetables, milk and butter seated on the bed. He was about to finish his dinner. I went in and touched his feet. He patted me on the back forcefully. The chief superintendent Kateli Sahib, a Parsi, was there. I immediately asked him about Ba's health. He told me that Ba was better but Mrs Naidu was rather unwell. As I touched Bapu's feet, Ba walked in and said, 'Behn! How are you? You are finally here!' I touched her feet and she blessed me, 'Be happy and serve well.' I could still feel the force of Bapu's pat on the back. Bapu made me his stick[350] and took me to Mrs Naidu and said, 'We did not take Manudi to the AICC, but she followed us here, such is the force of a person's desire.' I was very tired and had nothing to eat during the journey. Ba told Bapuji, 'Talk to her later, let her eat, bathe and wash. Her face

---

[348] Central Province, C.P. in English.

[349] English term in the original.

[350] It refers to the practice of leaning over a companion for support while walking. Manu Gandhi and Abha Gandhi became his 'sticks' in the last phase of his life.

has turned pale.' Bapuji immediately took me to the bathroom[351] and showed me everything. Ba was with us. My clothes were in the bag, which needed to be untied. Therefore, Ba gave her clothes to me. I wore Sushilabehn's blouse[352] and petticoat. I bathed hurriedly. Ba took me for the meal. Pyarelalji served me. That day the meal consisted of boiled vegetables, milk, butter, cream and fruits. During the course of the dinner, I spoke a great deal and talked with Ba. Ba said, 'Behn! How cruel can this Government get? They arrested you, a girl of fourteen, which the law prohibits.' Later, I talked with Bapu. Bapu said, 'During your two months' stay at Sevagram, you have won over Ba. Hence, she said no to those who have stayed with her for years and insisted that she wanted you. You have come here for Ba. You know her disposition. She could get angry in a moment. But she is so pure that her anger disappears the next moment. Therefore, your task is to win her over and make her better. You should not worry about any other task. You should do Ba's work with care and concern. You are affectionate by nature and hence Ba chose you over the others. Do not feel pain, should Ba get angry. You must be able to laugh about it.' I talked with Pyrelalji and Sushilabehn also. I asked Ba as to how she knew that I was lodged in the Nagpur prison? She replied that Bhai had come on a visit and he said that your eyes were being spoilt there and that we should have you over if that were possible. 'I also needed a nurse, you were the last one to serve me. We had adjusted well with each other. You are well acquainted with the work to be done for Bapuji and me, you have done that as well and Bapuji likes your work. Therefore, we called for you. Initially we considered giving names of Manibehn[353] and Premabehn[354] but their conversation with Bapu would be interminable. I prefer girls your age; I can even say a few words to you. She is after all Vallabhbhai's daughter and of a mature age and would be quick to

---

[351] English phrase in the original.
[352] English phrase in the original.
[353] Manibehn Patel.
[354] Premabehn Kantak.

take exception to my words. Therefore, you are the best. You would also get to learn here. It appears that I must have some claim over you. Otherwise, we had no inkling as to where you were.' We spoke about such other things till midnight as I sat pressing her feet. On the very first night Ba said that I should sleep beside her in her bed. Ba and I slept side by side. Three years after my mother's death I had the fortune of sleeping beside Ba, who was like a mother to me. In my childhood so long as my mother was alive, I slept in her bed. If I didn't, sleep would elude me. After her death, today I slept beside Ba. The joy of it could be known only by the one who was experienced it. I reached there on Saturday. Mrs Naidu was released on Sunday, 21st March 1943, due to her ill health. Now, Dr Guilder, Sushilabehn, Pyarelalji, Mirabehn, Ba, Bapuji and I remained.

Aga Khan Palace

The Aga Khan Palace is an enormous palace. The Aga Khan is regarded as divinity by Muslims. At present he is in England. The Muslims made a gift of this palace to him when he came to India. All around the palace there is a massive garden. But we are not allowed into all parts of the garden. The part in which we are allowed is a beautifully laid garden. At the entrance there are gun-wielding sergeants. There are our soldiers stationed near wire fencing. A third wire fencing leads to the steps of the verandah. All around the perimeter of the palace there are forty armed soldiers stationed at regular intervals. They seemed ready with their guns. But when? Only when their superior officers were on a round, otherwise they would sit at ease. The Government paid them a salary for doing nothing. The guards were stationed to ensure that Bapuji or the other prisoners did not run away and also to prevent outsiders from coming inside. The verandah is circular. Various rooms open into the verandah. The first room[355] was kept locked as furniture that was not required was kept in it. The

---

[355] The word 'room' is in English.

room after that is Mirabehn's room. She lives there. The third room is
our dining room, where dining tables[356] are placed. The fourth room
was Mahadevkaka's. After his passing Motiba, Sushilaben and I kept
our belongings there; some of Bapu's things were also in that room.
There were several cupboards in that room. We used to study there
as well. The fifth room was Bapu's. Mirabehn had inscribed 'Hey
Ram' on a calendar placed facing Bapu's sitting space. Motiba's bed
was also kept there. Adjoining the room are two large bathrooms[357]
equipped with bathtub[358] and other amenities. Bapu used one of
these bathrooms, while the other was used by Ba. All of us also
used Motiba's bathroom. Pyarelalji's room is next to these rooms. It
contains his library[359] of over two to three thousand books. All the
correspondence with the Government was also kept there. In this
sense, this was the office[360] of the Aga Khan Palace. Dr Guilder's
room is adjacent to this. There are two more floors above this one.
On the second floor our superintendent Kateli Sahib lived. It was
prohibited for us to go up to the floors above, lest someone should
see us! On the upper most floor the furniture[361] and other things of
the Aga Khan Palace were stored. The floor on which we lived was
used by the servants of the Aga Khan whenever he was in residence.
He preferred to stay on the third floor. There was a beautiful pool
where we learnt to swim during summer months. At some distance
from the wire fencing was the samadhi of Mahadevkaka. We had
made a space to play badminton[362] in the compound.[363] There were
three or four lovely mango trees in the garden, last year they gave
about 5000 mangoes. The mangoes were very sweet. Other plants

356 'Tables', in English.
357 'Calendar', in English.
358 'Bathtub', in English.
359 'Library', in English.
360 'Office', in English.
361 'Furniture', in English.
362 'Badminton', in English.
363 'Compound', in English.

and shrubs were decorative. We grew some vegetables during the monsoon as Bapuji liked it very much. Bereft of people the palace seemed ghostly, albeit we did not feel it to be so. Such is the palace. The furniture is of superior quality. This large palace lacked a kitchen. We cooked in the verandah and continued to do so for the duration of our stay.

Bapu's room had 'Hey Ram' inscribed on a calendar. Adjacent to his seat was a wooden case where books that he read regularly. These included Gitaji, the Bible, the Koran and similar such books. On his desk was a ceramic toy. This was the toy of three monkeys where one monkey has closed its eyes suggesting that one should not see evil, the other has closed its ears, so that one may not hear any evil and the third has shut its mouth so that one may speak no evil. This toy is placed so that it faces Bapu. Ba's cot was also in this room. Every room had carpets, but Bapuji had it removed from his room. Gradually, all the carpets from other rooms were also removed so that the floor could be cleaned well. We slept in the verandah. Bapuj's bed was made near the door of his room. Sushilabehn's bed was made to the left of Bapu's and Ba's bed was to the right. I slept to the right side of Ba. Pyarelalji's bed was made to the left of Suahilabehn's. Mirabehn did not like to sleep in the verandah and preferred to sleep in her room. Such were the sleeping arrangements.

Bapu's Diet

Bapu's diet consisted of boiled vegetables, wherein green leafy vegetables, beet root, potatoes, ladiesfinger, beans, pumpkin and other vegetables were boiled together. He took 8 oz. vegetables and vegetable broth. 1 oz. butter, 22 oz. milk, 6 oz fruit juice, 1 or 2 oz. jaggery, khakhra made from 4 oz. wheat flour or 1 oz. dates mixed with almonds and cashews and raw vegetables such as cucumber, raddish and coriander and methi.

At 7 in the morning he would take 16 ounces of orange juice mixed with juice of two lemons, some soda and water. He would also add 1 oz. of jaggery. The jaggery was prepared through a distinct process.

Jaggery was soaked in water till it dissolved completely and passed through a sieve. This jaggery water was mixed with three quarters of a kilo of goat's milk for each half kilo of jaggery and thickened. He would take 1 oz. of such jaggery. At 11:30 he would take a meal of vegetables, 12 oz. of milk, butter and if the food items did not include five items, he would take either fruits, khakhra, almonds and cashews or raw vegetables or tomato juice. He would take milk and 4 oz. of dates or just milk at 6 p.m.. This was his daily diet. I prepared all his meals.

Bapu's Routine

Bapu used to wake up at 5 a.m. and would wake us all. He would brush his teeth and would drink 12 oz. of warm water mixed with 1 and ½ oz. of honey. We would join him for prayers. Latest by 5:15 a.m. the prayers would commence. The first was the Japanese prayer followed by two minutes of silence. Then we would recite Isha Vasyam, followed by Pratah Swarami and recite ahimsa, satya, astheya followed by the Islamic and Parsi prayers. We would sing a bhajan and the dhun and end with the reading of the Gitaji.

Bapu would sleep after the prayers and wake up at 6:30. At 6:30 he would go to the latrine and take fruit juice and jaggery. He would write his diary or read for 10–15 minutes. Sometimes Mirabehn would read out the papers to him.

7:45 to 8:30: Bapu would take a walk. Sushilabehn and I would walk with him as his sticks. We would walk on either side of him with his hands on our shoulders for support. Hence, we were called sticks. Sometimes Pyarelalji would join us and sometimes not, but the three of us were regular. Mirabehn would walk fast, while we would walk slowly, talking. Bapuji would make us laugh, sometimes we would talk serious matters. We would walk at a pace slower than Mirabehn, hence she preferred to walk alone. Moreover, she is tall, so Bapu found it tiring to walk with hand over her shoulder. Motiba could not walk hence she stayed inside the house. During the walk we would spend 10 minutes at Mahadevkaka's samadhi and place flowers. This was usually between 7:45 and 8:30 that is during our walk. We would be back in the house by 8:30. 8:30 to 8:40, I would wash Bapu's feet and make preparations for his massage.

The massage would begin at either 8:50 or 9. Sushilabehn and Dr Guilder would give the massage. The massage would take 45 minutes, that is till either 9:45 or 10.

10 to 11: Bath. He would either read or would be read to during the hip bath. He would sit alternatively in cold and hot water for 10 minutes each and then would lie down in large tub. He would bathe under the shower also. This would take 45 minutes to an hour.

11 to 12: Meal. Bapu would teach Sushilabehn to translate the Sanskrit Ramayana into Gujarati. Sushilabehn would read the Bible to Bapu.

12 to 1: I would read the Valmiki Ramayana with Bapu.

After this Bapu would deal with correspondence with the Government, if any, or else would read in English books about Russia.

1 to 2: I would massage his feet with ghee while Bapu would sleep.

2 to 3: Reading or writing.

3 to 3:30: Bapu would teach Motiba one of the following subjects—Gitaji, English, Sanskrit, Gujarati or geography.

3:30 to 4: Reading newspapers.

4 to 4:30: Would teach me Gitaji in Sanskrit.

4:30 to 5: He would teach Sushilabehn either Margopadeshika or the Bible.

5 to 6: Spinning. Mirabehn would read to him passages marked in the newspapers. He would also discuss the writings. At 5 he would ring the bell and Dr Guilder, Sushilabehn, Pyarelalji, Kateli Sahib and I would go play either badminton, ping-pong or ring. [This was for exercise].

6 to 6:30: Evening meal or milk.

6:30 to 7: He would arrange and file newspapers cuttings.

7 to 7:45: Walk.

7:45 to 8: Evening prayers including Japanese prayer, Ishavasyam, verses of the Sthitpragna, Islamic and Parsi prayers, bhajan, dhun, two verses from Tulsi Ramayana. Sushilabehn would explain the meaning of these verses in Gujarati, while Bapu would correct her mistakes if any. He would write his diary or complete work that had remained incomplete and would go to sleep at 10. This was his usual routine, which changed during Motiba's illness and after her death.

Ba's Routine

Ba did not get up for the morning prayers. Her health had worsened after the fast. Sushilabehn would not allow her to wake up even if she wanted to. Hence she would wake up at 7 o'clock. She would brush her teeth and worship the basil plant and the sun after which she would have her tea. [Tea here implies a concoction of herbs pounded together and boiled with water and milk which had the hue of tea. This was for her asthma.] By this time we would have gone for our walk. She would read either the Bhajanavali or the Gita till we returned at 8:30. After the walk I would look after her needs.

8:30 to 9:- I would apply oil and comb her hair, from 9 to 9:30 or sometime 10 I would give her a full body massage, administer enema and bathe her. It would be 10:30 or 10:45 by the time this was over. After which I would cook for her, if she wanted to eat. Otherwise, she would have a cup[364] of milk with apricots, raisins and other dry fruits. She would have a cup of milk at 7:30 with her tea and another cup in the afternoon as well. Some days she would eat some vegetables, other times she would have khichadi, roti and if she felt like it she would get me to make theplas. But, she would invariably have palpitations in her heart after meals. For this reason she preferred to have milk, vegetables and hardly one, very small roti. I would serve Bapu his meals before serving Ba. Ba would sit with Bapu and often eat with him. We too, quite often would eat with him. On days we were delayed, we would eat later in the dining room.

---

364 'Cup' in English

Post lunch there would be recitation of the Ramayana in Bapu's room. She would listen to it and after which she would read, on her own, a book either in English or Hindi, Sanskrit, or Gujarati. She would sleep after I massaged her feet with ghee. She would get up at 2 o'clock and have warm water with honey or water mixed with soda.

At 2 o'clock I would read to her that day's newspapers or post. Monday was her day of writing letters. I would write letters for her. She would sign the letter. This would take up to 3 o'clock.

3 to 4: I would read to her Nanabhai's book on the characters of the Ramayana, we read the Valmiki Ramayana twice, also the Bhagavad and other religious books. She would also learn Gujarati writing from me. She was so much elder to me and of advanced age but she never felt any hesitation or shame about learning from a young girl like me. She learnt everything with great interest. One has to learn from her the enthusiasm for learning at the age of 75.

4 to 4:30: She would read the Gitaji with Sushilabehn and learnt her pronunciations from Bapu so that he would not have to spend much effort in teaching her. She was very careful and would read the chapter preceding and the ones to follow before every class. This is a very interesting fact about her that should be known.

She would do her 'lessons'[365] between 4:30 and 5.

We would go out and play between 5 and 6. She would come out to watch us at play. If I were found to be losing she would say throw the ring[366] on that side, or do your service[367] properly and you would win. She would watch us for a while and then go in to 'practice'[368] her carrom which we played at night. Her evening meal consisted of tea, like the one she had in the morning.

After our dinner, I would clean Bapu's utensils, after which we would sing bhajans, songs or I would play records on the gramophone. We would go out for our evening walk. She would at that time sit by

---

[365] 'Lessons' in English.
[366] 'Ring' in English.
[367] 'Service' in English.
[368] 'Practice' in English.

the tulsi plant and sing bhajans or join Mirabehn in her worship of the Bala Krishna. After the evening prayers she would have honey in warm water mixed with soda. From 9 to 10, for an hour, she would play carrom with Mirabehn, Dr Gilder and Kateli Sahib. For the duration of this play she would forget her pain, her severe asthma or the conviction that she was not to come out of the jail alive. This belief had grown stronger given the Government's attitude during the fast. But all of this would be forgotten. At 10 o'clock I would apply oil on her chest and some other ointments also. I would press her legs. Motiba would say, 'Behn! Change your clothes and let us go to sleep. Thus Ba and I would sleep together. During this jail term, and especially after Mahadevkaka's death, she was afraid of sleeping alone. Her asthma would worsen at night and she would have chest pain or require a spittoon. For these reasons, I would sleep with her.

Such were the routines of Bapu and Ba. Pyarelalji taught me and I read English books with Sushilabehn. Sushilabehn learnt German from Dr Gilder. She translated the Ramayana in the Gujarati and read a great deal and also spun. Both she and I studied for three hours daily. I cooked Ba and Bapu's meals, served them, cleaned utensils and performed petty chores for Ba. I also spun and washed Ba and Bapu's clothes. The day was filled with activities. Sushilabehn is M.D., she read medical books, taught me English, spun daily and studied with Bapuji, Pyarelalji and Dr Gilder. Sometime she would teach me nursing. She also taught me to embroider and knit. She could embroider even while walking. The *Dawn*[369] was the principal newspaper that Bapuji read. She would read it carefully and make cuttings of articles marked by him. Bapu has written 'Arogya Ni Chavi', which she translated in English and Hindi[370].

Dr Gilder's Routine

It was mainly reading. Later he and Sushilabehn were co-authoring a book on medicine. He taught me daily for an hour. He was very

---

[369] Spelt as 'Done'.
[370] Translated as 'Key To Health' and 'Arogy Ki Kunji'.

punctual. He taught me from 12 to 1. One day he began narrating his experiences of England. It went on till 1:30, even I lost track of time. He would bathe after teaching me. That day he did not take his bath so that he could keep to his pre-determined routine. He was so punctual.

Mirabehn's Routine

Mirabehn spent her mornings taking walks, bathing and washing her own clothes. She also gathered flowers and performed her worship. In the afternoon she read the Bible to Bapu and the newspapers in the evening. She prepared bath water for Bapu by mixing hot and cold water. I did all other work for Bapu. She also taught Sushilabehn. Her own reading was very vast. She intended to open an Ashram, and prepared plans for it. Her Hindi is so excellent. She also painted. She and Sushilabehn have made a beautiful painting of the landscape surrounding the Aga Khan Palace. Suahilabehn is also quite adept in the art of painting.

Such were our routines. If servants were brought in from the outside to the Aga Khan Palace, they might carry tales from outside and our stories to the world outside, hence each day two soldiers brought in several prisoners from Yeravada. They would come in by 7:30 in the morning and leave at 7 in the evening. The prisoners were very caring, devoted to service and emotional. We used to wash our clothes and also those of Bapuji and Ba. This pained the prisoners. One day a warder asked Bapuji, 'Why don't you allow us to serve you by washing your clothes?' Next day Bapu gave them clothes to wash. They served Bapu with devotion. All thirty of them would say that they might have committed a crime, but they had daily darshan of Bapuji. On auspicious days and national days like 15th August and 26th January we used to feed them, if nothing else, khichadi and vegetables. Bapu would serve the meals to them. These poor people were anyway tired of eating coarse food of the prison. This would give them joy. Bapu would also explain the reason for the special meals.

There were 10 soldiers on duty. They also served lovingly. The soldiers, the head constable and the superintendent were prohibited from going outside the premises, lest they should let out any stories. The head constable could go out to the market only with special permission, any slip on his part was certain to cost him his job. Our superintendent was an old guard. Every time Bapu has been imprisoned, he has been posted there on some duty or other. This time he was Bapu's superintendent.

Kateli Sahib

Any praise would be too little for this officer who was our superintendent. He was an officer but a devotee of Bapu; though an officer, he became for me both mother and father. On both occasions when we observed Bapu's birthday he offered Rs 75 each and did a sastang dandvat pranam to Bapu. He was a Parsi and a wonderful person. He invariably followed Bapu's command, he would unfailingly act on Bapu's words. He was jovial but he too was imprisoned with us. He had become one with us. He would even have his meals with us. He was 48 years of age. I was the youngest, and he and the others teased me a lot. Every day he would come up with a new prank. He was equally devoted to Motiba. At the time of Mahadevkaka's and Motiba's deaths he wept so much that Bapu had to console him. Such was the officer in whose charge we were placed.

Thus, our days were filled with activities. But Motiba would suffer palpitations of the heart frequently. The attack would last up to six hours. I would hold her close and sit by her. My eyes had welled up with tears during the first of such attacks. I feared that she would soon be gone. I asked Sushilabehn about Ba's condition. She assured me that the attack would pass before too long. Her heart beat so fast that each heartbeat could be heard distinctly. Each time, death appeared imminent. She would lie down when the palpitation occurred. As soon as they would pass and she regained some strength, she would get up. She was required to do no work but her disposition was such that she would not stay idle. She was always engaged in some activity. She used to spin 500 threads even in the prison. But as her heart became weaker, she was required to stop spinning.

Why Did Bapu Fast?[371]

One day I asked Bapuji, 'Bapuji why did you undertake the fast?' He replied, 'the Government had put terrible accusations on me which were all false. I had said at the time of my arrest that I would not be responsible for the actions of people after my arrest. But the accusations persisted. My conscience told me to fast, and if I had not undergone the fast I would not have found peace. The fast also told me whether god wanted work from me even after the imprisonment. Only for that reason He saved me from a fiery ordeal of 21 days. During those 21 days, I was face-to-face with god. I have no desire to live but I do hope to secure India's freedom. And for this reason my conscience advises me against the fast at the present time.'

Why Does Bapu Drink Goat's Milk? Why Not Any Other?

Bapu said, 'Once while touring Bengal, I saw that air was blown into the cow or buffalo so that she could be milked to the last. My heart trembled at the sight. I gave up milk that day and with that went butter and ghee as well. Soon thereafter I had severe diarrhoea, which continued for 50 days. The doctor insisted that I take milk. I declined; Ba was at that time standing by my bed. She said that I could take goat's milk as no such thing is done to goats. From that day I began to take goat's milk.'

Why is Non-Violence the Only Way to Obtain Swaraj? What is the Objection to Us Taking to Violence?

Bapuji replied, 'How much violence surrounds us in the world? Who has emerged victorious because of that? And even if they were to win, how many lives would be lost and what of other destruction?

---

[371] From 10 February 1943 to 3 March 1943.

A new constitution would be framed after efforts of many years, and someone would seek to oppose it. Non-violence is a new weapon. If not today, then tomorrow the world will have to adopt this means. Non-violence does not indicate cowardice but it signifies bravery. If a person were to slap us and we were to accept that, it is a sign of bravery. But if we were to retaliate, someone will die in the ensuing fight. That would create enmity and it would go on. In this way we can never move ahead. Non-violence has a special kind of bravery. How much can you hit me? At the most it can result in my death. Let him kill me. How many more will he kill? Eventually, he will grow weary of violence and adopt non-violence. If this were to find place and in the heart of every Indian, Swaraj is near. Today, the world has so much violence, only India has remained non-violent. India is a mere dot in the world, and yet I have no doubt that its non-violence moves more forcefully than weapons of violence.'

Bapu as Mother

Bapu is more than a mother. Bapu is adept in every way, but I had a complete experience of him as a mother. Bapu is Bapu and also a mother. After my mother's death many would say to me, 'Behn, mother is after all a mother, can father ever take place of the mother?' But after having lived with Bapu, this proved to be wrong. Bapu knows well how to do all that a mother does.

One morning I was fast asleep. Bapuji came to wake me up for the prayers. I sleep so deeply that I would not wake up unless shaken out of bed. If someone were to say 'Manu, Manu' softly, I would not even hear. Bapu came to wake me up at 5 o'clock. I have the habit of fastening the drawstrings of my salwar very tight. I had worn my Punjabi dress of salwar and kurta. Bapu placed his hand on me through the mosquito net. Bapu could see that I had fastened my salwar very tight. He woke me up and showed me how to fasten the drawstrings. He said, 'The drawstrings should not be fastened so tight, this could affect health adversely. Especially at night the knot should be loose, otherwise it prevents the flow of blood. Your mother died when you were young and therefore could not teach you such things; hence I teach them to you. Motiba at your age would wear the knot tight and Motiba and I had long standing quarrels about it.' From this day on, I would show Bapu the way I had tied my salwar. But the habit of fastening it tight took a long time to be remedied. Bapuji cares for me in many such small matters.

Bapu and Cleanliness

Bapu gives great attention to cleanliness. If there were to be any dirt, he prefers to clean it himself rather than point it out to someone else. An object had to be returned to its designated place; till it was done Bapu would be uneasy. Even if he were lying down, he would get up, and return the thing to its place.

In the last phase Motiba was rather unwell. Every five to ten minutes she would need to defecate. Sometimes even her clothes were soiled. I would wash her clothes each time they were soiled. One day I had stayed awake all night. Sushilabehn insisted that I should sleep. She said that if I did not sleep, I would not be allowed to do my 'duty'.[372] I went to sleep. Someone placed Ba's soiled petticoat in her bathroom. And that day, as fate would have it, Bapu went inside Motiba's bathroom[373] to wash his face, as Sushilabehn was bathing in his 'bathroom'. Bapu saw the soiled petticoat and began to wash it. Just then, I woke up and went to the bathroom to wash my face. I saw Bapu washing soiled clothes. I told Bapu, 'Bapuji are we all not here? I went to sleep against my wish. Why do you harass us so? Will this not cause us pain? We are so many of us, won't we have washed them?' Bapu replied, 'You were asleep. You need proper sleep. If you do not sleep, how are you going to be of service? It is not your fault in the least, but it appears that Ba's petticoat has been laying here for quite some time because faeces has spread and hardened. I do not

---

[372] 'Duty', in English.
[373] 'Bathroom', in English.

believe that so far no one has noticed it and that I am the first to see it. Sushila has been at her bath for some time now. Hence, neither you nor her are to be blamed. But, I believe that others have seen it. It is possible that my belief is wrong. But why has it not been cleaned? Not because people are averse to it, but because they have been careless. I asked around as to who had placed the petticoat in there. There was a female attendant who had done so. I asked the others if they had not seen the soiled clothes. Everyone admitted to having seen it but said that they did not realize that they were Ba's clothes.' Bapu said, 'It is sufficient for me to know that we are careless.'

One day after my studies, my books were strewn around. For some reason I had to go inside for some work of Ba. From one task to another I forgot to place the books at their designated place. The books were lying around in the middle room used by Mahadevkaka. Bapu was about to step out for his walk. I was with him. The pages of the 'Reader'[374] fluttered in the wind. Bapu said nothing to me, but he stepped inside. We wondered as to what had happened. I was ashamed; I took the books from him and placed them at their place. Bapu laughed, gave me an affectionate pat on the back and pulled my ear. He teaches us so much with good humour! And he also teaches us not to repeat the mistake. This is an art that he has. I take two to five minutes to eat my meals. Ba complained to Bapu that since I eat so hurriedly I do not put on weight. Bapu said that from the next day I should take my meals with him. Ba said that I was so shy that I would not be able to eat anything in his presence. She further said that sometimes I took stir fried vegetables from her portion as we sat eating on the table and that I would not do so in his presence. She told Bapu to advise me against eating hurriedly. Bapu asked me, 'Manu are you shy in my presence?' I replied, 'Bapu who can be shy in your presence? That is Ba's way of saying things.' Bapu said, 'I do not like that you eat in a hurry.' I said, 'Bapu, however much I try I end up eating fast.' Bapu said, 'These days it has become

---

[374] 'Reader', in English.

our way in the country not to care for our bodies. It seems to have become a fashion[375] to be a weakling and brittle bodied, isn't it?' I replied, 'Bapuji I know nothing about the fashion as for the past one year I have been with you. Don't you know whether I am simple or fashionable?' Bapu said, 'You are simple in every way, save in eating where you indulge in fashion.' I said, 'But Bapuji, my weight had gone up to 16, but this time I lost two pounds and I am berated by everyone, they tease me.' Bapu said, 'We wish to train you thus, unless we tease you, you will not learn to care for your body.' I told Bapu, 'But I have this habit of eating hastily for quite some time now.' Bapu replied, 'It pains me that no one cared to explain this to you.' There were many such small and subtle events and Ba and Bapu's care for me would come forth.

One day, I did not spin at all. I had resolved that the day I do not spin, I should forsake one meal as well. It was time for the evening meal. Sushilabehn and Motiba called me to eat. I told Motiba that I did not wish to eat as I had not spun that day. Ba said, 'You do not like to spin, and not eating is something that you like very much. So, you would neither spin nor eat!' I got up having decided to break my resolution. But before doing so, I asked Bapu's opinion. Bapuji said, 'Can resolutions be broken so easily? If we break resolutions, however small, how shall we keep large resolutions? You are correct in keeping the resolve on but there should be a fixed time for spinning. It cannot be that you spin in the morning on one day and in the evening on the other. But Ba would be pained if you do not eat. You should break your resolutions for her sake.' I broke my resolution.

I was made to drink 3 oz. of milk daily. I had distaste for milk. Ba would keep a tumbler of milk, with a lot of cream in it, ready on the table daily. I was required to drink it either in her presence or before anyone else who was on the table. I was required to drink the milk to obey Motiba and so as not to cause her pain. One day a tumbler full of milk was on the table, I cheated and poured the milk back into the container. As my luck would have it Sushilabehn came in just then,

---

[375] 'Fashion', in English.

'Poured the milk back, have you?' She asked. 'Reduced its quantity,' I replied. 'Beware, I will tell Ba.' I told her, 'Sushilabehn, please do not inform her today. I will drink it up but I get nausea when I drink milk. I just don't like it. Please excuse me today.' But she did not do so and I had to drink the milk. I told Bapu of my cheating that very evening. Bapu laughed and said, 'Does that happen while eating ghari sweet? If you persist with this I would surmise that you are lazy. Milk builds up the constitution of our body and we can serve only when we are strong in body. You are not lazy about your work, but it appears that you are becoming lazy.' After this incident I became more careful of my health.

I used to get fever every month despite taking 30 grams[376] of quinine. That fever left me after this. Bapu's words were etched in my mind.

Bapu began to teach me the Gita, before that he used to teach me geometry. On Mahadevkaka's death anniversary we had decided to recite the Gita. I did not know the correct pronunciations. For three days I did little else but to learn the Gita. I learnt five discourses in three days. From that day I was determined to learn the Gita and I learnt all the eighteen discourses from him.

During our evening walk Bapu would often relate episodes and experiences of his life.

One day, one thing led to another and Bapuji narrated experiences from South Africa. Bapu was taken to South Africa by a Muslim man.[377] Bapu was deeply perturbed by the all-pervading slavery there. On his second journey the whole Gandhi clan went with him. Bapu said, 'The second journey to South Africa proved to be immensely beneficial for the entire Gandhi clan. Even now many persons of the Gandhi family live there. Of all the people I took there Maganlal proved to be the best. He served ceaselessly till his death. Once there was an acute shortage of funds at the Sabarmati

---

[376] 'Grain', in English.
[377] Dada Abdullaha.

Ashram. The condition was such that there was no provision for food for the next month. Maganlal came to me and inquired, 'Bapu what will be our lot next month?' I replied, 'Have faith in god, just as He did Kuvarbai's Mameru, and kept the honour intact, we would do likewise for us and keep our honour. Just as we spoke of this a child came in and said Bapuji there is someone in the motor car and is calling you outside.' Bapuji went out and the Sheth asked him if he would accept a gift. Bapu replied, 'gladly'. The following day he came at 10 o'clock and gave a large sum of money. That person who made the gift was Sheth Ambalal Sarabhai. Even today he is a big mill-owner. He lives in Ahmedabad.

'One day I received a letter from Thakkar Bapa that there was a poor Harijan and I hope that you would keep this Harijan brother and his family. They will reach day after tomorrow. The family was about to come and no one, including Ba, were ready to touch a Harijan. But, they were being sent by Thakkar Bapa. Can one say 'no'? It was a real test but I kept my faith in god, I spoke to Ba. Ba said, 'I would neither touch them nor keep them.' When they came and drank water from a pot, Ba had the pot kept away, and Ba refused to touch them. When I came to know of this I told Ba that she was free to go wherever she liked. But if she wanted to live in the Ashram, such untouchability would not be tolerated. Poor Ba wept a lot. All they talked amongst themselves was that Bapu was committing a great sin. What is our duty? It is our duty to stay with our husbands even if they live with Harijans? Or is our duty in living separately from him! Ultimately they discussed the issue amongst them and decided that it was their duty to work for the uplift of Harijans and stay with the husband. Ba came to me, sought my forgiveness and adopted the Harijan girl as her daughter.'

That girl is Lakshmibehn. At present she is in Ahmedabad. Ba arranged her marriage. She lived with Ba till she was 18 to 20 years of age. Bapu narrated many such incidents from his life during our walks. One day Bapu told us about his first trip to England. How did Bapu go to England at the age of eighteen? Bapu said, 'My mother refused me the permission to go to England. I had never travelled alone. I did not know how to go to Porbandar from Rajkot. But I was determined to go to England.' I asked, 'Bapuji, who told you about going to England?' Bapuji said, 'There used to be a family priest who came to us since my father's time. He used to say that after our father's passing someone from the Gandhi family should retain the position of the Dewan. Both my elder brothers had given up the hope, but he had hopes from me. So he told me to go to England. But Ba said that my son would turn a meat eater in England and would turn bad in the company of whites; I cannot bear that. Just then a Jain monk came and said I have deep confidence in this boy. We should administer a pledge to him that he shall do no such thing. I have faith that this boy will not break a pledge. He placed a basil leaf and water in the palm of my hands with my mother, the sun and the priest as witness. Thus mother's permission was obtained. But where was the money coming from? I who had never travelled alone set out for Porbandar on a camel to obtain my uncle's permission. We halted for a day at Gondal and somehow reached Porbandar. This was my first journey and I felt as if I had travelled the world. It gave me such joy! I sought uncle's permission to travel to England. How was he to agree? He said, if you have your mother's blessings, mine are with you, but you must not go if it pains your mother. But money? He wrote a note to the ruler of Porbandar, but the Dewan said, 'We shall consider after you matriculate.'[378] I was thus disappointed and returned to Rajkot. We sold some ornaments of Motiba and my elder brother gave some money. I set out for Mumbai to eventually go to England. I asked one of my brothers-in-law about clothes and other things necessary for England, and I got clothes tailored. But the caste fellows of Bombay objected. At that time my elder brother showed great courage. He refused to pay a fine to the caste. Everything was ready for my departure. There was an acquaintance of my brother-in-law with whom I was to travel. Thus dilly-dallying, I boarded the

---

[378] As in the original, it should be 'graduate' at that time MKG was a first year B.A. student in Samladas College, Bhavnagar.

steamer. I knew no English or English customs. We were three of us in a cabin. My companion would go to the dining room and eat everything and would also insist that I do the same. But I had given a pledge to my mother. How was I to eat? When I told him so my companions got angry with me and then laughed. How will you survive a month and a half? He asked. But I ate only ganthia, mathia and other foodstuff that I had carried with me. I would go out of the cabin every morning and evening. No one spoke to me. I pined for my mother, somehow we reached Aden. I was subjected to torture there. They insisted that due to the cold I must eat meat and alcohol. The torture had reached its limit. Ultimately, I gathered courage and said even if you were to throw me into the seas I would not break the pledge given to my mother. After this their insistence stopped. I had carried with me study books—I spent my days reading those.' Bapu also narrated a funny incident. 'After Aden, London was at a distance of some days. I wondered how people can be so white, I felt as if I were to bathe and rub my skin hard with soap, I would also turn white like them. The water was salty and I rubbed the entire bar on my body. It caused such skin irritation that I felt like screaming. But who was I to share my stupidity with? I reached London. I had a letter of recommendation for Dr Pranjivandas Mehta. But there was no one to receive me at the port. I went to the Victoria Hotel. I washed and bathed and sat down to eat. I had never before used table and chair to eat and could not adjust to it all. Not just that, I used to eat at least six to eight wheat rotis. They asked me if I were a vegetarian. I said yes. They gave me eight or ten slivers of potato, small pieces bread, some butter and soup, pudding and billed[379] me five rupees for it. I was shocked. The food had left me hungry and so much money! But the custom there is that they charge for every item ordered. That evening I did not go down to eat. Dr Pranjivandas Mehta came to see me. There was an amusing incident that took place then. When he came to see me Dr Mehta had worn a beautiful

---

[379] 'Bill', in English.

hat,[380] which he placed on a table. We, the Indians, are known for our mischief. I picked up the hat and ran my hand over it. He immediately told me, "Mohandas, our ways don't work here. You are playing with it, which you will not do here. You would take one year to learn the customs and habits. You don't even know English. How will you become a Barrister in three years?" he also chided me sweetly that I would have to eat meat, etc.'

'Our way of eating is such that we dunk puri or roti in milk and eat. I had dunked the bread in the pudding causing much mirth and laughter around me. Dr Mehta gave me a book on the etiquette of eating, according to which bread and butter had to be eaten first using a knife, forks had to be used for food with skin. I had never seen a fork in our country. My condition was more pitiable than that of a villager. Soup and then last the pudding should be eaten. Thus Dr Mehta taught me rudimentary etiquette. He said, "You should lodge with a family." He asked me to meet him the following day at an appointed place. I somehow passed the night. Early next morning Dr Mehta came to fetch me. My baggage was still at the port, which we fetched. He arranged for me to stay with a family. In about eight days, I began to be acquainted with the basics. One day I set out to walk about London. I felt like going to the areas where the poorest of the poor lived. There I saw a vegetarian hotel.[381] I went in and that day for six pence I ate my fill. I relished it mere than the meals at Victoria Hotel. My "Land lady"[382] had two daughters. According to their custom the land-lady's daughter would take the lodgers like us around. I was very shy and would not so much as speak with the daughters. They would insist that I eat meat and drink alcohol. It was a daily quarrel. I was on the lookout for another lodging and while on my walk I found this place. I not only found food but also cheap lodging. I went to Dr Pranjivandas Mehta and said I would manage

---

[380] 'Hat', in English.
[381] 'Hotel', in English.
[382] 'Land-lady', in English.

everything. He tried to dissuade me. But I hired this set of rooms. My expenses were halved. I would eat one meal in the hotel initially. But later I managed with soya beans, bread, which I bought, and milk. I would eat bananas or some other fruits in the evening.'

'I began to learn dancing and playing the violin, but that did not hold my interest for long. I had a European tutor who helped me with my studies of matriculation examination. I appeared and passed at the first attempt.[383] I used to walk everyday four to five miles. I enjoyed my walks immensely and also saw new places. One Sunday I went for a walk and lost my way. What was I to do? I asked the police. I narrate this incident to demonstrate to you as to how helpful the police there are. The policeman telephoned the place where I lived. He helped me cross over to the other side and gave me directions to the other side and gave me directions to the next police post. He also phoned them to say that such and such person would come there and he has to be given directions to such and such place. I reached the police post and they sent me to a third one, from where I was escorted to my lodging. They also phoned to inquire if I had reached! They were so careful. In six months I made some acquaintances. I became a member of the "vegetarian"[384] society. I sometime wrote articles for its journal on vegetarianism. My knowledge of English was quite adequate now. I studied Latin and French also. I also had to attend dinners at the Inn. The food was largely non-vegetarian and I was the only vegetarian, hence I could hardly eat. But I was required to make speeches and participate in debates. And they created a good impression, given my young age.'

Thus Bapu became a barrister. But before he returned to India, his mother, who had worked so hard to send him to England and who had deep affection for Bapu, passed away. She did not live to see his return.

---

[383] MKG passed it at the second attempt.

[384] The original has 'vegetable'.

Diary 3

Sevagram Ashram
20.10. 1944

I have decided to commence writing from today. I asked Bapu this morning, what if I go to Karachi and study? I wish to study. Bapu replied that if I wished to study, it can be done privately. 'Even if you wished later to appear for examinations, you would be able to do so, as if it were a mere game. But if you were to study only for the sake of passing examinations, you will not be able to learn anything. Munnalal has obtained B.A., L.L.B—of what use is that? Pyarelal is M.A., what use is that? But they have decided, very wisely, to serve the people. But which school did Krishnadas and Prabhudas go to? But how well are they discharging their duties? I want you to give up this infatuation. I would prefer that you stay here and become a nurse. You would be under my watch and I would not have to worry on your account. I am confident that you would go far on this path.'

From today I have joined work in the dispensary from 9 to 11 a.m.. Johrabehn is with me as well. Today we had classes up to 10 o'clock, after we learnt to clean wounds, apply bandages and sterilise[385] instruments. For the rest of the time I was with Bapu. Today, Sushilabehn replied to a letter as instructed by Bapu. I also wrote one. Bapu said, 'What if I do not attend to the correspondence at all?' Pyarelal bhai said, 'Bapu, you will have to see to some correspondence. That would satisfy people. You will also have to see to it in order to take certain decisions.'

I read a little and slept after lunch. I studied with Bhansali bhai. I studied again after 3 o'clock. I cooked theplas. I could not attend to spinning, as I returned at six. Bapu has stopped the practice of leaning on us as walking sticks. These days Sita[386] is here and so he made her his stick. On the way back I was the stick. Bapu warned

---

[385] 'Sterilise', in English in the original.
[386] Sita Gandhi, daughter of Manilal and Sushila Gandhi.

Leelavatibehn, 'Have you spoken to her about studies?' But the desire for study persists. Wrote some at night and slept thereafter.

21.10.1944 Saturday

I spent 9 to 11 today at the dispensary. I got up early and bathed so that I could assist Mataji. Otherwise I feel bad that I am not able to perform properly the tasks of service assigned by Bapu. So, I have decided to wake up and get ready early so that I can give tea, etc. at the correct time. After the work at the dispensary we sat in Bapu's room for some time. At the bell for lunch, I ate and checked the post. There was a letter from Vijayabehn, I received a letter after many days, felt good. I wrote a reply to her. I studied for an hour with Bhansali bhai. Dr Sayeed Mohmmad came at 3.30 p.m.. He is to stay here. As I sat fanning Bapu, the workers from Kathiawad were narrating the situation of Bhavnagar. They discussed about the monopoly[387] over ghee. The Maharaj hears everyone but frankly admits that he can do nothing. That worker asked, 'What are we to do?' Bapu replied, 'Revolt.' The worker asked, 'Would it be proper for one man to revolt?' Bapu said, 'If one person is passionate, he should go to jail, much will be achieved by it. I am very firm about this. And Pattani[388] and I have discussed this matter at length. You give me in writing and I will write to Pattani.' Another worker described the condition of Rajkot after Verrawala,[389] the others who have come to occupy that position are much worse than him. The present Prime Minister is the father-in-law of the ruler. Three Dewans have been changed.

Bapu conversed with Dr Sayeed Mohmmad after this. Bapu did not say anything to me while spinning. I spun, ate and went to Kakiba's home. I went for a walk thereafter. After the prayers Munnalal bhai

---

[387] 'Monopoly', English term in the original.

[388] Sir Prabhakar Pattani, Dewan of Bhavnagar state.

[389] Durbar Verrawala, Dewan of Rajkot, MKG fasted against him in 1939.

said, 'Bapu called and asked me as to who was looking after the two girls from Chimur?' Munnalal replied that Prabhakarji was charged with the responsibility. Bapu asked, 'Why are any of the women not looking after them? I asked Vasumati and she said that no one had given her the responsibility so who is caring for them?'

Munnalalbhai replied, 'As I said Prabhakar looks after them.' Bapu said, 'There are so many women at the Ashram. And why no one cares? Kanchan should have looked after them.'

Munnalalbhai, 'Last year during the holidays, the matter of looking after these girls came up, at that time all the women declined. Hence, this year we did not ask any of them.' Prabhakarji has looked after Bhansalibhai with great care and Bhansalibhai has brought the girls here so he must be looking after them, they thought.

This angered Bapu even more and he said, 'The women who have been with us for so many years do not understand their responsibility. What am I to do, if not disband the Ashram? Perhaps, if I were to break up the Ashram everyone will recognize their responsibility. If Ramdas' or Devadas' daughter had come many would have shown willingness to look after them. And no one for them? My heart is sighed. For the first time today I saw their hair clean. I saw these girls clean and neat today. For all these days the girls were dirty. Today, all of a sudden they came and stood before me, my heart burnt. I called them and asked affectionately, they replied that Prabhakar cares for them. Place this matter before the women.' Bapu having said this began to read a newspaper. Bapu's blood was on boil.

Tomorrow is 22nd and hence this evening we made a list of all those who were to spin through the day without a break. Gave a massage to Kakiba and now I write this.

Bapu has been speaking of a fast, which is a cause of concern. Bhansalibhai said, 'Behn! There is nothing to be worried about. We are bound by love. But it is better to die than tolerate such an environment. When I fasted Chimanlalbhai and Ramdasbhai came and reasoned with me that I should give up the fast. When our mothers and daughters were being dishonoured, were they not ashamed to say so? How could that be? They came to reason with me! Such is the situation.'

One thing led to another and we said that Bapu gives solace even to a mad man. He speaks to him with such love. There is a man here who is called mad by everyone. Bhansalibhai said, 'Some 8-10 years ago I had fasted for 55 days. At that time in my madness I told Bapu to write to me every day of my fast. Bapu agreed to write. Everyday a letter of his arrived.' I asked, 'Where are those letters?' Bhansalikaka replied, 'Lilavati tore up all those letters. She did not spare even one.' He spoke with pain, 'Behn you will not understand this. Let bygones be bygones. But each day a letter came. Thus, Bapu understands the suffering of a madman and tries to provide solace.' This morning I had a talk with Krishnachandraji. Earlier there were three administrators at the Ashram. One of them, Ramdas Gulati, has left. Krishnachandraji is like any ordinary member. Bapu said, 'I am not interested in such forced outward decorations. It is better to break up the Ashram.' We were told that yarn spun by us has been woven and has reached the Ashram. Mridulabehn left for Mumbai today.

22.10.1944 Sunday

Today is 22nd—Motiba's death anniversary. I woke up for the prayers. The Gita was recited in the prayer. After the recitation I went for a walk. After which I cleaned the house and bathed, I went to the dispensary at 9 and returned at 11:30. Bathed again and went to Kakiba and helped her make rotis. Santok Kakiba is here these days. After lunch, I looked at the post. There were letters from Bhai and Umiyabehn. Umiyabehn wrote to Bapu, 'You will have to take the case in your hands, because you have become my mother. You are bound by promise. If I had known I would not have allowed such a thing to happen to me. I would have been like Vinod. But I did so because of the fear of being shamed in public and to protect the honour of my parents.' I gave this letter to Bapu. There was a letter from Faiba as well, which too I gave Bapu. Bapu laughed when he read Umiyabehn's letter. When I went to fan him in the afternoon he gave me a letter for Umiyabehn.

Sevagram 22.10.44[390]

CHI. UMIYA,

Why do you scold? Did I not give a good husband to you? If you don't like him, I can arrange for a divorce. Life has both highs and lows that form us. If you feel defeated, the shame would be mine. You would cause pain to Jamanalalji and shame Jaysukhlal. Why are you being cowardly? I consider you to be very brave. Let the fruits of the New Year be with both of you.

Blessings
Bapu

Bapu gave me the letter. He also said that there was a meeting[391] at 9 o'clock that evening. I spent the rest of the day studying and reading newspapers. I spun from 4:30 to 5:30. During the evening walk Bapu made Sita his stick. He looked for me, but I was struggling at the back. It appears that Bapu has resumed the practice of leaning on us during walks.

Meeting at 9 o'clock:

Vasumatibehn, Johrabehn, Shakrimasi, Dudhibehn, Kanchanbehn, Durgamasi and I among other women participated. Almost all the women were present. Bapu said to the women, 'Today I wish to speak to you about three matters. First regarding my experiments. The experiments that I wish to conduct are correct from my point of view. I had long talks with Devadas and Kishorelal. The family is pained by it. Hence, for the time being, I have given up the idea. Second, about attire. Manu has made this attire her own. This attire is very good for those who have to work. This is the best.

---

[390] Not in the *CWMG*.

[391] 'Meeting', English word in the original.

Gujarati attire is the worst, especially for doing any work. Yes, the Raniparaj women have an attire of their own. But none among you would wear those clothes. Mirabehn did adopt that attire, but finally she has adopted Punjabi clothes. That attire is the best and covers the full body. Third, it is about what happened yesterday. All of you are aware of it. I saw the two girls day before yesterday; compared to that today they were cleaner and neater. Their hair was combed. They were also trimmed. I smiled to myself that though late someone has awakened. Whoever among you did this would receive a great deal of thanks from me. I asked the girl happily, who cleaned your hair? She hesitated. I joked with her and asked again. She said, Prabhakarbhai cleaned them. I was angry from head to toe. What no one is willing to do, Prabhakar does. Prabhakar is really an ornament of the Ashram. He does any task given to him diligently. But I was pained. There are so many women and no one looked in their direction! These girls will not be a burden on anyone. Just then Vasumati crossed my path. I asked her, to which she said, "No one told me to. If I had been told, I would have most certainly done so." This made me even angrier. I asked Prabhakar and he said that he had asked each of the women but he was forced to look after the girls as all the women declined. This is really painful. It is a matter of great wonder that those who have lived with me for so long would not comprehend such an insignificant matter. Your contribution should be large. However, I had believed that the Ashram would not survive the struggle but all of you sustained it and come together in moments of crisis; and yet you also fought a great deal amongst you. This too I know. But I am content that you sustained the Ashram. I tell you that you should set me free. There is a kitchen in Bajaj Vadi, I will not be a burden there. But I am a burden here. Do I any more have the strength to carry buckets? I desire to live up to 125 years, but that is arrogance. Each of the women here have an art, but we have failed to raise Sevagram higher. I have said that if you raise Sevagram higher the seven lakh villages of India can easily be uplifted. I have no doubt regarding that.' The women said, 'Bapu our health is such that we cannot do all this.' Bapu said, 'In that case your first duty is to improve your

health. I have said what I had to. You let me know of your decision.'
The meeting lasted till 10 p.m..

24.10.1944, Monday

Today was Bapu's day of silence. Bapu has a lot of fun with children while on his walks. The routine remained the same. 9 to 12, I spent in the dispensary. Wrote a letter to Bhai. I gave a massage to Kakiba in the evening. These days Kanubhai does not talk to me. I do not know the reason.

25.10.1944

This morning I had a talk with Bapu. Bapu said, 'You need not worry. Is it possible to put filters on the mouths of the entire village?' There was a meeting today from 4 to 5. Bapu said, 'You should allow me to go away to Bajaj Vadi or you should all join some activity. Otherwise, you should set me free. Because the Ashram is heavily burdened. I can accommodate my guests in the Bajaj Vadi. That entire place is empty and available to me. My secretarial staff[392] and I can live there.'

Koshorlalbhai: 'Even if you were to move there, another Ashram will come up there. And who would you then ask to leave. The same thing has happened here. Initially there were only five persons and now we are so many.'

Bapu: 'It is likely that another fast will come upon me. Assuming that I survive that I would travel through all of India. Even if I do not fast I have this strong urge to go to Calcutta. If the Government prohibits that I would go to jail. I wish to stay in one region for 3 months or at least 2 months. I can live in 4 to 6 places in 12 months and mingle among people.

---

[392] English phrase in the original.

Letter to Dr Sangani

16.11. 1944[393]

'BHAI SANGANI,

I got your letter. You have given Sanyuktabehn excellent treatment and nursing. She was in great agony. May God repay you. Tell Chi. Samyukta that I had her letter. She can come over when you allow her to leave.

Blessings from Bapu.'

4.12.1944

Bapu has stopped all work for a month, that is up to 31.12.1944. It is a work fast.

---

[393] *CWMG*, vol 78, p. 306. Dr Sangani was at Harkissondas Hospital, Bombay.

About the Translator

Tridip Suhrud is a scholar, writer, and translator who works on the intellectual and cultural history of modern Gujarat and the Gandhian intellectual tradition. As the director and chief editor of the Sabarmati Ashram Preservation and Memorial Trust (2012-2017), he was responsible for creating the world's largest digital archive on Gandhi—the Gandhi Heritage Portal. His books, as an editor and translator, include the critical edition of *Hind Swaraj* (co-editor and co-translator, Suresh Sharma, 2010), Narayan Desai's four-volume biography of Gandhi, *My Life is My Message* (2009), and the four-volume epic Gujarati novel, *Sarasvatichandra* (2015). His most recent work is a critical edition of Gandhi's autobiography *My Experiments with Truth* (2018) in two languages: Gujarati and English.

Tridip Suhrud is presently translating the diaries of Manu Gandhi, covering the period between 1942 and 1948, compiling a series 'Letters to Gandhi'—of unpublished correspondence to Gandhi—and working on an eight volume compendium of testimonies of indigo cultivators of Champaran, Bihar. He is professor and director, Archives, CEPT University, and Director of Lalbhai Dalpatbhai Institute of Indology, Ahmedabad, and serves as Chairman of the Governing Council of MICA.